Index to the
LEGON OBSERVER
volumes two through nine, 1967-1974

Bibliographies
and
Guides
in
African Studies

James C. Armstrong
Editor

Index to the
LEGON OBSERVER

volumes two through nine, 1967-1974

THERESA DADSON

G.K.HALL &CO.
70 LINCOLN STREET, BOSTON, MASS.

Library of Congress Cataloging in Publication Data
Dadson, Theresa.
   Index to the Legon observer, volumes two through nine,
1967-1974.

   (Bibliographies and guides in African studies)
   Index to v. 1 of the Legon observer published by the Legon
Society on National Affairs in 1971.
   1. The Legon observer — Indexes.   I. Legon Society on
National Affairs.   II. Title.   III. Series.
DT510.A1L4333   309.1'667'05   78-26414
ISBN 0-8161-8294-9

This publication is printed on permanent/durable acid-free paper
MANUFACTURED IN THE UNITED STATES OF AMERICA

Contents

Preface

The Legon Observer was published from July 1966 until July 1974 when it ceased publication. (A special statement was issued as explanation of the cessation in October 1974.) During this period, the journal was the leading organ of social, economic and political commentary in Ghana.

In 1971, The Legon Society on National Affairs published an index to volume one. The present index covers the contents of volumes two to nine, and thus completes the indexing of all the issues of Legon Observer ever published. To ensure uniformity the arrangement of the earlier index has been followed as far as possible. More subject headings and form headings have been added, naturally, due to the volume of material handled in the current index. For a complete list of subject headings, <u>see</u> p. 1.

INFORMATION FOR USERS

The index is presented in four sections in one continuous paging. These are: the Main Index, Correspondence, News Summary, and Reviews.

1. Main Section

This first section is composed of all the serious articles, editorials and Observer Notebook entries appearing in the issues indexed. These articles are indexed by author, subject and title (where necessary) in one alphabetical sequence. Sample entries follow:
(a) DADSON, J. A. Strategy for economic recovery: The 1967/68 budget. II:17:13-15.
(b) ECONOMY
    DADSON, J. A. Strategy for economic recovery. The 1967/68 budget. II:17:13-15.
(c) Strategy for economic recovery: The 1967/68 budget. J. A. Dadson. II:17:13-15.

Explanation

Full information with regard to author, title and reference is given under every entry.

Author's surname appears first (in capital letters) followed by initials of forenames or given names.

Title is given as on page cited and not as appears on cover page. All three entries (a), (b) and (c) are interfiled. Most articles, therefore, can be approached through author, subject or title, whichever is known by the user.

Reference (II:17:13-15)
The Roman numerals indicate the volume number; this is separated from the issue number (Arabic numerals) by a colon: The last set of figures separated by a dash (-) indicates the inclusive paging of the article in the Legon Observer.

The year of publication is omitted from the reference. It is hoped that users can easily correlate the volume number and the year of publication:-

Volume	I/1966
"	II/1967
"	III/1968
"	IV/1969
"	V/1970
"	VI/1971
"	VII/1972
"	VIII/1973
"	IX/1974

2. Correspondence

The second section gives an author and title alphabetical listing of all the letters that appeared in the issues indexed.

3. News Summary

This "selective historical record" is presented as an alphabetical title listing. Some titles had to be permuted to aid reference.

4. Reviews

This is an author, or title listing in alphabetical order of all the books, films, plays, etc., that were reviewed in the issues indexed.

ACKNOWLEDGMENTS

I wish to thank the Balme Library and its current Librarian, Mr. J. M. Walpole, for financial assistance and encouragement, and also the Africana Library Staff who contributed in no small measure to the work, especially Misses Margaret Vowotor and Vivian Aminarh, and also Mr. Nartey. Mr. Essandoh and Mr. Afrane who typed the work deserve mention and last, but not the least, Bob Dadson who helped in every way imaginable to produce this work. My mistakes, however, are wholly mine.

Preface

ABBREVIATIONS USED IN THE INDEX

(ON) . . . . Observer Notebook entry.

(Ed.) . . . . Editorial or leading article.

(jt. au.) . . . . .Joint author.

Main Index

1

Main Index

A.A.S.U. launched in Kamasi. M. Mgxashe. VII:16:384-385.
ABABIO, L. N. K. Animal production in Ghana. 1) II:23:8-9; 2)
    II:24:5-7.
ABBAN, J. B. Fixed versus flexible exchange rates. VI:19:9-13.
ABBAN, J. B. and A. G. BLOMQVIST. More price controls in Ghana?
    VI:2:2-6.
ABBEY, J. L. F. The National Service Corps. V:4:5-7.
_____. The 1969 elections--A preliminary analysis: IV:19:2-4.
ABBEY, J. L. S. A country of two worlds. VI:14:x-xii.
ABBEY, J. L. S. and K. BREW. The unemployment problem. V:26:11-13.
Abbott case: A test of statesmanship. III:1:9-10. (ON).
Abbott-Ghana Agreement. See Ghana-Abbott Agreement.
Abe Fortas affair. IV:11:14-15. (ON).
Accra-Health or beauty. IV:5:14. (ON).
Accra-Tema City Council Area. II:17:17-18. (ON).
Accusation of extravagance at Legon. E. O. Dodoo. IV:8:16-18.
ACHAMPON-MANU, K. Ghana's economic problem and the new regime.
    V:2:3-4.
_____. The task ahead. IV:10:10-11.
ACHAMPONG, A. P. Africa's cultural freedom. VIII:8:184-185.
_____. Educating the "Masses." VII:20:470-474.
ACHEAMPONG, I. K. National Redemption Council Budget Statement
    1972/73. VII:19:459-462.
_____. Revaluation of the cedi and Ghana's external debts.
    VII:3:60-64.
ACKOM-MENSAH, I. Bouncing Cheques and the economy. V:22:10-15.
_____. Chieftaincy in crisis. II:7:9-10.
_____. Educational administration in Ghana. II:16:7-9.
ADALI-MORTTY, G. Change of government to the spoils system again?
    IX:4:79-80.
_____. The changing views on sovereignty. VII:3:49-50.
_____. Criteria and tests for measuring cabinet productivity.
    V:20:8-9.
_____. Danger signals before and after civilian take-over.
    II:20:17-19.
_____. Ideologies on sale--response to rejoinders. VIII:14:332-334.
_____. Ideologies on sale--whose do we buy? VIII:10:232-234.

_____. The incredible prosperity of Lebanon. VI:23:9-12.
_____. Industrial productivity: Soviet style. V:13:2-6.
_____. Old age discredited? VII:4:74-76.
_____. On "The Changing Views on Sovereignty." VII:6:144.
_____. Organising civil servants. VII:12:283-285.
_____. Our stand in the Arab-Israeli conflict. VIII:22:530-531.
_____. Reply to Dr. P. A. V. Ansah's rejoinder. IX:5:116.
_____. Reply to Kwabena Manu's rejoinder to "Change of Government to the spoils system again?" IX:7:166.
_____. The significance of President Losconczi's visit. VIII:24:566-568.
ADAM, B. Capital punishment--time to abolish it? V:3:7-8.
ADDAE, F. F. Collective security in Africa. VI:22:12-13.
ADDO, E. AKUFO. See Akufo-Addo, E.
ADDY, P. A. K. What the public should know about rabies. VII:26:615-618.
ADEGOROYE, V. A. Peace prospects in Nigeria. III:4:17-18.
ADEMOAWA, K. Conversations with Joe Apalahala: Of cricket and politics. V:13:29-30.
_____. Introducing Joe Apalahala. V:12:16-18.
ADJEI, B. The future of fee-free education in Ghana. IV:17:7-10.
ADJEI, K. Are we saving enough foreign exchange? III:18:4-6.
_____. The businessman and the "Little Budget." II:15:12-14.
_____. Implications of the 1970 Surcharge. V:22:2-10.
_____. Should unions be allowed to strike? III:20:12-14.
_____. The utilization of executive talents in a developing Ghana. II:16:10-12.
_____. Wage and salary increases--are they necessary? (and our economy). III:14:16-17.
ADJEI-BRENYAH, D. China and world peace. V:25:21.
_____. Dialogue and world peace. VI:4:16-17.
ADJIKU, W. K. Dialogue and world peace. VI:7:19-20.
Administering the bitter pill or lessons in government--A Correspondent. IX:13:298-302.
ADMINISTRATION
    ADALI-MORTTY, G. Organising Civil Servants. VII:12:283-285.
    ADJEI, K. The utilization of executive talents in a developing Ghana. II:16:10-12.
    ATSU, E. S. Regional planning practice in Ghana. V:21:8-11.
    Great purge. V:5:1-2. (Ed.).
    KUDIABOR, C. A new organization for development planning in Ghana. III:1:7-9.
    KWAMINA, A. Public servants or masters? II:16:14-15.
    NANOR, A. T. K. The training of local council staff in Ghana. V:16:9-10.
    NKRUMAH, S. A. The civil service and its masters. VIII:7:150-152.
        _____. Who advises the government? VIII:6:129-131.
    OFORI, I. M. Regional development planning in Ghana. III:8:5-6.

3

(ADMINISTRATION)

      Our civil servants. V:3:1-2. (Ed.).

      OWUSU, J. Y. Electoral registration system: its programme and principles. IV:2:7-9.

      PEASAH, J. Ministry of Rural Development. IV:9:12-13.

      Public Service. II:8:3-5.

      RADIX, A. Report of the Commission on the structure and remuneration of the Public Services in Ghana. 1) III:15:20-24; 2) III:16:13-16; 3) III:17:3-6.

      SAFO, D. B. Department of Post and Telecommunications. IV:11:6-7.

      ZUOLO, C. T. Civil servants and pay increase. VIII:11:251-253.

ADOMAKO, A. Ghana's foreign debts. II:19:8-10 [23-25].

ADOMAKO-BONSU. Some aspects of population growth and economic development in Ghana. VI:26:12-16.

ADU, K. SAFO. See Safo-Adu, K.

ADUAMAH, E. Y. The big dam. VI:4:20-22.

_____. The press after the coup. V:17:14-15.

Advanced Teacher Training College Course: A rejoinder. S. W. A. Rizvi. IV:5:7-9.

Advanced Teacher Training Course--Another stop-gap. G. K. Bluwey. III:26:19-20.

Advisory Committee. VII:4:88. (ON).

ADZOBU, C. DORM. See Dorm-Adzobu, C.

AFFUL, K. N. Unemployment in Ghana. 1) VII:11:254-258; 2) VII:12:279-282.

AFREH, K. An arsenal of laws for a would-be dictator. III:25:4-8.

_____. The Busia administration and the law. V:20:20-24.

_____. The exercise of discretionary powers under the new Constitution. IV:25:2-4.

_____. The future of the opposition. V:1:14-18.

_____. Law reform--Mr. Adade's formidable task. IV:9:8-11.

_____. The law's delays--and the high cost of litigation. IV:6:8-10.

_____. The laws of apartheid. VI:1:15-20.

_____. Lawyers in nation building. IX:5:104-111.

_____. Liberty of the press. VIII:8:178-181.

_____. Lt. General Afrifa and the constitution. V:17:2-8.

_____. The N. L. C. and the law. IV:22:11-14.

_____. The need for legal aid in Ghana. V:4:2-5.

_____. Organisational problems facing the opposition. V:23:13-18.

_____. The proof of corruption. IV:11:2-4.

_____. The role of the president under the constitution. V:12:2-5.

_____. The role of trade unions in Ghana. VII:11:258-261.

_____. Some factors which impede progress. VII:9:209-213.

_____. Some legal trends since the coup. VI:5:16-21.

_____. Some trends in criminal legislation since independence. 1) VIII:17:397-403; 2) VIII:18:427-435; 3) VIII:19:448-454.

_____. What does the N. R. C. stand for? VII:18:420-428.

Main Index

AFRICA
ACHAMPONG, A. P. Africa's cultural freedom. VIII:8:184-185.
ADDAE, F. F. Collective security in Africa. VI:22:12-13.
ANSAH, P. A. V. Francophone Africa after DeGaulle. IV:10:4-6.
ASAMOAH, O. Y. Towards the dignity of blackness. II:20:8-9.
ASANTE, S. K. B. Politics of confrontation: Background to
Africa's break with Israel. VIII:24:562-566.
ASSIMENG, M. Minority parties in Africa. V:23:3-6.
AYISI, A. A. Archaeology, anthropology and African history.
V:10:3-8.
Banda betrays Africa. II:7:14-15. (ON).
CAVANAGH, T. K. Rewriting African history. V:7:4-6.
Ghana's African friends. V:10:1-3. (Ed.).
GREENFIELD, R. Africanist after-thoughts and incidentalia --
Part I: Origins. III:4:10-11.
_____. Africanist after-thoughts and incidentalia -- Part II:
Dakar. III:5:3-6.
HESSE, F. Dr. Mondlane and the Mozambique liberation movement.
IV:4:22-25.
_____. The explosion of African studies. IV:20:8-12.
JONES-QUARTEY, K. A. B. One-Party States and the role of op-
position in contemporary Africa. V:26:4-8.
_____. Report from the West Coast -- personal account.
VI:9:14-18.
KUMAH, O. M. France and her African allies 1972-73: towards
disenchantment? VIII:25:586-591.
Lessons of the Middle East war for Africa--Correspondent.
IX:3:59-62.
LEWIS, A. The process of modernization. III:13:3-6.
_____. Socialism in Africa. III:12:7-10.
Mgxashe, M. A.A.S.U. launched in Kumasi. VII:16:384-385.
OBICHERE, B. I. Collective security in contemporary Africa.
VI:6:10-14.
PEASAH, J. A. Africa 1966. II:14:10-11.
PIPIM, A. Lessons in tolerance for Africa. IV:9:6-7.
SAFFU, Y. O. What has changed in Ghano-Ivoirien relations?
III:12:4-7.
Urgency of Co-operation in Africa. VIII:8:169-170. (Ed.).
Africa and relief for Biafra. IV:16:12-13. (ON).
Africa and the E. E. C. VIII:4:73-74. (Ed.).
Africa, Ghana and the Olympics. III:23:6-7. (ON).
Africa, Lonrho and Rowland. VIII:10:230-231. (ON).
African Airspace. VIII:9:202. (ON).
African in Latin-America. E. Ofori-Akyea. V:12:5-8.
African Ministers at Addis-Ababa. II:6:14. (ON).
African Theatre. J. S. Kennedy. IV:15:18-20.
African Theatre at the Algiers festival. J. S. Kennedy. IV:19:14-17.
African Universities and the Western tradition. L. H. Ofosu-Appiah.
1) II:22:7-9; 2) II:23:11-14.
Africanist after-thoughts and incidentialia--Part I: Origins. R.
Greenfield. III:4:10-11.

Africanist after-thoughts and incidentalia--Part II: Dakar. R.
    Greenfield. III:5:3-6.
Africa's cultural freedom. A. P. Achampong. VIII:8:184-185.
AFRIFA, A. A. Budget statement for 1967-68. II:17:7-12.
_____. The future of politics in Ghana (Supplement). II:22:ii-iv.
AFRIFA, [A. A.]. Interviewed. II:4:iv-vi.
Afrifa, Busia. "1966 before and after"--comment. A. A. Boahen.
    II:8:iv-vii.
Afrifa's economic philosophy. III:6:10-11. (ON).
Aftermath of Gbedemah's press conference. IV:7:18-19. (ON).
Aftermath of the Leventis deal. II:21:11-12. (ON).
AFUM-KARIKARI. My kind of leader. IV:5:6.
_____. The need for self-reliance. IV:12:5-6.
AGAMA, G. K. Alternative economic policy for Ghana. VI:21:4-10.
_____. Foundations of economic policy: 1) The State Enterprises.
    II:10:5-8.
_____. Foundations of economic policy: 2) Private Enterprises.
    II:13:6-8.
_____. Foundations of economic policy: 3) Foreign Aid. II:16:5-6.
_____. Ghanaian business today. II:19:17-19.
_____. On devaluation of the new cedi. II:15:3-6.
_____. A policy for the fishing industry. 1) II:1:2-3; 2) II:6:8-9.
_____. The trade fair and the economy. II:3:9-10.
AGAMA, K. The rains and the economy. III:19:3-4.
Agama. Congrats and sympathy. IV:25:12-13. (ON).
AGBEMAWOKLA, W. S. K. Shortages--what are the causes? VIII:5:105-106.
AGBLE, W. K. A look at Ghanaian agriculture today: the requirements,
    strategies and prospects. VII:14:322-330.
AGBOZO, K. Rural development and economic development. VII:10:231-233.
AGRICULTURE
        ABABIO, L. N. K. Animal production in Ghana. 1) II:23:8-9;
            2) II:24:5-7.
        AGBLE, W. K. A look at Ghanaian agriculture today: The re-
            quirements, strategies and prospects. VII:14:322-330.
        Agricultural mechanization in Ghana? V:19:2-4. (Ed.).
        Agriculture downwards again. IV:20:14. (ON).
        ATA, J. K. B. A. Food preservation--Use simple methods.
            VII:19:444-448.
        BORTEI-DOKU, E. Agricultural Education and extension in Ghana's
            economic development. VII:17:396-400.
            _____. Our agricultural extension service. III:1:2-3.
            _____. Reorganisation of the Ministry of Agriculture: posts,
            salaries and motivation. VIII:5:100-102.
        BUXTON, T. K. Ghana's agricultural policy and rural develop-
            ment. VI:7:9-11.
        DADZIE, K. G. Agriculture under the N. R. C. VIII:2:32-36.
            _____. Agriculture under the N. R. C.--Retrospect and prospect.
            IX:3:54-56.
        DOKU, E. V. Crop production in Ghana. II:21:7-9.
        DOKU, E. V. and MANTE, E. F. G. The "Oriental Cow"--Can't it
            also become the "Cow" of Tropical Africa? VIII:15:351-354.

AIDOO, E. S. The law's delays and the high cost of litigation--A re-
joinder. IV:9:20-22.
_____. Organising mass education. VIII:6:138.
_____. Slow justice: an introduction to a problem. V:5:4-12.
Aidoo report. VIII:20:481. (ON).
Aircraft vandals. IV:7:19-20. (ON).
Air-Marshall M. A. Otu's case. III:25:14-16. (ON).
Air-Marshall Otu. III:26:21-22. (ON).
AKPATA, T. Tragic illusions. III:3:2-4.
AKROFI, E. ASIEDU. See Asiedu-Akrofi, E.
AKUAMOAH-NKOUM, R. The I. L. O. and Ghanaian women workers. 1)
VII:1:9-11; 2) VII:7:161-165.
AKUFO-ADDO, E. Draft Constitution for Ghana. III:3:12-15.
AKYEA, E. OFORI. See Ofori-Akyea, E.
ALIENS
Early economic consequences of "quit" order. IV:26:18-21. (ON).
Grappling with aliens. IV:26:1-2. (Ed.).
HAKAM, A. N. Economic implications of the aliens order. V:6:2-4.
Immigrant population and the national interest. IV:2:1-2. (Ed.).
KONTOPIAAT, K. Who is a Ghanaian? V:3:16-19.
Who is an alien? VI:27:16-17. (ON).
All West Africa Media Seminar. VI:16:12-15.
Allowances, Salaries and hidden persuaders. VII:13:304-305. (ON).
Almost mobbing African unity away. VIII:4:88-89. (ON).
Alternative economic policy for Ghana. G. K. Agama. VI:21:4-10.
Alvin Ailey American Dance Theatre. M. Bossman. II:23:25-26.
AMAAH, G. K. A. OFOSU. See Ofosu-Amaah, G. K. A.
Ambassador Hotel. II:1:14. (ON).
AMEGASHIE, R. S. The Ghana-Abbott Agreement. II:25:18-25.
Amending the Constitution-Political Correspondent. 1) II:17:3-6;
2) II:18:3-4.
America at the Cross-roads--Political Correspondent. III:9:4-10.
American Negroes, Western radicals, African students and Nkrumah's
overthrow. II:22:10. (ON).
AMIN, IDDI DADA
ANSAH, P. A. V. Big Dada's histrionics. VIII:22:520-523.
President Amin, the Asians and Britain--A Political Correspon-
dent. VII:21:490-494.
el AMIN, R. N. The Asians in Uganda. VII:17:392-394.
AMONOO, R. F. Negritude in the 1970s. VI:19:i-viii.
AMPENE, E. First year Anniversary of "Legon Observer"--"The Social
Scene." II:14:12-13.
AMPENE, K. The third U.N.E.S.C.O. International conference on adult
education--Tokyo, July 25 to 7th August, 1972. VII:19:455-456.
AMPOFO, D. A. Ghanaian culture and the concept of small family-size.
IV:22:14-20.
AMPOMAH, R. A. Self-reliance and expatriate missionaries.
VIII:20:484-486.
AMPONSAH, F. Is there any salvation left? VII:5:102-104.
And it came to pass.... See Santrofi Epistles.

ANGOLA
      The M. P. L. A. and the Struggle in Angola. R. Lobban.
      VII:8:186-190.
Animal health and disease control in Ghana. E. N. W. Oppong.
   II:22:5-6.
Animal production in Ghana. L. N. K. Ababio. 1) II:23:8-9; 2)
   II:24:5-7.
ANKRAH, J. A. Broadcast...at the launching of the Centre for Civic
   Education. II:13:i-ii.
ANNAN, C. K. Implications of rural water development. III:19:4-6.
Anniversary Message--Four years of the "Legon Observer." V:14:1-2.
Anniversary of the Bolshevik Revolution. V:24:16-17. (ON).
Another attack on Ghana. IV:17:14. (ON).
Another round of debt negotiations? VIII:24:568-570. (ON).
Another view of family planning. K. Brew. VII:26:610-615.
ANSAH, P. A. V. Big Dada's histrionics. VIII:22:520-523.
_____. The Case of identity cards. VII:10:236-238.
_____. The constitutional impasse in Dahomey. III:15:24-28.
_____. Francophone Africa after DeGaulle. IV:10:4-6.
_____. Instant justice, rough and ready. IV:4:76-80.
_____. On party brigandage or the spoils system--A rejoinder to G.
   Adali-Mortty. IX:5:114-116.
_____. The press scene since February 1966. VIII:14:316-320.
_____. Registration and return to civilian rule. II:21:10-12.
ANSERE, J. K. The role of local government in nation building.
   V:3:i-viii.
ANSONG, C. LAWSON. See Lawson-Ansong, C.
Anti-bribery Commission. V:7:12-13. (ON).
Anti-Mosquito campaign. II:1:14. (ON).
APARTHEID
      ADJEI-BRENYA. Dialogue and world peace. VI:4:16-17.
      ADJIKU, W. K. Dialogue and world peace. VI:7:19-20.
      AFREH, K. The laws of apartheid. VI:1:15-20.
      APRONTI, J. Resistance to apartheid. VI:1:10-12.
      ASAMOAH, O. Y. Dialogue with South Africa--The Opposition's
         view. VI:1:29-32.
      Banda and apartheid. VI:11:24. (ON).
      BUSIA, K. A. Statement on South Africa...at the National
         Assembly. VI:1:20-23.
      Dialogue on dialogue. V:26:1-2. (Ed.).
      GREENFIELD, R. The early roots of apartheid. VI:1:4-9.
      JONES-QUARTEY, K. A. B. Houphouetism and the dialogue debate--
         A commentary. VI:10:i-iv.
      _____. "Houphouetism" and dialogue II. VI:11:8-10.
      MANTE, E. F. G. What is respect? VI:7:18-19.
      OBICHERE, B. I. Apartheid in Zimbabwe (Rhodesia). VI:1:12-15.
      OPPON-AGYARE, J. South Africa's apartheid: an invitation to
         blood-bath. V:15:7-10.
      WIREDU, J. E. "Dialogue" as a problem. VI:1:23-29.
Apartheid and the U. N. III:24:10. (ON).
Apartheid brutalities. VI:23:20. (ON).

Apartheid wages. VIII:7:159-160. (ON).
Apathy in Armed Forces and Police? IV:1:9. (ON).
APPIAH, J. The fall of the curtain and some reflections on a constitution for Ghana--an extract. IX:9:208-211.
APPIAH, L. GYESI. See Gyesi-Appiah, L.
APPIAH, L. H. OFOSU. See Ofosu-Appiah, L. H.
Appointment of commissioners and assignment of portfolios. II:14:18.
Appollo 13 episode. V:9:15. (ON).
Approaching sell-out. VI:24:18. (ON).
APRONTI, J. The debate on ideology. VIII:19:461-463.
_____. The fate of non-alignment. V:9:8-10.
_____. India, Ideology and hunger. VI:5:21-24.
_____. Nkrumah and the building of Socialism. VII:9:208.
_____. Racial discrimination in America. V:22:16-18.
_____. Resistance to apartheid. VI:1:10, 12.
_____. Taxi rates: a bad case of capitulation. VIII:9:208-210.
_____. To Uli and back. VII:22:530-532.
Archaeology, anthropology and African history. A. A. Ayisi. V:10:3-8.
ARCHAMPONG, K., et al. K. A. Gbedemah's press conference--a report and analysis. IV:7:15-17.
ARCHER, J. P. Reform of the law of succession. IX:13:302-308.
Are some books being banned? (ON). III:25:16.
Are the Abbott criticisms really sincere? P. T. K. Aidam. II:26:10-11.
Are we saving enough foreign exchange? K. Adjei. III:18:4-6.
ARHIN, K. Behind the Asantehene's Majesty. V:21:5-8.
_____. Institutionalized sycophancy--gains and costs. IX:14:330-334.
_____. Joe Appiah's future constitution. IX:10:238-240.
_____. Kwadwo Kwa's manifesto. II:22:20-21.
_____. Mr. Kwesi Lamptey and the P. D. A. threat. VI:3:2-4.
_____. Urgently needed--a genuine revolution. VI:24:4-6.
_____. Why should we let sleeping dogs lie? IV:23:11-12.
_____. Withdrawal of scholarships. II:7:20-21.
Aristotle on Ghana (African) Politics. B. D. G. Folson. III:2:22-23.
ARKU, D. (jt. au.). See Ghartey, A.
Arms and the Commonwealth. VI:3:7-8. (ON).
Army changes. Kontopiaat. II:10:21.
Arrogance of power. V:4:14-15. (ON).
Arsenal of laws for a would-be dictator. K. Afreh. III:25:4-8.
ASAMOAH, E. K. What type of teacher? II:22:17-18.
ASAMOAH, O. Y. America in agony. III:8:6-8.
_____. Czechoslovakia raped again. III:18:6-7.
_____. Dialogue with South Africa--The Opposition view. VI:1:29-32.
_____. The O. A. U. Achievements and failures. II:18:4-6.
_____. Policy differences between government and opposition. V:23:6-13.
_____. South east Asian trial of strength. III:4:21-22.
_____. Towards the dignity of blackness. II:20:8-9.
ASANTE, S. K. B. Africa in the United Nations. VII:22:514-519.
_____. The birth of the O. A. U.: the early years. VIII:10:218-223.
_____. A decade of the O. A. U. Liberation Committee. VIII:2:36-38.

_____. The Garveys and the Back-to-Africa Movement: A retrospective view. VIII:21:506-508.
_____. The O. A. U. at 10: Progress and problems. VIII:11:242-247.
_____. Pan-Africanism revisited: The road to Addis-Ababa. VIII:9:194-198.
_____. The policy of non-alignment in the changing world. VIII:19:447-448.
_____. Politics of confrontation: Background to Africa's break with Israel. VIII:24:562-566.
_____. Politics of racial discrimination: fourteen years after Sharpeville. IX:7:161-164.
_____. The significance of the tenth anniversary Summit meeting of the O. A. U. VIII:12:266-269.
_____. Twenty-five years of the United Nations and human rights: an African viewpoint. VIII:25:591-596.
_____. The United Nations: twenty-eight years of trial. VIII:22:514-518.
_____. Year of African solidarity: The O. A. U. at eleven. IX:12:278-283.
Asantehene's funeral. VI:26:17-18. (ON).
Ashiaman--Eyesore and opportunity. M. Peil. V:18:4-6.
ASHITEY, G. A. The Report of the Committee on the health needs of Ghana (1968). IV:24:16-18.
_____. What I think. III:21:18-19.
ASHUN, C. K. The High cost of imported goods. VI:25:17-18.
_____. Problems of an incomes policy in Ghana. VII:25:594-596.
_____. The Role of the church in development. VII:7:158-161.
Asians in Uganda. R. N. el Amin. VII:17:392-394.
ASIEDU-KROFI, E. Cape Coast University--A rejoinder. V:13:16-18.
Aspects of political behaviour. P. Gamesu. VI:5:10-16.
Assassination--an American art. J. Bruchac. III:13:6-8.
ASSIMENG, M. The Budget and social justice. VI:17:8-12.
_____. Catholic laity in search of role. VI:23:15-18.
_____. The Colonel's dispensation. IV:21:4-8.
_____. Confusion among the Saints: The Aladura controversy. VI:15:13-16.
_____. The Dilemma of Christian missions in Africa. II:5:17-19.
_____. Dilemma of unfulfilled prophecies. IV:25:9-10.
_____. Edward Heath and Africa. V:14:12-14.
_____. The Electoral panorama. IV:18a:3-6.
_____. Ghana's political "Sects"--and their mission. IV:11:4-6.
_____. The Great experiment. IV:18:4-8.
_____. Is Busia a politician? V:20:5-8.
_____. Jehovah's witnesses and the millenium. V:2:12-14.
_____. Kwame Nkrumah: the incredible Messiah. VII:9:205-206.
_____. Legon: the frustrated tribe. V:7:8-10.
_____. Minority Parties in Africa. V:23:3-6.
_____. The Parties testaments. IV:17:3-5.
_____. Politics and ideological portraits. IV:13:6-8.
_____. The Prospects of the Parties. IV:16:2-6.

Beer bottles and conditional sales. II:13:12. (ON).
Behave or else. III:18:8-10. (ON).
Behind the Asantehene's Majesty. K. Arhin. V:21:5-8.
BEKOE, D. A. Legon's role in the development of Geological studies
    in Ghana--A rejoinder. VIII:9:206-208.
Belief in God--replies (1) P. Barker. II:1:9-10.
Belief in God--replies (2) F. I. D. Konotey-Ahulu. II:1:10-13.
Belief in God--reply to my critics. J. Thrower. II:3:16-18.
BEN-JIB, M. K. Clear course for Ghana. VII:16:388-390.
BENTSI-ENCHILL, K. Institution-building in Ghana and Nigeria: A
    summary of proceedings. 1) II:13:3-6; 2) II:15:7-8; 3) II:17:15-17;
    4) II:18:8-10.
Bentsi-Enchill on the institutional challenges of our time--A Corre-
    spondent. 1) VI:8:4-6; 2) VI:9:2-4; 3) VI:10:2-6.
BENZANSON, K. A. Educational reforms--A rejoinder. VII:24:581-583.
Berry Cure for diabetes?--Don't believe it. K. K. Oduro. VI:20:9-10.
Biafra--a peoples' right to exist. K. Bediako. IV:2:4-6.
Biafra--a peoples' right to exist--A rejoinder. K. Marfo. IV:6:4-6.
Biafra and Nigeria--facts on territorial integrity. S. O. Nwafor.
    IV:23:13-14.
Biafra: the politics of relief agencies. E. Ofori-Akyea. V:4:8-9.
Big Dada's histrionics. P. A. V. Ansah. VIII:22:520-523.
Big Dada's histrionics--A comment. K. Jonah. VIII:23:558-559.
Big dam. E. Y. Aduamah. VI:4:20-22.
Bing on education. Serpentarius. IV:1:4-7.
BIOBAKU (S. O.) interviewed. V:12:i-viii.
Birth of the O. A. U.: the early years. S. K. B. Asante.
    VIII:10:218-223.
Bishops and rebels in Rhodesia. V:9:15-16. (ON).
BISUE, I. The devaluation of the New Cedi: Whose responsibility?
    VI:27:4-5.
_____. The Economic Community of West Africa. II:19:12-15.
Black folks--discovering each other's humanity. J. S. Kennedy.
    IV:14:21-22.
Black power and the Caribbean. Political Correspondent. V:10:12-14.
Black Stars and Sudan Affair. V:5:20. (ON).
Black tourists among us. VIII:14:326-327. (ON).
BLACKIE, N. These charter flights. VIII:6:141-142.
_____. The youth and the national revolution. VII:8:190-192.
BLANKSON, C. C. T. Development from the grass-roots. VII:22:520-522.
_____. Urban planning: towards better city centres. VIII:12:269-271.
BLOMQVIST, A. G. (jt. au.) See Abban, J. B.
_____. (jt. au.) See Kwarteng, K.
BLUWEY, G. K. The Advanced Teacher Training Course--Another stop-gap.
    III:26:19-20.
BOAFO, S. T. The press, the government and the people. IX:7:150-156.
_____. Road safety: some facts and figures. IX:10:225-226.
BOAHEN, A. A. Afrifa, Busia, "1966 before and after"--comment.
    II:8:iv-vii.
BOAHEN, A. The Changing views on sovereignty--A rejoinder. VII:4:70-73.

_____. The new crop of politicians and the military. IV:18a:6-20.
BOATENG, J. K. Bouncing cheques and the economy--A comment.
V:24:14.
BONSU, ADOMAKO. See Adomako-Bonsu.
BOOHENE, E. H. A reply to your Editorial dated 23 June-6 July 1967.
II:14:17-18.
Border Guards. II:16:12. (ON).
BORTEI-DOKU, E. Agricultural education and extension in Ghana's
economic development. VII:17:396-400.
_____. Our Agricultural extension services. III:1:2-3.
_____. Re-organisation of the Ministry of Agriculture: posts,
salaries and motivation. VIII:5:100-102.
BOSSMAN, M. The Alvin Ailey American Dance Theatre. II:23:25-26.
_____. Tribalism in Ghana? II:15:20-21.
Bouncing Cheques and the economy. I. Ackom-Mensah. V:22:10-15.
Bouncing Cheques and the economy--A comment. J. K. Boateng. V:24:14.
BOYE, C. Soccer league system needs recasting. VIII:13:304-305.
Brain crisis in the teaching profession. N. K. Dzobo. III:6:3-4.
"Brain Drain" conference. II:18:12-13. (ON).
Brain drain from the less developed countries. J. A. Agyare.
III:23:11-12.
Brazil, Portugal, Africa and the U. N. VII:24:570. (ON).
BRENYAH, D. ADJEI. See Adjei-Brenyah, D.
BREW, K. (jt. au). See Abbey, J. L. S.
BREW, K. Another view of family planning. VII:26:610-615.
BREW, K. Misconceptions about family planning--Some observations.
V:24:20-21.
_____. Preview of the budget. V:18:2-4.
Bribery and corruption. VII:3:55-56. (ON).
Brigadier Afrifa's 'Cabinet'. IV:9:13-14. (ON).
Brigadier Afrifa's comment. III:3:15-16.
Brigadier Afrifa's salary increases. III:10:8. (ON).
Britain and Ian Smith. IV:13:13-14. (ON).
Britain: the last days of a Giant. IV:7:19. (ON).
BRITISH COMMONWEALTH
Astronomy according to Austin or the Commonwealth in Eclipse.
Political Correspondent. 1) VII:6:130-134; 2) VII:10:233-234.
Commonwealth in recurrent crisis. VI:2:1-2. (Ed.).
Commonwealth: myth and reality. VIII:17:393-394. (Ed.).
KARIKARI, K. A. Britain's central position within the multi-
racial Commonwealth. V:17:15-17.
MUANGE, E. A. A sketch of the growth of the British Common-
wealth. III:19:18-19.
The Phoney Conference? IV:3:10. (ON).
British probity, Corruption and the Nkrumah Regime. II:3:12-13. (ON).
BRITWUM, A. On having learnt to serve one's masters. (A. N. Mensah
"Talking about Jawa's Poem"). VII:13:314.
Broadcast by Lt. Gen. J. A. Ankrah...at the launching of the Centre
for Civic Education on 7th June, 1967. II:13:i-ii.
Broadcast speech by the Chairman of the National Liberation Council on
22nd May, 1968. III:12:22.

BROOKS, R. G. Financing health services. VIII:25:596-601.
_____. The Hospital fees report. VIII:23:538-544.
BRUCE, I. K. The problem of unemployment in Ghana. 1) IV:4:11-21;
    2) IV:5:2-4.
BRUCE, K. The import surcharge and the economic administration of
    Ghana. IV:6:6-8.
BRUCE-KONUAH, W. G. Interviewed by K. Arhin. VI:20:i-viii.
BRUCHAC, J. Assassination--An American art. III:13:6-8.
BRUGGER, C. The conversion of the journalists: A legend of modern
    times. II:14:22-23.
Budget and public morality--A Correspondent. VI:20:8-9.
Budget and social justice. M. Assimeng. VI:17:8-12.
Budget and taxation. G. A. Donkor. IV:16:8-9.
Budget and the Surcharges--A rejoinder. K. Ahiakpor. V:24:10-14.
Budget statement for 1967-68. A. A. Afrifa. II:17:7-12.
BULLEY, A. K. University entrance and guidance in schools.
    VIII:23:544-546.
Bush fires in Ghana. J. M. Lock. IX:12:270-274.
BUSIA, K. A. One year after the coup. (main points). II:8:ii-iv.
_____. [P. M.'s fiscal and monetary measures.] VII:1:16-17.
_____. Press Conference on the Centre for Civic Education.
    II:13:ii-iv.
_____. Statement on South Africa...at the National Assembly on
    Thursday, 10th December, 1970. VI:1:20-23.
BUSIA, K. A.
    AFREH, K. Busia administration and the law. VI:20:20-24.
    ASSIMENG, M. Is Busia a politician? V:20:5-8.
    BOAHEN, A. A. "Afrifa, Busia, 1966 before and after"--comment.
        II:8:iv-vii.
    Busia [K. A.] interviewed. III:15:12-20.
    Busia's overseas trip. IV:23:14.
    DORVLO, K. Nkrumah and Busia. VII:4:76-78.
    EDUCAT. Gbedemah, the N.L.C., Busia and the Volta Region.
        IV:22:6-11.
    GAMESU, P. An open letter to Dr. Busia. V:9:22.
    HESSE, F. Busia's style of administration. V:1:8-12.
    KONTOPIAAT, K. Busialogy. V:20:28-30.
    _____. Which way Dr. Progress Busia? V:25:18-22.
    OFORI-AKYEA, E. Busia and the youth. V:20:4-5.
    P. M. and the judges. V:9:10-12. (ON).
    P. M. and the rule of law. V:8:16-17. (ON).
    P. M. in London and New York. V:23:18-19. (ON).
    SARPONG, K. A. Busia and the new politics. V:20:9-13.
BUSINESS EDUCATION
    ACKOM-MENSAH I. Educational administration in Ghana.
        II:16:7-9.
    AIDAM, P. T. K. Some misgivings about the present state of the
        Accountancy profession in Ghana--A rejoinder. IX:1:14-16.
    DANIEL, E. Business education in Ghana. VIII:14:328-332.
    _____. Business education in Ghana--A reply to Messrs. Arku
        and Ghartey. VIII:17:414-415.
    GHARTEY, A. and D. ARKU. Business education in Ghana--A com-
        ment. VIII:17:411-414.

(BUSINESS EDUCATION)
> GHARTEY, A. Education for Accountancy in Ghana.
> > VIII:21:498-501.
> > _____. The fourth year Accounting course at Legon. IX:336-340.
> > _____. Report of the Committee on the establishment of a School
> > for training Accountants and other related professionals--A
> > comment. VIII:20:473-478.
> > _____. Some misgivings about the present state of the Accoun-
> > tancy profession in Ghana--Reply to a rejoinder. IX:3:70-71.

BUSINESS MANAGEMENT
> DOVLO, M. Is the corporate image necessary? VIII:16:376-378.

Businessman and the "little budget." K. Adjei. II:15:12-14.
BUXTON, T. H. Ghana's one-year development plan: July 1970 to June
> 1971. VI:2:6-7.
BUXTON, T. K. Ghana's agricultural policy and rural development.
> VI:7:9-11.
> _____. The increase in producer prices: A comment. VIII:22:523-524.
> _____. The increase in the cocoa producer price--A comment.
> VIII:21:497-498.
C. I. A. and Western intellectuals. II:7:12-14. (ON).
Cabinet reshuffle: A commentary. P. Gamesu. VI:4:5-8.
Caetano's visit to Britain. VIII:15:357-358. (ON).
CAIQUO, B. W. K. The devaluation debate: stronger evidence needed.
> VIII:13:299-300.
Cairo Conference. II:8:10. (ON).
Call for the return of the Regalia. IX:4:84-86. (ON).
Campbell and the N. L. C. IV:9:14. (ON).
CAPE COAST UNIVERSITY
> ASIEDU-AKROFI, E. Cape Coast University--A rejoinder.
> > V:13:16-18.
> The Cape Coast University affair. IV:17:12-14. (ON).
> Cape Coast University College again. V:1:7-8. (ON).
> KARIKARI, K. A. University of Cape Coast: A unique experiment.
> > V:8:9-11.
> OBESE-JECTY, K. A. B.Sc. Degree Examination results in the
> > University College of Cape Coast. IV:17:11.
> SAFO, D. B. The economic impact of the University on Cape
> > Coast town. VIII:16:373-376.
Capital punishment--time to abolish it? B. Adam. V:3:7-8.
Capitalism, Socialism and Ghana--Political Correspondent.
> VIII:15:358-362.
Careless driving. II:4:21-22. (ON).
Case for a press trust again. J. Oppong-Agyare. VII:13:294-297.
Case for disfranchisement and disqualification. L. H. Ofosu-Appiah.
> II:24:7-9.
Case for identity cards. P. A. V. Ansah. VII:10:236-238.
Case for increasing Cocoa producer price in Ghana. P. Osei-Kwame and
> G. N. Murphy. VIII:20:466-473.
Case of Seyoum Sabat. II:12:13-14. (ON).
Case of the dismissals. V:5:2-3 (L. S. N. A. Communication).

16

CASTAGNO, M. F. The Third Woman. IV:4:iii-vii.
Catholic laity in search of role. M. Assimeng. VI:23:15-18.
Caution on the creation of a national youth organization. A. Koi-Larbi. VIII:24:581-583.
Cautionary hints on state take-over bids. Gematuxo. VII:20:474-476.
CAVANAGH, T. K. Rewriting African history? V:7:4-6.
Cedis, pesewas and £ s. d. III:3:6-7. (ON).
CENTRE FOR CIVIC EDUCATION
    ANKRAH, J. A. Broadcast...at the launching of the Centre for Civic Education. II:13:i-ii.
    BUSIA, K. A. Press Conference on the Centre for Civic education. II:13:ii-vi.
    Centre for Civic Education. II:14:13-14. (ON).
    Centre for Civic Education. V:2:11-12. (ON).
    OPPON-AGYARE, J. The Centre and its critics. III:22:24-26.
CHAMBERS, G. On the implications of the devaluation. VII:1:2-5.
Change of government to the spoils system again? G. Adali-Mortty. IX:4:79-80.
Changes in Poland. VI:2:9-10. (ON).
Changes in policies. K. Manu. VII:5:98-100.
Changing views on sovereignty. G. Adali-Mortty. VII:3:49-50.
Changing views on sovereignty--A rejoinder. A. Boahen. VII:4:70-73.
CHAUDHURY, D. S. A note on rehabilitation in leprosy. VI:7:20-21.
CHE GUEVARA. See Guevara, Ernesto Che.
Czechoslovakia and world public opinion. K. Nkansa-Kyeremateng. IV:5:9-10.
Chief Justice on the rule of law. A. Koi-Larbi. VIII:21:491-493.
Chieftaincy. VIII:1:16. (ON).
Chieftaincy disputes in Bolgatanga. B. L. J. Kumasi. VI:3:16-17.
Chieftaincy in crisis. I. Ackom-Mensah. II:7:9-10.
Chieftaincy in crisis. S. O. Gyandoh. II:2:6-8.
China and world peace. D. Adjei-Brenyah. V:25:21.
Chinese representation question in retrospect and prospect. R. Simmonds. VI:23:4-9.
Choice of Freedom. J. Kwadu. II:5:15-17.
Choreography in traditional dances. F. Nii-Yartey. VIII:6:126-129.
Christian thinks aloud at Christmas. C. R. Gaba. IV:26:10-14.
Christmas in Kontopiaatkrom. Kontopiaat. V:1:21-22.
CHUKWUKERE, B. I. Conflict of idealism and realism: Nigeria-Biafran war. II:24:2-5.
_____. Nigeria--the utopian case in Ghana. III:19:10-12.
Church and education in Ghana. N. K. Dzobo. III:22:4-6.
Church and state in school management. N. K. Dzobo. IV:11:7-10.
CIVIC EDUCATION
    GEMATUXO, A. Problems of meritocracy. II:14:21.
Civil Commissioners. II:14:13. (ON).
CIVIL ENGINEERING
    BLANKSON, C. C. T. Urban planning towards better city centres. VIII:12:269-271.
    VORKEH, E. K. Solving the transport problem in Accra. 1) VIII:13:294-296; 2) VIII:15:348-351; 3) VIII:16:378-382.
Civil servants and pay increase. C. T. Zuolo. VIII:11:251-253.

Civil service and its masters. S. A. Nkrumah. VIII:7:150-152.
Civil Service week. IX:14:340-342. (ON).
Civilian coup in Lesotho. V:4:17-18. (ON).
Clash of personalities in Africa. II:1:13. (ON).
Clear course for Ghana. M. K. Ben-Jib. VIII:16:388-390.
Closure of the A. T. T. C. IV:7:17-18. (ON).
Cocoa marketing. R. A. Kotey. VI:24:14-15.
Code of conduct for Commissioners. IV:15:11-12. (ON).
Cold war and agriculture. III:18:8. (ON).
Collective security in Africa. F. F. Addae. VI:22:12-13.
Collective security in contemporary Africa. B. I. Obichere.
    VI:6:10-14.
Colonel's dispensation. M. Assimeng. IV:21:4-8.
Colonial mentality or inferiority complex? VII:16:379. (ON).
Colonialism reappraised? IV:20:13-14. (ON).
Combating Crime. V:25:16-17. (ON).
Coming famine season. M. Ray. III:24:16-18.
Coming search in Ghana. I. M. Ofori. VII:5:100-102.
Commanding heights of the economy and the mineral industries.
    L. A. K. Quashie. VII:16:366-371.
Comment on the current cocoa price. J. N. Seward. VI:10:13-14.
Comment on the current economic situation--A Correspondent.
    VII:2:26-30.
Commentary: J. H. Mensah's "The wealth of the nation." VI:18:2-5.
Commission on Land Tenure. I. M. Ofori. II:21:10.
Commonwealth games results. V:16:17. (ON).
Commonwealth of Nations. See British Commonwealth.
Communist world. III:19:8. (ON).
Comprehending Comprehensive education. D. M. Paintin. VII:13:298-300.
Confederation of Arab Republics. VI:19:14. (ON).
Conference report: Agriculture within and without the groves of
    academe. J. Gordon. VI:12:9-10.
Conflict of idealism and realism: Nigerian-Biafran war. B. I.
    Chukwukere. II:24:2-5.
Conflicting statements on public policy. V:4:14. (ON).
Confusion among the Saints: the Aladura controversy. M. Assimeng.
    VI:15:13-16.
Congo again. II:14:15. (ON).
Congo in turmoil again. II:17:18-19. (ON).
Congratulations, Chief Electrical Engineer. II:6:15. (ON).
Congratulations, Mister Ian Smith! V:6:10. (ON).
Conscience on trial. VI:25:19. (ON).
Consequences of Repudiation. VII:7:165-166. (ON).
Constituent Assembly. II:26:20-21. (ON).
Constitutional impasse in Dahomey. P. A. V. Ansah. III:15:24-28.
CONSTITUTIONS
        AKUFO-ADDO, E. Draft Constitution for Ghana. III:3:12-15.
        Amending the Constitution. Political Correspondent. 1)
            II:17:3-6; 2) II:18:3-4.

APPIAH, J.   The fall of the curtain and some reflections on a
   Constitution for Ghana--An extract.   IX:9:208-211.
ARHIN, K.   Joe Appiah's future Constitution.   IX:10:238-240.
Constitutional Proposals.   III:3:1-2.   (Ed.).
Decentralization and local government.   Political Correspondent.
   1) II:11:2-4; 2) II:16:3-4.
Executive.   Political Correspondent.   II:6:3-6.
FOLSON, B. D. G.   Ratifying the Draft Constitution.   IV:16:6-8.
Fundamental rights.   Political Correspondent.   1) II:4:2-4; 2)
   II:5:3.
Ghana's constitutional milestones.   V:17:1-2.   (Ed.).
GYANDOH, S. O.   Judicial review under the proposed Constitution:
   A critique.   III:5:6-8.
_____.   On a future Constitution for Ghana.   IX:11:254-256.
_____.   The President and the delegation of power.   VI:7:2-6.
KOILLARBI, A.   Joe Appiah on a Constitution for Ghana--A review.
   IX:8:178-182.
KONTOPIAAT.   Rule of law and a regime of judges?   III:6:17-20.
KONTOPIAAT, K.   An open letter to the members of the Constituent
   Assembly.   1) IV:2:21-22; 2) IV:3:18-20; 3) IV:4:30.
Legislature.   Political Correspondent.   II:10:3-4.
PEASAH, J. A.   The presidency under Ghana's new constitution.
   IV:19:5-7.
Presidency under the proposed Constitution.   1) III:5:1-2.
   (Ed.); 2) III:6:1-2.   (Ed.).
Public Service.   Political Correspondent.   II:8:3-5.
SAFFU, Y. O.   The proposed constitution--A riposte to the Re-
   publican Constitution.   III:5:8-12.
Suggested amendments to the Draft Constitution.   III:26:8-16.
Three Constitutional decrees.   A. Radix.   III:4:5-9.
Consulting public opinion.   VII:26:620-622.   (ON).
Containing Dubcek.   V:3:8-10.   (ON).
Control of the Economy and Ghanaian Entrepreneurs.   VII:12:285-286.
   (ON).
Conversation or confrontation.   K. Yawson.   IV:24:4-6.
Conversations with Joe Apalahala.   I. of Cricket and politics.   K.
   Ademoawa.   V:13:29-30.
Conversion of the journalists: a legend of modern times.   C. Brugger.
   II:14:22-23.
Correlation equal to one?   IV:5:13-14.   (ON).
Cost of owning a vehicle.   III:20:20.   (ON).
Costs, prices and profits.   VI:12:20.   (ON).
Country of two words.   J. L. S. Abbey.   VI:14:x-xii.
Courtesy calls.   II:2:11.   (ON).
Crime.   II:3:15.   (ON).
Crime Problem.   D. N. A. Nortey.   V:25:9-13.
Crime wave.   III:20:17-18.   (ON).
Criminal Code (Amendment) Bill, 1971:   An exercise in excessive
   caution?   1) VI:19:2-6; 2) VI:20:4-5.
Crisis in Arts subjects in Ghana.   L. H. Ofosu-Appiah.   IV:2:10-13.

Crisis in Pakistan. A. Kumar. VI:8:6-9.
Crisis of British policy in Southern Rhodesia. Y. Manu. VII:4:78-80.
Criteria and tests for measuring Cabinet productivity. G. Adali-
    Mortty. V:20:8-9.
Critics and sycophants. VI:21:14. (ON).
Crop production in Ghana. E. V. Doku. II:21:7-9.
Crusade on indiscipline. VI:5:24-25. (ON).
CUDJOE, J. E. The minerals industry in Ghana. II:16:18-20.
CUKWURAH, A. O. We have no alternative. V:1:3-4.
Czechoslovakia raped again. O. Y. Asamoah. III:18:6-7.
DADSON, J. A. Strategy for economic recovery: The 1967/68 budget.
    II:17:13-15.
DADZE, K. G. Agriculture under the N. R. C. VIII:2:32-36.
_____. Agriculture under the N. R. C.--Retrospect and prospect.
    IX:3:54-56.
DAHOMEY
        ANSAH, P. A. V. The Constitutional impasse in Dahomey.
            III:15:24-28.
Dahomey: Now a Presidential Troika. V:11:22-24. (ON).
Dahomey's chain of coups. IV:26:22. (ON).
DAKE, J. M. The road to African Unity. II:22:19-20.
DAKUBU, S. Atomic energy in Ghana: A review of the Report of the
    Review Committee of Enquiry into the Atomic Reactory Project.
    IX:4:92-94.
DAMPTEY, N. W. Physical planning in Ghana at the crossroads.
    VI:13:5-8.
Danger signals before and after civilian take-over. G. Adali-Mortty.
    II:20:17-19.
Dangers of tribalism. W. E. A. Osei. V:17:8-10.
DANIEL, E. Business education in Ghana. VIII:14:328-332.
_____. Business education in Ghana--A reply to Messrs. Arku and
    Ghartey. VIII:17:414-415.
DANQUAH, J. B.
        J. B. Danquah--an appreciation. L. H. Ofosu-Appiah.
            IV:4:i-viii.
Date of a return to civilian rule. II:11:9. (ON).
DATE-BAH, E. The need for sociological research in Ghanaian industries.
    VI:3:4-6.
DATE-BAH, S. K. The matrimonial causes bill 1971. VI:12:2-5.
D'AUROCH, C. The Mali coup. III:25:12-14.
_____. O. A. U. Summit Conference 1968. III:20:14-16.
Day Kontopiaatkrom stood still. K. Kontopiaat. VII:3:65-66.
Death of a hero. IV:10:13-14. (ON).
Death of Karume. VII:8:192. (ON).
Death sentence for armed robbers. VII:3:58. (ON).
Debate on ideology. J. Apronti. VIII:19:461-463.
Debate on Press trust. V:25:16. (ON).
Debt repudiation and some allied measures. VII:5:116. (ON).
Decade of the O. A. U. Liberation committee. S. K. B. Asante.
    VIII:2:36-38.
Decentralization and local government--Political Correspondent. 1)
    II:11:2-4; 2) II:16:3-4.

Declaration of Assets. VI:2:11-12. (ON).
Decline in Ghana sports. III:12:12. (ON).
DEKU, (A. K.) Interviewed. 1) III:16:6-12; 2) II:4:iii-iv.
Demographic situation and Ghana population policy. S. K. Gaisie.
 IV:12:i-iv.
Department of Post and Telecommunications. D. B. Safo. IV:11:6-7.
Departmental heads and international conferences. II:21:11. (ON).
Devaluation and economic growth: A comment. N. Ahmad.
 VIII:10:223-226.
Devaluation and our students overseas. II:21:12. (ON).
Devaluation and the economy. VI:27:15-16. (ON).
Devaluation debate. M. D. Steur. VIII:12:273-274.
Devaluation debate--A few questions to Steur and Ahmad--Economic
 Correspondent. VIII:11:254-257.
Devaluation debate--A reply. N. Ahmad. VIII:12:274-279.
Devaluation debate: Stronger evidence needed. B. W. K. Caiquo.
 VIII:13:299-300.
Devaluation gives me a blow. Kontopiaat. II:19:26.
Devaluation of the Franc. IV:17:16-17. (ON).
Devaluation of the New Cedi: Whose responsibility? I. Bissue.
 VI:27:4-5.
Devaluation revisited. Economic Correspondent. VIII:13:300-304.
Development from the grass roots. C. C. T. Blankson. VII:22:520-522.
Development in Kontopiaatkrom. K. Kontopiaat. V:8:22.
Development planning. A. Lewis. III:11:3-6.
Development through self-help. VI:9:21-22. (ON).
Development without Planning--Correspondent. VII:5:104-108.
DIALOGUE (with S. Africa).
 For more articles on this subject - See Apartheid.
 Dialogue and world peace. D. Adjei-Brenya. VI:4:16-17.
 Dialogue and world peace. W. K. Adjiku. VI:7:19-20.
 Dialogue as a problem. J. E. Wiredu. VI:1:23-29.
 Dialogue on discipline. K. Kontopiaat. VI:12:23-24.
 Dialogue with South Africa--the Opposition's view. O. Y.
 Asamoah. VI:1:29-32.
DICKSON, A. Teachers and the Secondary Schools. II:15:8-10.
DICKSON, K. B. Need for a comprehensive land-use plan. II:4:10-11.
Dictatorship of referees. Kontopiaat. III:17:14-15.
Dilemma of Christian missions in Africa. J. M. Assimeng. II:5:17-19.
Dilemma of Ghanaian journalists. K. Poku. IX:14:326-330.
Dilemma of Israel--Political Correspondent. V:15:10-12.
Dilemma of unfulfilled prophesies. M. Assimeng. IV:25:9-10.
Discoverer of Aggrey. II:15:15. (ON).
Disfranchisement and disqualification--Radix answered. Y. Kobli.
 II:24:23-27.
Disgorging ill-gotten gains. II:8:9. (ON).
Disqualification and public office. III:15:5. (ON).
Disqualification issue resolved. III:3:5-6. (ON).
Disqualification of C. P. P. officials. II:18:10. (ON).
Dissipating the Lincolnite's Lincoln. II:18:12. (ON).
Distribution of the wealth of the nation. Q. Pepee. VI:14:ix-x.

District and Local Councils. S. N. Woode. VI:6:8-10.
Dr. Kaunda and Ghana again. IV:19:9. (ON).
Dr. Mondlane and the Mozambique liberation movement. F. Hesse.
    IV:4:22-25.
DODOO, E. O. The accusation of extravagance at Legon. IV:8:16-18.
DODOO, J. N. French and language studies in the proposed educational
    system. IX:9:201-204.
DOKU, E. BORTEI. See Bortei-Doku, E.
DOKU, E. V. Crop production in Ghana. II:21:7-9.
DOKU, E. V. and E. F. G. MANTE. The "Oriental Cow"--Can't it also
    become the "Cow" of Tropical Africa? VIII:15:351-354.
Dollar crisis. A. Kumar. VI:18:12-15.
Donkey and our agriculture. Kontopiaat. IV:24:28-30.
DONKOR, G. A. The Budget and taxation. IV:16:8-9.
    _____. Ghana's unemployment problems. V:8:4-8.
DORM-ADZOBU, C. Handicraft industries: A tool for rural development
    in Ghana. VI:12:5-9.
DORVLO, K. Nkrumah and Busia. VII:4:76-78.
DOVLO, M. Is the Corporate image necessary? VIII:16:376-378.
    _____. The nature and purpose of public relations. VI:25:13-17.
Draft Constitution for Ghana. E. Akufo-Addo. III:3:12-15.
DRAMA
    BOSSMAN, M. The Alvin Ailey American Dance Theatre.
        II:23:25-26.
    JONES-QUARTEY, K. A. B. Music and drama; The recent offerings.
        IV:6:13-18.
    KENNEDY, J. S. African theatre. IV:15:18-20.
        _____. African theatre at the Algiers festival. IV:19:14-17.
        _____. Black folks--discovering each other's humanity.
        IV:14:21-22.
        _____. Drama and theatre in Ghana. IV:20:20-21.
        _____. Music and theatre at Legon. IV:7:24.
    NII-YARTEY, F. Choreography in traditional dances.
        VIII:6:126-129.
    SENANU, K. E. Preserving our culture--The Adzido Dance Troupe.
        II:22:22-23.
        _____. Thoughts on creating the popular theatre. 1)
        II:20:25-26; 2) II:21:22-23.
    WILLIAMS, D. The horse's mouth: Adzido. III:1:22-23.
DUODU, C. Erskine May in Busia's parliament. V:2:4-6.
    _____. The Legon Observer through outside eyes. VI:14:8-10.
    _____. The literary critic and social realities. IV:6:24-26.
    _____. The revised programme for a return to civilian rule.
    III:24:3-4.
    _____. Wole Soyinka: his talent and the mystery of his fate.
    III:16:17-18.
DUVALIER, DR. FRANCOIS
    OBICHERE, B. I. Dr. Francois Duvalier: A political postmortem.
        VI:11:10-14.

DZAKPASU, C. C. K. Origins of the Rhodesian crisis. V:9:7-8.
DZOBO, N. K. The brain crisis in the teaching profession. III:6:3-4.
_____. The Church and education in Ghana. III:22:4-6.
_____. Church and State in School management. IV:11:7-10.
Early economic consequences of "quit" order. IV:26:18-21. (ON).
Early roots of apartheid. R. Greenfield. VI:1:4-9.
East African Community: crisis or confidence? G. F. A. Sawyerr.
   VI:9:9-14.
East African Community: crisis or confidence? T. Gatabaki.
   VI:6:15-17.
Economic Community of West Africa. I. Bissue. II:19:12-15.
Economic Community of which West Africa? VIII:9:201-202. (ON).
Economic impact of the University on Cape Coast town. D. B. Safo.
   VIII:16:373-376.
Economic implications of the aliens order. A. N. Hakam. V:6:2-4.
Economic measures for 1973-74--Strengths and Weaknesses--E. Treve.
   1) VIII:18:418-422; 2) VIII:19:442-447; 3) VIII:21:493-502.
Economic recovery--A precondition of civilian rule?--A fallacy.
   II:23:14-15. (ON).
Economics and human nature. K. A. B. Jones-Quartey. IV:7:11-14.
Economics of education. A. Lewis. III:10:4-6.
Economics of the Pakistani prisoners-of-war case. B. B. Quraishy.
   VIII:13:290-294.
ECONOMY
        ABBAN, J. B. and A. G. BLOMQVIST. More price controls in
           Ghana? VI:2:2-6.
        ABBEY, J. L. S. A country of two worlds. VI:14:x-xii.
        ACHAMPON-MANU, K. Ghana's economic problems and the new regime.
           V:2:3-4.
        _____. The task ahead. IV:10:10-11.
        ACHEAMPONG, I. K. National Redemption Council budget statement
           1972/73. VII:19:459-462.
        ACKOM-MENSAH, I. Bouncing Cheques and the economy. V:22:10-15.
        ADJEI, K. Are we saving enough foreign exchange? III:18:4-6.
        _____. The businessman and the "little budget." II:15:12-14.
        _____. Implications of the 1970 Surcharge. V:22:2-10.
        _____. Wage and salary increases--Are they necessary?
           II:14:16-17.
        ADOMAKO, A. Ghana's foreign debts. II:19:8-10 and [23-25].
        AFRIFA, A. A. Budget statement for 1967-68. II:17:7-12.
        After devaluation, What? VI:27:1-2. (Ed.).
        AGAMA, G. K. Alternative economic policy for Ghana.
           VI:21:4-10.
        _____. Foundations of Economic policy: The State Enterprises.
           1) II:10:5-8; 2) II:13:6-8; 3) II:16:5-6.
        _____. Ghanaian business today. II:19:17-19.
        _____. On devaluation of the new cedi. II:15:3-6.
        _____. A policy for the fishing industry. 1) II:1:2-3; 2)
           II:6:8-9.
        _____. The trade fair and the economy. II:3:9-10.

N. R. C's. economic policy. VII:13:293-294. (Ed.).
National self-reliance or dependence? II:23:1-2. (Ed.).
1968/69 Budget. III:15:3-4. (Ed.).
1969/70 Budget--A Correspondent. IV:15:2-4.
1969/70 Budget--A delayed appraisal--A Correspondent.
    IV:20:5-8.
Note on Annual estimates: 1971/72--Part I. VI:19:13-14. (ON).
NTIM, S. M. Raising minimum wages? V:17:10-14.
NYANTENG, V. K. The need for a consumer union in Ghana.
    VI:13:2-5.
OMABOE, E. N. The state of the economy today. II:19:3-8.
Operation Asutsuare. VII:6:139. (ON).
ORLEANS-LINDSAY, J. K. Ghana's policy for economic rehabilita-
    tion. II:11:5-6.
OSEI-KWAME, P. and G. NEWLYN MURPHY. The case for increasing
    cocoa producer price in Ghana. VIII:20:466-473.
Our economic plight and the non-patriots. IV:25:11-12. (ON).
Our external debts. VII:1:1-2. (Ed.).
Our external debts. IV:12:8. (ON).
Our international indebtedness. III:20:3-4. (Ed.).
Our national debts. IV:20:1-2. (Ed.).
P. M's. fiscal and monetary measures. VII:1:16-17.
Path to economic development. II:1:1. (Ed.).
PEPEE, K. A. Stock Exchange for Ghana. VI:6:5-6.
PEPEE, Q. The distribution of the wealth of the nation.
    VI:14:ix-x.
Petrol crisis in Ghana. VIII:25:602-604. (ON).
Planning Ghana's economic development. VIII:19:441-442. (Ed.).
Plight of importers. V:19:19-20. (ON).
Plight of poverty. V:18:1-2. (Ed.).
Preview of the budget. II:16:2. (Ed.).
Price differentials. IX:13:316-317. (ON).
Problem car. II:22:10. (ON).
Problem of shortages. VIII:25:585-586. (Ed.).
Profit and loss in state enterprises. IX:12:284. (ON).
QUAIDOO, P. K. K. Ghanaian business today. II:19:15-17.
QUARSHIE, L. A. K. The Commanding heights of the economy and
    the mineral industries. VII:16:366-371.
_____. The future of the minerals industry in Ghana.
    II:10:8-11.
_____. The future of the petroleum industry. VII:17:394-396.
Recent economic measures. VIII:18:417-418. (Ed.).
Regional Development Corporations. VIII:2:38. (ON).
SAFO, D. B. The economic impact of the University on Cape
    Coast town. VIII:16:373-376.
SEWARD, J. N. Manipulating the budgets. V:7:2-3.
Some reflection on the performances of the economy since the
    Coup. A Correspondent. VI:5:8-10.
State enterprises. VII:2:37. (ON).
STEUR, M. D. The devaluation debate. VIII:12:273-274.

Main Index

Between May and September. IV:9:1-2.
Beyond Biafra. V:2:1-2.
Bread and breath of life. II:14:1.
Brinkmanship in the Middle East. II:11:1-2.
Business in the Constituent Assembly. IV:3:1-2.
Change in name and emphasis. II:5:1-2.
Chieftaincy on trial. V:12:1-2.
Civilian rule in Sierra Leone. III:10:1-2.
Clause 71. IV:14:3-4.
Closing down the Universities. IX:4:77-78.
Cocoa and the economy. VII:20:465-466.
Cocoa and the nation. IV:22:1-2.
Cocoa in continuing boom. VIII:10:217-218.
Cocoa still our life-blood. VII:4:69-70.
Combating subversion. II:2:1-2.
Commonwealth in recurrent crisis. VI:2:1-2.
Commonwealth: myth and reality. VIII:17:393-394.
Constitutional proposals. III:3:1-2.
Control of the national press. VI:4:1-2.
Coup d'etat in Uganda. VI:3:1-2.
Coups in Africa and the Ghana coup of the 13th January, 1972.
    VII:2:21-26.
Courts for chiefs. VI:22:2.
Crumbling Alliances. V:16:1-2.
Declaration of assets. IV:15:1-2.
Dialogue on dialogue. V:26:1-2.
Dilemma of the United Nations. V:14:3-4.
Duplication in our Universities. IX:10:221-222.
Economic Co-operation in West Africa. II:10:1-2.
Economic Planning Council. IX:7:149-150.
Educating children abroad. VII:22:513-514.
Education and its many problems. VIII:6:121-122.
Education in Ghana. III:21:1-2.
Ending the Nigerian war. III:22:1-2.
Extravagance at Congregations. IV:6:1-2.
Failure of the Ghanaian elite. VI:24:2-4.
Fifth Anniversary message: The Observer is for all. VI:14:2.
Five years after the coup. VI:5:2.
Foreign aid for Ghana's economic recovery. II:19:1-2.
Foreign participation in the economy. II:24:1-2.
"Freedom" Acts of government. VIII:5:98.
Future of our mines. VII:25:585-586.
Future of our public press. IV:11:1-2.
Future of the U. N. V:22:1-2.
General Amin and the Asians. VII:17:389-390.
General Ankrah's "honourable" resignation. IV:8:1-2.
General Gowon in London. VIII:12:265.
Ghana Airways: Loss of faith in Ghana and Ghanaians.
    II:13:1-2.

Main Index

Nigeria. II:17:1-2.
Nigerian tragedy. III:16:3-4.
1968/69 Budget. III:15:3-4.
Nixon and the Golden Fleece. III:17:2.
Nkrumah passes away. VII:9:201-202.
O. A. U. and African problems. II:18:1-2.
O. A. U. and Rhodesia. VII:11:249-250.
O. A. U. "celebrations." VIII:11:241-242.
O. A. U. in crisis? VI:12:1-2.
On national integration. VI:26:1-2.
On national integration and unity. IV:7:1-2.
One year of freedom and sanity. II:4:1-2.
One year of the N. R. C. VIII:1:1-4.
Our civil servants. V:3:1-2.
Our external debts. VII:1:1-2.
Our international indebtedness. III:20:3-4.
Our national debts. IV:20:1-2.
Our Second Anniversary. III:14:3-4.
Our Stand. VII:14:317-318.
Party and the government. IV:25:2.
Path to economic development. II:1:1.
Peace prospects in Nigeria? III:1:1-2.
Planning Ghana's economic development. VIII:19:441-442.
Plight of poverty. V:18:1-2.
Police and Courtesy. V:19:1-2.
Political Detainees. VII:8:177-178.
Political parties decree. IV:10:3.
Political scene. IV:12:1-2.
Politics and economics in Southern Africa. II:21:1.
Politics and the Judiciary. V:9:1-3.
Politics of intolerance. IV:17:1-2.
Power in reserve. IV:24:1-2.
Power politics and the small nation. III:18:3.
Preparations for the take-over. IV:19:1-2.
Presidency under the proposed Constitution. 1) III:5:1-2; 2)
   III:6:1-2.
President Banda's gamble. VI:18:1-2.
Preview of the Budget. II:16:2.
Price of solidarity. VIII:24:561-562.
Problem of building a democracy and the issue of disfranchise-
   ment. II:20:1-2.
Problem of shortages. VIII:25:585-586.
Problems of the farmer. IX:12:269-270.
Proposed Educational reforms. VII:12:273-274.
Protecting our mining industries. VII:16:365-366.
Reappraising O. F. Y. IX:3:53-54.
Recent economic measures. VIII:18:417-418.
Registration of voters. IV:10:3-4.
Removal of the Subsidy and social justice. VIII:3:49-50.
Retirement of the 3,000. VIII:23:537-538.
Return to civilian rule? II:8:1-2.

Main Index

(EDITORIALS)

      Safety on our roads. IX:9:197-198.
      Salute to Guinea-Bissau. VIII:20:465-466.
      Seven years ago. VIII:13:289-311.
      Should freedom be "guarded?" V:6:1-2.
      Sierra Leone: soldiers and politicians. II:7:1-2.
      Social revolution in our countryside? V:24:1-2.
      Stabilization of fish supply. VII:15:341-342.
      Strikes and economic development. IV:13:1-2.
      Students in revolt. VI:13:1-2.
      Task ahead in the New Year. IV:1:1-2.
      Tasks for Busia government. V:2:2.
      Threatening war clouds in Nigeria. II:12:1-2.
      Time for an enquiry into crime. VI:11:1-2.
      Time table for return to civilian rule. III:12:1-2.
      To have or not to have a Jury. IX:8:173-174.
      Towards changing the guards. III:23:1-2.
      Towards economic independence. V:4:1-2.
      Towards party politics. IV:4:3-4.
      Tradition, public policy and the law. III:7:1-2.
      Turning point in Anglo-Ghana relations. II:3:1-2.
      25 years of Adult Education. IX:1:1-2.
      Two years of the N. R. C. IX:2:25-26.
      Two years of post-coup Ghana. III:4:1-2.
      Undercurrents in the Ghana-Abbott debate. II:25:1-2.
      "Unemployment has become a major national problem." VI:15:1.
      United we stand. IV:18a:1-2.
      University and Society. VII:23:537-538.
      Urgency of Cooperation in Africa. VIII:8:169-170.
      Using local talent. VII:24:561-562.
      Vandalism, anarchy and world order. V:8:1-2.
      Vorster's Trojan horse. VI:7:1-2.
      Wanted: A new approach to social problems. V:25:1-2.
      Wanted: A single national day. VIII:5:97-98.
      What sort of opposition? V:23:2-3.
      When are strikes legal? V:15:1-2.
      Winning the Commanding heights of the economy. VII:10:225-226.
      Withdrawal of the subsidies. IX:13:297-298.
      Work permits. III:13:1-2.
      Year in retrospect. II:26:3-4.
EDJAH, K. Association with the E. E. C.--Relationship of junior partnership and exploitation. VIII:3:50-55.
_____. Production drive in Ghana--Some preliminary reflections on crop insurance. VII:13:300-304.
EDUCAT. Education Review Committee and Ghanaian languages. IV:2:13-16.
_____. Gbedemah, the N. L. C., Busia and the Volta Region. IV:22:6-11.
_____. Give us a soul. IV:8:6-8.
_____. Why we study or not study the classics. IV:17:10-11.

EDUCATION

ACHAMPONG, A. P. Educating the "Masses." VII:20:470-474.

ADJEI, B. The future of fee-free education in Ghana. IV:17:7-10.

AIDAM, P. T. K. The University loan scheme. VI:16:9-10.

AIDOO, E. S. Organising mass education. VIII:6:138.

AMPOMAH, R. A. Self-reliance and expatriate missionaries. VIII:20:484-486.

ASAMOAH, E. K. What type of teacher. II:22:17-18.

ASSUON, B. K. Reflections on higher education in Ghana. VI:9:24-26.

BAFI-YEBOAH, V. Educating the mentally retarded. IX:11:246-250.

BENZANSON, K.A. Educational reforms--rejoinder. VII:24:581-583.

BLUWEY, G. K. The Advanced Teacher Training course--Another stop-gap. III:26:19-20.

BULLEY, A. K. University entrance and guidance in schools. VIII:23:544-546.

Development without planning--A Correspondent. VII:5:104-108.

DICKSON, A. Teachers and the secondary schools. II:15:8-10.

DODOO, J.N. French and language studies in the proposed educational system. IX:9:201-204.

DZOBO, N. K. The brain crisis in the teaching profession. III:6:3-4.

_____. The Church and education in Ghana. III:22:4-6.

_____. Church and State in school management. IV:11:7-10.

EDUCAT. Education Review Committee and Ghanaian languages. IV:2:13-16.

_____. Why we study or not study the classics. IV:17:10-11.

Education and its many problems. VIII:6:121-122. (Ed.).

Education in Ghana. III:21:1-2. (Ed.).

GARDINER, R. K. A. Education in Rural areas. V:11:18-22.

_____. The Structure of Education in rural areas. V:13:6-14.

GHANAPAT. Once again: Teachers' Uniform. V:13:20-22.

GYESI-APPIAH, L. Why we study the Classics. IV:15:12-14.

HAIZEL, E. A. Education under the N. R. C.--the first year. VIII:1:11-16.

_____. Proposed system of education for Ghana: Teacher Training--The need for more information. VII:12:274-278.

_____. The report of the Education Review Committee. 1) III:25:8-12; 2) III:26:16-18.

_____. The right to be under-educated. VI:20:6-7.

HARTLEY, E. M. On being educated. II:15:10-11.

HAREWARD, D. Four stages of Education. VII:15:350-351.

HESSE, F. The right to practise medicine in Ghana: Some implications and a corollary. III:5:12-21.

IDAN, L. K. Research in the Universities. 1) VII:5:108-111; 2) VII:6:134-138.

JACKSON, O. Y. Scientific manpower in Ghana--Crisis in supply and demand. VII:1:6-9.

JONES-QUARTEY, K. A. B. The teacher and Ghanaian Education in search of an orientation. VII:16:374-377.

VARTANIAN, G. A. Medical education in the U. S. S. R.--A re-
joinder. VIII:2:43:46.
Educational administration in Ghana. I. Ackom-Mensah. II:16:7-9.
Educational Reforms in Ghana. VII:11:262-263. (ON).
Edward Heath and Africa. M. Assimeng. V:14:12-14.
Effecting economy in education in Ghana. J. K. Atta. VIII:10:226-230.
Effects of the new devaluation. A. N. Hakam. VI:27:5-8.
EGYPT
Inside Egypt--Political Correspondent. III:4:11.
EKPEBU, L. B. The minorities and the Nigerian crisis. 1)IV:6:2-4;
2) IV:7:4-8; 3) IV:8:8-13.
[Election results]. IV:18a:7-19.
Electoral panorama. M. Assimeng. IV:18a:3-6.
Electoral process. J. A. Peasah. 1) III:7:3-4; 2) III:8:2-4; 3)
III:11:6-10.
Electoral registration. III:19:6. (ON).
Electoral registration and return to civilian rule. III:20:18. (ON).
Electoral registration system: its programme and principles. J. Y.
Owusu. IV:2:7-9.
ELEGBO, A. Nigeria's dubious friends: Ghana and Gambia. II:21:21-22.
Element of repetition in Ghanaian elections: 1956 and 1969. N.
Uphoff. V:1:19.
Elite and the masses. T. A. Kofi. VII:8:178-182.
Elite and the state chest. II:18:12. (ON).
ENCHILL, K. BENTSI. See Bentsi-Enchill, K.
Encouraging exports. VII:4:88-89. (ON).
Enquiry into the P. D. A. II:7:12. (ON).
Environment: Comment on some pollution problems in Ghana. K. O. A.
Mensah. IX:12:274-276.
Erskine May in Busia's parliament. C. Duodu. V:2:4-6.
Escalation in Vietnam. VII:10:238-240. (ON).
Escape of Mr. Ayeh-Kumi. IV:13:12. (ON).
ESEDEBE, P. O. Why international opinion supports Biafra. IV:16:9-10.
Ethnocentricism, not Tribalism. VII:7:166. (ON).
Events in Sierra Leone. VI:8:17. (ON).
EWUSI, K. Ghana's economic prospects. V:19:4-8.
_____. The transport problem reconsidered. VI:9:5-8.
Examination Leakages. V:23:20-21. (ON).
Excerpts from the budget. VI:16:15-20. (ON).
Exchange control decree. VIII:23:555. (ON).
EXCHANGE RATES
ABBAN, J. B. Fixed versus flexible exchange rates. VI:19:9-13.
Executive Sovereignty? V:7:10-12. (ON).
Exercise of discretionary powers under the new constitution. K. Afreh.
IV:25:2-4.
Exit permits. VII:3:56-58. (ON).
Expediting Committee. II:2:8-9. (ON).
Explosion of African studies. F. Hesse. IV:20:8-12.
Export bonus scheme. A Correspondent. VI:4:9-10.
Export promotion. VII:16:379. (ON).

Ex-public officers and patriotic duty. V:4:15-16. (ON).
Expulsion of Ghanaian fishermen from Sierra Leone. C. Lawson-Anson.
    IV:5:4-5.
Extensions to the Ministerial Buildings. VI:10:18. (ON).
Facing economic realities. A Correspondent. VII:3:46-49.
Facts, criticism and the public good. VII:26:619-620. (ON).
Fall of the curtain and some reflections on a constitution for Ghana--
    An extract. J. Appiah. IX:9:208-211.
Fallen trees and our Highways. III:13:10. (ON).
FAMILY PLANNING
    AMPOFO, D. A. Ghanaian culture and the concept of small
        family-size. IV:22:14-20.
    BREW, K. Another view of family planning. VII:26:610-615.
    _____. Misconceptions about family planning. V:24:20-21.
    FISCIAN, C. E. Voluntary sterilisation as a component of a
        family planning programme. VIII:11:247-251.
    GAISIE, S. K. Demographic situation and Ghana population
        policy. IV:12:i-iv.
    KPEDEKPO, G. M. K. Misconceptions about family planning. 1)
        V:22:20-22; 2) VI:2:20-22.
    SAFO, D. B. Population growth and family planning. V:8:8-9.
Famous last words. VII:2:39. (ON).
Farewell to arms and batons. Kontopiaat. IV:21:17-18.
Farewells, inaugurals and policy statements. IV:21:13. (ON).
Fate of non-alignment. J. Apronti. V:9:8-10.
February 24th celebrated. IV:5:11-12. (ON).
Feeding the people. VI:13:17. (ON).
Festival of Arts. IV:4:27-28. (ON).
FIADJOE, A. K. The Law Week: 24th February--3rd March--A comment.
    IX:5:102-104.
Fight against cholera. V:26:16. (ON).
Financing health services. R. G. Brooks. VIII:25:596-601.
Firestone Agreements. III:14:18-19. (ON).
First Anniversary messages. II:14:2-5.
First anniversary resolutions. Kontopiaat. II:14:23-25.
First flush. IV:10:13. (ON).
First Session of Ghana's Parliament. V:14:4-6.
First year anniversary of Legon Observer--"The Social Scene." E.
    Ampene. II:14:12-13.
FISCIAN, C. E. Management and the liberal arts graduate. VI:23:13-15.
    _____. The uses and abuses of drugs. 1) VI:7:11-14; 2) VI:8:9-15;
    3) VI:9:19-21.
    _____. Voluntary sterilisation as a component of a family planning
    programme. VIII:11:247-251.
500 years of European contact. VI:20:10-12. (ON).
N¢5 million for British Headmasters. VI:24:16-18. (ON).
Five per cent tax. IV:6:12. (ON).
Fixed versus flexible exchange rates. J. B. Abban. VI:19:9-13.
Flare-up in the Arab World. V:20:25. (ON).
Focus on Nigeria. IV:6:11. (ON).

FOLSON, B. D. G. Aristotle on Ghana (African) politics. III:2:22–23.
_____. Ratifying the Draft Constitution. IV:16:6–8.
_____. The sale of, and private participation in State Enterprises.
    II:25:9–14.
FOLSON, K. The public executions—A national disgrace. II:11:21–22.
Food, nutrition and agriculture. F. T. Sai. 1) II:20:5–7; 2)
    II:21:5–7.
Food preservation—Use simple methods. J. K. B. A. Ata.
    VII:19:444–448.
Football slump. Sports Correspondent. II:5:19–21.
Foreign aid and world trade. II:12:20–22.
Foreign banks again. III:14:19–20. (ON).
Foreign banks in Ghana. III:9:11. (ON).
Foreign currency. II:2:12–13. (ON).
Foreign currency escape value. II:11:9. (ON).
Foreign enterprise in Ghana—The case of Ghana Sanyo. II:4:16. (ON).
Foreign experts. VII:2:37–38. (ON).
Foreign participation in State Enterprise—The case of Abbott Labora-
    tories (Ghana) Ltd. A. Radix. II:23:2–7.
FOREIGN RELATIONS
        BEN-JIB, M. K. Clear course for Ghana. VIII:16:388–390.
        Ghana and the world—two years of realism—Political Corre-
            spondent. IX:2:27–30.
        Ghana's foreign affairs. VI:20:2–4. (Ed.).
        KARIKARI, K. A. Ghana and the world. II:14:9–10.
        _____. Ghana's external relations since the coup. II:4:13–16.
        _____. Ghana's foreign policy under Busia. V:20:13–18.
        _____. The new administration and foreign policy. V:1:12–14.
        Turning point in Anglo-Ghana relations. II:3:1–2. (Ed.).
Formal education and conflict in Ghanaian society. B. S. Kwakwa.
    VIII:6:124–126.
Foundations of economic policy: (i) The State Enterprises. G. K.
    Agama. II:10:5–8.
Foundations of economic policy: (ii) Private Enterprises. G. K.
    Agama. II:13:6–8.
Foundations of economic policy: (iii) Foreign aid. G. K. Agama.
    II:16:5–6.
Four stages of Education. D. Hereward. VII:15:350–351.
Fourth year accounting course. A. Ghartey. IX:14:336–340.
France and her African allies 1972–73: towards disenchantment? O. M.
    Kumah. VIII:25:586–591.
France's new President. IV:13:12–13. (ON).
Francophone Africa after De Gaulle. P. A. V. Ansah. IV:10:4–6.
Free speech: A brief comment on an ambiguity. J. E. Wiredu.
    V:6:6–7.
"Freedom day" acts of Government. VIII:5:98. (Ed.).
Freedom of the Press. VII:2:36–37. (ON).
Freedom of whose Press? VII:14:334–336. (ON).
Frelimo and the struggle in Mozambique. R. Lobban. VII:7:150–154.
French and language studies in the proposed educational system. J. N.
    Dodoo. IX:9:201–204.

French grip on Africa weakening? VIII:16:383. (ON).
French Somaliland. II:8:11. (ON).
FRIMPONG, K. N. R. C. and the standard rent. VIII:3:57-59.
'Fringe benefits'. VI:13:18. (ON).
From Ghostland--with a cross. V:20:25. (ON).
Fundamental rights. Political Correspondent. 1) II:4:2-4; 2) II:5:3.
Future of fee-free education in Ghana. B. Adjei. IV:17:7-10.
Future of our public press: some suggestions. G. K. A. Ofosu-Amaah
    and J. E. Wiredu. III:7:ii-vii.
Future of the independence of the press. II:19:19-20. (ON).
Future of the mineral industry in Ghana. L. A. K. Quashie.
    II:10:8-11.
Future of the opposition. K. Afreh. V:1:14-18.
Future of the petroleum industry. L. A. K. Quashie. VII:17:394-396.
FYNN, J. K. The Middle East crisis--An historical perspective.
    III:24:4-7.
_____. The role of history in a developing country. III:2:9-11.
G. B. C.--Television. V:13:24. (ON).
G. B. C.--T. V. and Sports. VI:4:15. (ON).
G. N. T. C. and distribution. VII:18:429. (ON).
G. N. T. C. services. II:20:15-16. (ON).
GABA, C. R. A Christian thinks aloud at Christmas. IV:26:10-14.
_____. Your God is too small. 1) II:15:16-17; 2) II:18:17.
GAISIE, S. K. Demographic situation and Ghana's population policy.
    IV:12:i-iv.
_____. How anti-intellectual is Ghana? III:6:15-17.
GAMESU, P. Aspects of political behaviour. VI:5:10-16.
_____. The Cabinet reshuffle: A commentary. VI:4:5-8.
_____. The Ghanaian Scene--A personal view. VI:2:22.
_____. Leadership in Ghana--A personal view. III:21:2-10.
_____. Mercantilist politics and Rachmanism in Ghana--Effah Commis-
    sion on the Housing Corporation. III:7:20-21.
_____. An open letter to Dr. Busia. V:9:22.
_____. An open letter to party leaders. IV:13:8-10.
_____. Parliamentary debate on "Tribe and all its parts of speech"
    Extracts. V:11:2-4.
Gammalin and the cocoa industry. D. Leston. VIII:12:280-282.
GARBRAH, E. Health and national development planning. III:17:17-18.
GARDINER, R. K. A. Education in Rural areas. V:11:18-22.
_____. The structure of Education in Rural areas. V:13:6-14.
Garveys and the Back-to-Africa Movement: A retrospective view.
    S. K. B. Asante. VIII:21:506-508.
GATABAKI, T. East African Community: crisis or confidence?
    VI:6:15-17.
Gaullism without DeGaulle. V:24:17-18. (ON).
Gbedemah, the N. L. C., Busia and the Volta Region. Educat.
    VI:22:6-11.
Gbedemah's [K. A.] Press Conference--A report and analysis. K.
    Archampong (et al). IV:7:15-17.
GBORDZO-MATOKU, K. The invasion of Guinea. VI:3:16.
GEMATUXO. Cautionary hints on State take-over bits. VII:20:474-476.

38

Main Index

GEMATUXO, A. Kotoka is dead: What of the future? II:9:12-14.
_____. Problems of meritocracy. II:14:21.
_____. Toll for the cowardly. II:1:21.
GENERAL ELECTIONS
    ABBEY, J. L. F. The 1969 election: A preliminary analysis.
        IV:19:2-4.
    ASSIMENG, M. The electoral panorama. IV:18a:3-6.
    _____. Prospects of the parties. IV:16:2-6.
    [Election results.] IV:18a:7-19.
    KONTOPIAAT. Reflections and refractions on the election
        results. IV:18a:21-22.
    List of Candidates and their Constituencies for the August 29
        General Elections. IV:18:9-21.
    PEASAH, J. A. The electoral process. 1) III:7:3-4; 2)
        III:8:2-4; 3) III:11:6-10.
    TWUMASI, Y. The political failure of Gbedemah--myths exploded?
        1) IV:20:3-5; 2) IV:21:8-10.
    UPHOFF, N. An element of repetition in Ghanaian elections;
        1956 and 1969. V:1:19.
General Idi Amin's offer to the O. A. U. VI:26:17. (ON).
GEOLOGICAL STUDIES
    ATOBRA, K. Legon's role in the development of geological
        studies in Ghana--the discussion so far. VIII:11:257-258.
    AYETEY, J. K. Geological training at Legon: A view on the
        controversy. VIII:11:259.
    BEKOE, D. A. Legon's role in the development of geological
        studies in Ghana--A rejoinder. VIII:9:206-208.
    The Future of our mines. VII:25:585-586. (Ed.).--Rejoinders.
        1) VIII:1:19; 2) VIII:3:59-62; 3) VIII:3:65-66.
    KWASHIE, A. P. Geological training. VIII:11:259.
    OCRAN, V. Legon's role--Comments on Dr. Bekoe's rejoinder.
        VIII:11:258-259.
    _____. Legon's role in the development of geological studies
        in Ghana. VIII:9:204-206.
George Padmore, black revolutionary. S. I. A. Kotei. II:21:18-21.
GERRITSEN, R. Nima and the revolution--An open letter to Col.
    Acheampong. VIII:13:299.
Getting agriculture moving. B. E. Rourke. VIII:16:370-373.
GHANA
    Ghana: A visitor's view. B. Streek. VI:14:16-22.
    Ghana-Abbott Agreement. (The Contract). II:25:25-27.
    Ghana-Abbott Agreement. A. Woode. II:25:14-15.
    Ghana-Abbott Agreement. B. D. G. Folson. II:25:9-14.
    Ghana-Abbott Agreement. J. Ofori-Atta. II:25:15-18.
    Ghana-Abbott Agreement. P. T. K. Aidam. II:26:10-11.
    Ghana-Abbott Agreement. R. S. Amegashie. II:25:18-25.
    Ghana-Abbott Agreement. W. Ofori-Atta. II:25:9.
    Ghana-Abbott Agreement: Statement by the Legon Society on
        National Affairs. II:25:27-28.
    Ghana-Abbott Agreement: Symposium and comment. II:25:9-28.
    Ghana Airways controversy. A Correspondent. IV:3:11-14.

39

Ghana's external relations since the coup. K. A. Karikari.
    II:4:13-16.
Ghana's financial woes. V:15:14. (ON).
Ghana's foreign debts. A. Adomako. II:19:8-10; [23-25].
Ghana's foreign debts. K. Manu. V:10:8-9.
Ghana's foreign policy under Busia. K. A. Karikari. V:20:13-18.
Ghana's national Commercial Bank. VIII:11:253-254. (ON).
Ghana's new Cabinet. IV:8:14. (ON).
Ghana's one-year development plan July 1970 to June 1971. T. H.
    Buxton. VI:2:6-7.
Ghana's political "Sects"--and their missions. M. Assimeng.
    IV:11:4-6.
Ghana's ties with East and Central Africa. V:10:18-19. (ON).
Ghana's unemployment problems. G. A. Donkor. V:8:4-8.
GHARTEY, A and D. ARKU. Business education in Ghana--A comment.
    VIII:17:411-414.
GHARTEY, A. Education for accountancy in Ghana. VIII:21:498-501.
_____. The fourth year accounting course at Legon. IX:14:336-340.
_____. Report of the Committee on the establishment of a School for
    training accountants and other related professionals--A comment.
    VIII:20:473-478.
_____. Some misgivings about the present state of the accountancy
    profession in Ghana. VIII:26:618-624.
_____. Some misgivings about the present state of the accountancy
    profession in Ghana--Reply to a rejoinder. IX:3:70-71.
GIBBS, J. Nationalism and the cultural revolution. VI:8:20-21.
Gift of a Presidency. VI:27:17-18. (ON).
Gift of Brazilian football--Correspondent. V:14:24-26.
Give us a soul. Educat. IV:8:6-8.
GLOVER, J. N. A. KPAKPOE. See Kpakpoe-Glover, J. N. A.
"Goal" (Globe cinema). III:14:32. (ON).
God and the coup. VII:2:38. (ON).
Good neighbourliness and national self-interest. VII:19:452-453. (ON).
GORDON, J. Conference report: Agriculture within and without the
    groves of academe. VI:12:9-10.
Government and Cargo Handling Company. III:14:21. (ON).
Government and Ghanaian business. III:15:4-5. (ON).
Government and opposition in Sierra Leone: The clouds reform.
    K. A. B. Jones-Quartey. V:23:i-viii.
Government, Press and journalists. IX:10:226-230. (ON).
Government rent control policy. J. N. A. Kpakpoe-Glover.
    VIII:5:102-105.
Government, the press and the masses. O. Okai. VIII:8:183-184.
Great experiment. M. Assimeng. IV:18:4-8.
Green revolution in India. V:19:8-13.
GREENFIELD, R. Africanist after-thoughts and incidentalia--Part I:
    Origins. III:4:10-11.
_____. Africanist after-thoughts and incidentalia--Part II: Dakar.
    III:5:3-6.
_____. The early roots of apartheid. VI:1:4-9.

_____. Lord Pearce and Zimbabwe: The report of the Commission on Rhodesian opinion. VII:11:250-254.

_____. Politics and religion in the Sudan. V:8:2-4.

_____. Some impressions of Mogadishu--June 1974. IX:13:308-316.

Growing data shortage. M. D. Steur. IX:3:58-59.

Growing over-crowding in our cities. J. Opare-Abetia. V:25:6-9.

Guarding and preserving public documents. III:25:16. (ON).

Guarding and preserving public documents. Librarian. R. L. A. A. IV:1:16-17.

Guerillas in Latin American politics. E. Ofori-Akyea. V:16:12-16.

Guessing game. D. Hereward. II:18:19.

GUEVARA, ERNESTO CHE
  NYARKO, K. The man that was "Che Guevara." III:23:12-14.

Guidelines for agricultural development.--Special Correspondent. 1) IX:5:111-112; 2) IX:6:126-128; 3) IX:10:222-224.

GUINEA-BISSAU
  HADJOR, K. B. A background to the revolution in Guinea-Bissau. VIII:23:546-554.
  LOBBAN, R. The P. A. I. G. C. and the Struggle in Guinea (Bissau). VII:5:111-115.
  Salute to Guinea-Bissau. VIII:20:465-466. (Ed.).

Guaranteed price of maize. VII:26:622. (ON).

GYANDOH, S. O. Chieftaincy in crisis. II:2:6-8.

_____. Judicial review under the proposed Constitution: A Critique. III:5:6-8.

_____. Legal aid: A plea for rationalisation. VII:23:538-542.

_____. On a future constitution for Ghana. IX:11:254-256.

_____. The party game in Ghana. IV:4:4-8.

_____. The President and the delegation of power. VI:7:2-6.

_____. The Proposed Constitution--paradoxes of diagnosis and pre-scription. III:4:3-5.

_____. Towards civilian rule. II:8:6-8.

_____. Watergate, law and commonsense. VIII:22:518-520.

GYESI-APPIAH, L. Why we study the Classics. IV:15:12-14.

GYINAYE, J. Plight of our rural communities. VI:4:17-18.

H. M. S. spineless. III:22:12. (ON).

HADJOR, K. B. A background to the revolution in Guinea-Bissau. VIII:23:546-554.

HAINES, R. W. Modernising agriculture. VI:3:15.

HAIZEL, E. A. Education under the N. R. C.--The first year. VIII:1:11-16.

_____. Proposed system of education for Ghana: Teacher Training--the need for more information. VII:12:274-278.

_____. The report of the Education Review Committee. 1) III:25:8-12; 2) III:26:16-18.

_____. The right to be under-educated. VI:20:6-7.

HAKAM, A. N. Economic implications of the aliens' order. V:6:2-4.

_____. The effects of the new devaluation. VI:27:5-8.

_____. Ghana and the European Economic Community. VI:22:4-6.

HINIDZA, R. KIYA. See Kiya-Hinidza, R.
History and Lt. Gen. Ankrah. II:9:16-17. (ON).
Home truths about the Ghanaian businessman. E. K. Kumi.
    VIII:7:155-157.
Honours list. III:6:11. (ON).
Hop step and Jump! IV:11:15-16. (ON).
Horse's mouth: Adzido. D. Williams. III:1:22-23.
Hospital conditions in Ghana. II:20:14. (ON).
Hospital fees report. R. G. Brooks. VIII:23:538-544.
Houphouet-Boigny's envoy in Pretoria. VI:21:14. (ON).
Houphouetism and the dialogue debate--A commentary. K. A. B. Jones-
    Quartey. 1) VI:10:i-iv; 2) VI:11:8-10.
Housing the Police. II:7:15. (ON).
How anti-intellectual is Ghana? S. K. Gaisie. III:6:15-17.
How can rents be controlled? G. Woodman. VII:20:466-470.
How cold is budget fever? V:18:10-12. (ON).
How relevant is devaluation to Ghana's economic situation? J. C. W.
    Ahiakpor. VII:2:30-36.
How to build a dictatorship again. H. Ofori. III:2:3-4.
How to build a dictatorship again in Ghana. J. E. Wiredu. III:1:4-6.
Hypocrites and Company, Inc. VII:23:551. (ON).
I. L. O. and Ghanaian women workers. R. Akuamoah-Nkuom. 1) VII:1:9-11;
    2) VII:7:161-165.
IDAN, L. K. Research in the Universities. 1) VII:5:108-111; 2)
    VII:6:134-138.
Ideological conflict in Ghana. J. F. S. Hansen. V:26:8-11.
Ideologies on sale--rejoinders. (a) Apronti, J., 1) VIII:12:279; 2)
    VIII:19:461-463; (b) Idrissu, A. VIII:12:280; (c) Otuteye, S. C.
    VIII:12:280.
Ideologies on sale--response to rejoinders. G. Adali-Mortty.
    VIII:14:332-334.
Ideologies on sale--whose do we buy? G. Adali-Mortty. VIII:10:232-234.
IGNORAMUS. The rest vs. Volta--A reply to Educat. 1) IV:24:6-12; 2)
    IV:25:5-8.
Impasse in India. III:6:10. (ON).
Implications of rural water development. C. K. Annan. III:19:4-6.
Implications of the 1970 Surcharge. K. Adjei. V:22:2-10.
Ingredients of an African ideology...For other articles in the series
    see Muntu, O.
Ingredients of an African ideology--The texture of unity. O. Muntu.
    V:2:6-9.
Ingredients of an African ideology--The way of good fellowship. O.
    Muntu. V:8:14-16.
Inside Egypt--Political Correspondent. III:4:11.
Inside the apartheid Kingdom--Letter to a friend. V:11:10-18.
Inside the Northern and Upper Regions. J. O. M. Pobee. 1) IX:4:98-99;
    2) IX:11:260-262.
Inside the Western Region. J. O. M. Pobee. 1) VIII:4:94-95; 2)
    VIII:5:112-116.
Instant fines. IX:1:7-8. (ON).
Instant justice--rough and ready. P. A. V. Ansah. VIII:4:76-80.

Institution-building in Ghana and Nigeria. K. Bentsi-Enchill.
II:18:8-10.
Institution-building in Ghana and Nigeria: A summary of proceedings.
K. Bentsi-Enchill. 1) II:13:3-6; 2) II:15:7-8; 3) II:17:15-17.
Institutionalized corruption. J. A. Peasah. II:4:11-13.
Institutionalized sycophancy--gains and costs. K. Arhin.
IX:14:330-334.
Insurrectionists and students. II:9:15-16. (ON).
Integrated approach to rural development in Ghana. I. M. Ofori.
V:24:9-10.
Intellectual non-alignment--who wants it? J. Oppong-Agyare.
II:26:25-26.
Intellectuals. II:2:2-3.
International Book Fair. IV:6:12-13. (ON).
International Cocoa Agreement of October, 1972. A Correspondent.
VIII:8:173-177.
International V. I. P.s in Africa. V:5:17-18. (ON).
Interview with Brigadier Ocran--A correction. II:5:8. (ON).
INTERVIEWS
    AFRIFA, A. A. II:4:iv-vi (Supplement).
    BIOBAKU, S. O. V:12:i-viii (Supplement).
    BRUCE-KONUAH, W. G. VI:20:i-viii (Supplement).
    BUSIA, K. A. III:15:12-20.
    DEKU, A. K. II:4:iii-iv (Supplement).
    _____. III:16:6-12.
    HARLLEY, J. W. K. III:15:6-12.
    _____. II:4:i-ii (Supplement).
    KOTOKA, E. K. II:4:vi-vii (Supplement).
    MATE-KOLE, NENE AZU. III:18:10-16.
    OCRAN, A. K. II:4:vii-viii (Supplement).
    OWUSU, V. III:14:8-16.
    SAFO-ADU, K. VI:17:16-20. (ON).
    SCHECK, S. III:20:4-12.
    SENGHOR, L. S. VI:10:i-iv (Supplement).
    STEVENS, S. IV:4:i-viii (Supplement).
    YAKUBU, B. A. III:14:4-8.
    _____. II:4:viii (Supplement).
Intestate succession in Ghana. IX:13:317. (ON).
Introducing Joe Apalahala. K. Ademoawa. V:12:16-18.
Invasion of Guinea. K. Gbordzo-Matoku. VI:3:16.
Invasion of Guinea. V:25:17-18. (ON).
Investigate import prices. II:4:16-19. (ON).
IRELE, A. The Nigerian civil war and international opinion. 1)
IV:13:2-6; 2) IV:14:11-14.
_____. The Nigerian situation--A personal view. II:26:5-7.
IRELE, A. and Y. TWUMASI. Press freedom on trial in Uganda.
IV:4:25-26.
Is Busia a politician? M. Assimeng. V:20:5-8.
Is Christmas for Christians? S. Yeboah. IV:26:14-18.
Is Mali sitting on a powder keg? III:1:11. (ON).

Is the Corporate image necessary? M. Dovlo. VIII:16:376-378.
Is the top incapacitated? A. Trebla. V:19:14-15.
Is there any salvation left? F. Amponsah. VII:5:102-104.
J. B. Danquah--An appreciation. L. H. Ofosu-Appiah. IV:4:i-vii.
JACKSON, E. Does Ghana need the Atomic Reactor? II:20:23-25.
JACKSON, O. A. Y. Scientific manpower in Ghana--Crisis in supply
    and demand. VII:1:6-9.
JECTY, K. A. OBESE. See Obese-Jecty, K. A.
Jeff Holden Affair. VI:11:2-5.
Jehovah Witnesses and the Millennium. M. Assimeng. V:2:12-14.
JENKINS, P. In praise of Cape Coast. VI:26:21-24.
_____. Judicial review--the American experience. IV:3:2-3.
Jiagge Report and after. IV:11:15. (ON).
JIB, M. K. BEN. See Ben-Jib, M. K.
Job for "Job 600." III:25:14. (ON).
Job well done. IV:18a:20-21. (ON).
Joe Appiah on a constitution for Ghana--A review. A. Koillarbi.
    IX:8:178-182.
Joe Appiah's future constitution. K. Arhin. IX:10:238-240.
Joi Bangla! VII:1:12. (ON).
JONAH, K. Big Dada's histrionics--A comment. VIII:23:558-559.
JONES-QUARTEY, K. A. B. Economics and human nature. IV:7:11-14.
_____. Government and Opposition in Sierra Leone--The clouds reform.
    V:23:i-viii.
_____. "Houphouetism" and the dialogue debate--A commentary. 1)
    VI:10:i-iv; 2) VI:11:8-10.
_____. Music and drama: The recent offerings. IV:6:13-18.
_____. The National language question. IV:1:16.
_____. Nationalism and the cultural revolution. VI:4:10-13.
_____. Nigeria's Agony. II:6:6-7.
_____. One-Party States and the role of Opposition in Contemporary
    Africa. V:26:4-8.
_____. Report from the Regions. VI:19:6-8.
_____. Report from the Regions. VI:25:10-13.
_____. Report from the Regions. VI:27:8-12.
_____. Report from the West Coast--Personal account. VI:9:14-18.
_____. The Russian phenomenon. II:23:10-11.
_____. Sierra Leone after the "non-coups" 1) II:26:8-10; 2) III:2:2-3.
_____. Sierra Leone: explosion in a Constitutional crisis. II:4:8-9.
_____. Sierra Leone: explosions of a Constitutional crisis.
    II:5:4-6.
_____. Sierra Leone--Recent changes and present trends. 1)
    III:10:i-vi; 2) III:13:i-viii.
_____. Sierra Leone: Return to turmoil. V:21:11-16.
_____. Sierra Leone: The role of the Press. V:25:i-viii.
_____. Sierra Leone: Tensions of a Constitutional crisis. II:3:5-8.
_____. Sierra Leone's turn. II:7:3-4.
_____. The teacher and Ghanaian education: In search of an orienta-
    tion. VII:16:374-377.
_____. The view from Washington. VIII:18:424-427.

_____. A Kontopiaatkrom Philosopher on Scholars and Politics. VII:6:145-146.

_____. Kontopiaatkrom revisited. V:19:22.

_____. Kontopiaatkrom revisited. 1) IX:2:48-50; 2) IX:4:94-98; 3) IX:7:166-170; 4) IX:9:211-214; 5) IX:11:264; 6) IX:13:322-323.

_____. The last Easter in Kontopiaatkrom. VII:9:219-220.

_____. The merry wives budget. VI:17:22-24.

_____. The new cedi--an Obituary. VI:27:19-20.

_____. An open letter to the members of the Constituent Assembly. 1) IV:2:21-22; 2) IV:3:18-20; 3) IV:4:30.

_____. Our New Year Honours List. VI:3:17-18.

_____. Our New Year Resolutions. VI:1:32-34.

_____. What will go wrong. VII:4:93-94:

_____. Who is a Ghanaian? V:3:16-19.

KONTOPIAAT, KWAME. Developments in Kontopiaatkrom. V:8:22.

_____. The Judiciary and the law school in Kontopiaatkrom. V:11:30.

_____. The Return of Kwadwo Kontopiaat. V:18:20-22.

KONUAH, W. G. BRUCE. See Bruce-Konuah, W. G.

KOO BRO. A letter from the citizens of Kontopiaatkrom to Hon. Kwadwo Kontopiaat. V:26:21.

KORANTENG, A. Sugar industry in Ghana. VI:3:6-7.

KORANTENG, W. R. Trends in the Cocoa trade. II:19:10-12.

Korle-Bu and Guggisberg. VIII:21:502. (ON).

KOTEI, S. I. A. George Padmore, black revolutionary. II:21:18-21.

KOTEY, N. and R. C. WILLIAMS. Scientific manpower crisis in Ghana-- rejoinder. VII:4:80-86.

KOTEY, R. A. Cocoa marketing. VI:24:14-15.

_____. High costs and price control. VI:10:6-9.

_____. Standardization of vehicle imports and the economy. VII:24:562-566.

KOTO, K. B. Report of Ghana by the [expert] ugly American. II:23:20-21.

KOTOKA [GEN. E. K.] interviewed. II:4:vi-vii.

KOTOKA, LT. GEN. E. K. Tributes to. II:9:3-5.

Kotoka is dead: What of the future. A. Gematuxo. II:9:12-14.

KPAKPOE-GLOVER, J. N. A. Government rent control policy. VIII:5:102-105.

KPEDEKPO, G. M. K. Misconceptions about family planning. 1) V:22:20-22; 2) VI:2:20-22.

KUDIABOR, C. A new organization for development in Ghana. III:1:7-9.

_____. Planning for rural development in Ghana. V:24:6-9.

_____. What kind of candidates for the next Parliament? III:6:6-8.

KUDIABOR, K. Literacy and development. V:14:6-8.

KUMAH, O. M. France and her African allies 1972-73: Towards disenchantment? VIII:25:586-591.

KUMAR, A. Crisis in Pakistan. VI:8:6-9.

_____. The dollar crisis. VI:18:12-15.

_____. The Indo-Pakistani war. VI:26:9-12.

KUMASI, B. L. J. Chieftaincy disputes in Bolgatanga. VI:3:16-17.

_____. The Ghanaian Student Society. VI:18:10-12.

KUMI, E. K. Home truths about the Ghanaian businessman.
    VIII:7:155-157.
_____. Wake up P. and T. Department. VII:24:568-570.
KWADU, J. The choice of freedom. II:5:15-17.
Kwadwo Kwa's manifesto. K. Arhin. II:22:20-21.
KWAKU, K. The United Nations as an instrument of peace--An African
    viewpoint. VII:24:566-568.
KWAKWA, B. S. Formal education and conflict in Ghana society.
    VIII:6:124-126.
KWAME, P. OSEI. See Osei-Kwame, P.
Kwame Nkrumah, the incredible Messiah. M. Assimeng. VII:9:205-206.
KWAMINA, A. Public servants or masters. II:16:14-15.
KWANSA, K. B. Educational reforms--rejoinder. VII:24:583.
_____. Ghana's educational reform. VII:15:342-350.
KWAPONG, A. A. Report on the University of Science and Technology,
    Kumasi. III:8:20-22.
KWARTENG, K. and A. G. BLOMQVIST. Ghana and the E. E. C.: Some
    further thoughts. VIII:7:152-155.
KWASHIE, A. P. Geological training. VIII:11:259.
Kwesi Armah and Britain. II:3:13-15. (ON).
KYEMFE, S. Some factors in the growth in agricultural output.
    VI:15:2-4.
KYEREMATENG, K. NKANSA. See Nkansa-Kyeremateng, K.
L. S. E. Closed down. IV:3:10-11. (ON).
L. S. N. A. Communications from our 5-year book of memories.
    VI:14:4-6.
LA-ANYANE, S. A note on Land Tenure. II:21:10-11.
_____. Three leading issues in Agricultural policy. II:20:3-5.
LABOUR PROBLEMS
    ABBEY, J. L. S. and K. BREW. The unemployment problem.
        V:26:11-13.
    ADJEI, K. Should unions be allowed to strike? III:20:12-14.
    AFFUL, K. N. Unemployment in Ghana. 1) VII:11:254-258; 2)
        VII:12:279-282.
    AFREH, K. The role of trade unions in Ghana. VII:11:258-261.
    AKUAMOAH-NKOUM, R. The I. L. O. and Ghanaian women workers.
        1) VII:1:9-11; 2) VII:7:161-165.
    BRUCE, I. K. The problem of unemployment in Ghana Part I.
        IV:4:11-21.
    _____. The problem of unemployment in Ghana Part II. IV:5:2-4.
    BRUCE-KONUAH, W. G. Interviewed. VI:20:i-viii.
    DONKOR, G. A. Ghana's unemployment problems. V:8:4-8.
    Strikes and economic development. IV:13:1-2. (Ed.).
    TWUM, S. Strikes and industrial harmony. V:16:2-8.
    When are strikes legal? V:15:1-2. (Ed.).
Labour Relations in Ghana. V:14:20. (ON).
Lagos V. C. 10 tragedy. IV:25:13-14. (ON).
LAING, W. N. Medical laboratory technologists--A case for recognition.
    VIII:24:571-574.
Lamizana in Ghana. III:18:8. (ON).

(LAW AND SOCIETY)
      Supreme Court and the Ghana Bar Association. VII:9:213-214.
      (ON).
      Taking higher justice to the regions. VIII:5:106-107. (ON).
      Traditional courts. IV:14:16-17. (ON).
      TWUM, S. Industrial relations and the high court. VI:24:6-10.
      WOODMAN, G. How can rents be controlled? VII:20:466-470.
      _____. Land law reform; Reducing insecurity of title. 1)
      III:22:6-9; 2) III:23:7-11.
      _____. Making land available for agriculture. VII:14:i-viii.
      _____. The recent rent control legislation. VIII:9:198-201.
      _____. Sale of land in Ashanti. VI:11:5-8.
LAWSON-ANSON, C. The expulsion of Ghanaian fishermen from Sierra
    Leone. IV:5:4-5.
_____. The significance of income-tax in developing countries.
    IV:13:10-11.
_____. The struggle of youth for emancipation. IV:11:11-14.
Leadership in Ghana. A personal view. P. Gamesu. III:21:2-10.
Leadership in Local Government. S. N. Woode. V:26:i-viii.
Learning Ghanaian languages. V:9:16. (ON).
Leave Mali alone. IV:1:9-10. (ON).
Legal aid: A plea for rationalism. S. O. Gyandoh. VII:23:538-542.
Legal gymnastics. J. Oppong-Agyare. III:17:6-7.
Legalisation of Abortion. E. M. Otchere. V:26:19-21.
Legend of Nkrumah properties. VII:10:238. (ON).
Legislature. Political Correspondent. II:10:3-4.
Legon: The frustrated tribe. M. Assimeng. V:7:8-10.
LEGON OBSERVER
      DUODU, C. The Legon Observer through outside eyes. VI:14:8-10.
      Our benefactors. II:14:7-8.
      Our stand. VII:14:317-318. (Ed.).
      Select and annotated chronological history of Legon Society on
          National Affairs and the "Legon Observer." II:14:6.
      Seven years of history: Highlights from the columns of the
          "Legon Observer." VIII:14:322-324.
      Special statement on Legon Observer (Special Issue). October
          3, 1974.
      The State Vs. The Legon Observer. III:2:23. (ON).
      To our detractors. VII:14:318-322.
LEGON SOCIETY ON NATIONAL AFFAIRS
      Change in name and emphasis. II:5:1-2. (Ed.).
      Members of the Legon Society on National Affairs. II:14:7.
Legon's own priorities. V:19:20. (ON).
Legon's role in the development of geological studies in Ghana. V.
    Ocran. VIII:9:204-206.
Legon's role in the development of geological studies in Ghana--A re-
    joinder. D. A. Bekoe. VIII:9:206-208.
Legon's role in the development of geological studies in Ghana--the
    discussion so far. K. Atobrah. VIII:11:257-258.
Legon's role--Comments on Dr. Bekoe's rejoinder. V. Ocran.
    VIII:11:258-259.

Lenin's legacy. V:9:12-14. (ON).
Lessons in tolerance for Africa. A. Pipim. IV:9:6-7.
Lessons of history. II:2:13.
Lessons of the insurrection of the 17th April. Kontopiaat. II:9:22.
Lessons of the Middle East war for Africa. Correspondent. IX:3:59-62.
Lest we forget. VIII:19:456. (ON).
LESTON, D. Gammalin and the Cocoa industry. VIII:12:280-282.
Letter from Britain. January 1972--Special Correspondent. VII:3:51-55.
Letter from the citizens of Kontopiaatkrom to Hon. Kwadwo Kontopiaat.
   K. Bro. V:26:21.
LEWIS, A. Development planning. III:11:3-6.
_____. The economics of education. III:10:4-6.
_____. The process of modernisation. III:13:3-6.
_____. Socialism in Africa. III:12:7-10.
_____. Two decades of growth. III:9:3-4.
Liberators and the Revolution. II:4:i-viii (Supplement).
LIBERIA
      Liberia: the sacked minister. VIII:9:202-203. (ON).
      OBICHERE, B. I. William Vacanarat Schadrach Tubman, President
         of Liberia. 1943-1971. VII:18:5-10.
      RICKS, J. C. Liberia's role in Africa. II:26:22-24.
      SAFFU, Y. Liberia's role in Africa. II:22:3-4.
Liberty of the press. K. Afreh. VIII:8:178-181.
Liberty Press Limited. II:14:8.
Libraries in Ghana's Schools and Training Colleges. L. H. Ofosu-
   Appiah. V:5:13-17.
Lt. General Afrifa and the Constitution. K. Afreh. V:17:2-8.
Lifting the ban on May 1st. IV:8:16. (ON).
LINDSAY, J. K. ORLEANS. See Orleans-Lindsay, J. K.
List of Candidates and their Constituencies for the August 29 General
   Elections. IV:18:9-21.
Literacy and development. K. Kudiabor. V:14:6-8.
Literary critic and social realities. C. Duodu. IV:6:24-26.
Little local affairs: The G. N. T. C. shop at Legon. VI:9:22-23.
   (ON).
Livestock production under O. F. Y. II. E. N. W. Oppong. VIII:4:84-86.
Loans and foreign aid. II:18:11-12. (ON).
LOBBAN, R. Frelimo and the Struggle in Mozambique. VII:7:150-154.
_____. The M. P. L. A. and the Struggle in Angola. VII:8:186-190.
_____. The P. A. I. G. C. and the Struggle in Guinea (Bissau).
   VII:5:111-115.
LOCAL GOVERNMENT
      ANSERE, J. K. The role of local government in nation building.
         V:3:i-viii.
      Decentralization and local government--Political Correspondent.
         1) II:11:2-4; 2) II:16:3-4.
      NANOR, A. T. K. Local government reforms, II. IV:17:5-7.
      _____. The local government service in post-coup Ghana.
         IV:8:4-6.
      _____. Suggested local government reforms for post-coup Ghana.
         IV:15:8-10.

(LOCAL GOVERNMENT)
    _____. The training of local council staff in Ghana.
     V:16:9-10.
    NKRUMAH, S. A. Some reflections on local government in Ghana.
     VIII:1:10-11.
    QUIST, M. D. Industrialization and local government.
     II:21:16-18.
    WOODE, S. N. District and local councils. VI:6:8-10.
    _____. Leadership in local government. V:26:i-viii.
LOCK, J. M. Bush fires in Ghana. IX:12:270-274.
Logistics Committee suspended. VIII:16:382-383. (ON).
Lonrho and Africa. IV:7:18. (ON).
Look at Ghanaian agriculture today: The requirements, strategies and
    prospects. W. K. Agble. VII:14:322-330.
Lord Pearce and Zimbabwe: The report of the Commission on Rhodesian
    Opinion. R. Greenfield. VII:11:250-254.
Lufthansa at the Airport. II:26:13. (ON).
Luxury cars. III:12:10. (ON).
M. P. L. A. and the Struggle in Angola. R. Lobban. VII:8:187-190.
M. T. U. and the Annual (and Quarter) Motor Licence. II:1:14-15.
    (ON).
MACDONALD, A. D. The U. S. foreign aid debate. VI:25:8-10.
Making land available for agricultural development. G. Woodman.
    VII:14:i-viii.
Making Saints of culprits. VII:3:56. (ON).
MALI
    D'AUROCH, C. The Mali coup. III:25:12-14.
Mallam Shitta case. VIII:5:107. (ON).
Man that was "Che" Guevara. K. Nyarko. III:23:12-14.
MANAGEMENT
    Criteria and tests for measuring Cabinet productivity. G.
     Adali-Mortty. V:20:8-9.
Management and the liberal arts graduate. C. E. Fiscian. VI:23:13-15.
Management Committees and party politics. IV:15:11. (ON).
Management of the Ghanaian economy--The reliance on controls. E.
    Treve. IX:6:130-134.
Managing Ghana's economy--The illusions of success--A Correspondent.
    VIII:4:80-83.
Mandate for perfidy. II:6:14-15. (ON).
Manipulating the budgets. J. N. Seward. V:7:2-3.
MANTE, E. F. G. (jt. au.). See Doku, E. V.
MANTE, E. F. G. What is respect? VI:7:18-19.
MANU, K. Changes in Policies. VII:5:98-100.
    _____. The distribution of social facilities. A reply to G. Adali-
    Mortty. IX:5:118-120.
    _____. Ghana's foreign debts. V:10:8-9.
    _____. Import Licensing in Ghana. II:1:3-4.
    _____. The N. R. C. and the economy. IX:2:32-36.
    _____. The N. R. C. Budget. VII:19:443-444.

_____. New deal for Ghana. IV:3:6-8.
_____. Problems in import licensing. II:5:7-8.
_____. Should Ghana join the E. E. C.? VII:21:494-496.
_____. The year's economic review. VIII:1:4-6.
MANU, K. ACHAMPON. See Achampon-Manu, K.
MANU, O. Rural development and our chiefs. VI:2:16-20.
MANU, Y. The crisis of British policy in Southern Rhodesia.
    VII:4:78-80.
Many people want to teach. M. Peil. III:9:17-20.
MARFO, K. Biafra--A peoples' right to exist--A rejoinder. IV:6:4-6.
Martin Luther King and the American Political Scene. III:8:9. (ON).
Mass Literacy and Rural Development. VII:26:622-623. (ON).
'Match' they did not miss. VIII:5:108. (ON).
Mate-Kole, Nene Azu, interviewed. III:18:10-16.
Mathematics--Ancient and modern. S. I. K. Odoom. VIII:26:615-618.
MATOKU, K. GBODZO. See Gbodzo-Matoku, K.
Matriculation address delivered by the Vice-Chancellor.
    VIII:23:548-552.
Matrimonial causes bill 1971. S. K. Date-Bah. VI:12:2-5.
Measuring public opinion in Ghana. II:26:12. (ON).
Meat problem. C. K. Mintah. VIII:12:282.
Medical education in the U. S. S. R.--A rejoinder. G. A. Vartanian.
    VIII:2:43-46.
[Medical education in the U. S. S. R.... reply.] J. O. M. Pobee.
    VIII:2:46-47.
Medical laboratory technologists--A case for recognition. W. N. Laing.
    VIII:24:571-574.
Members of the Legon Society on National Affairs. II:14:7.
MENDS, E. On Prof. Bentsi-Enchill's idea of "Abusuabo." VI:16:2-5.
_____. Traditional values and bribery and corruption. V:25:13-14.
MENSAH, A. N. The language of Ghanaian newspapers. VI:22:6-12.
_____. Sincerity and poetry (A reply to A. Britwum and Ama Atta
    Aidoo). VII:13:314-315.
MENSAH, I. ACKOM. See Ackom-Mensah, I.
MENSAH, J. H. The wealth of the nation. VI:14:i-ix.
MENSAH, K. O. A. The environment: Comment on some pollution problems
    in Ghana. IX:12:274-276.
Mercantilist politics and Rachmanism in Ghana--Effah Commission on the
    Housing Corporation. P. Gamesu. III:7:20-21.
Mercedes Benzes and Historical Ironies. VII:13:305. (ON).
Merry wives budget. K. Kontopiaat. VI:17:22-24.
Mfodwo's Headaches. V:17:18. (ON).
MGXASHE, M. A. A. S. U. Launched in Kumasi. VII:16:384-385.
_____. South Africa. VI:7:15-16.
Middle East crisis--An historical perspective. J. K. Fynn.
    III:24:4-7.
Middle East: Peace Prospects. V:17:21. (ON).
Middle East War. II:14:19.
Middle East War. VIII:21:501-502. (ON).
Middle East: War and Peace. II:13:11. (ON).

Military intervention in Politics. J. A. Peasah. II:9:6-10.
Military politics in Sierra Leone. VI:14:14. (ON).
Mills-Odoi Report and Pharmacists. J. R. Tekyi [et-al.]. III:13:16.
MINING INDUSTRY
> The Ata-Bedu Report: New wine in old bottles. VI:23:2. (Ed.).
> CUDJOE, J. E. The Minerals Industry in Ghana. II:16:18-20.
> The future of our mines. VII:25:585-586. (Ed.).
> Protecting our mining industries. VII:16:365-366. (Ed.).
> QUASHIE, L. A. K. The commanding heights of the economy and
> the mineral industries. VII:16:366-371.
> _____. The future of the minerals industry. II:10:8-11.
> _____. The future of the petroleum industry. VII:17:394-396.
> _____. [Mr. Q. writes to the Editor]. II:18:21-23.
Ministerial peregrinations. VI:24:16. (ON).
Ministers' salaries. IV:24:22. (ON).
Ministry of Rural Development. J. A. Peasah. IV:9:12-13.
Minor miracle. III:2:13. (ON).
Minorities and the Nigerian crisis. L. B. Ekpebu. 1) IV:6:2-4; 2)
> IV:7:4-8; 3) IV:8:8-13.
Minority Parties in Africa. M. Assimeng. V:23:3-6.
MINTA, C. K. The meat problem. VIII:12:282.
Misconceptions about family planning. G. M. K. Kpedekpo. 1)
> V:22:20-22; 2) VI:2:20-22.
Misconceptions about Family Planning—Some observations. K. Brew.
> V:24:20-21.
Missions of cultural Freedom. V:2:10. (ON).
Mr. Duncan Sandys: whites and blacks. III:15:5. (ON).
Mr. Franklin Hall Williams. III:10:6-8. (ON).
Mr. Harlley's retirement as I. G. P. IV:20:13. (ON).
Mr. John Mathew Poku: The new Asantehene. V:13:23-24. (ON).
Mr. Kwesi Lamptey and the P. D. A. threat. K. Arhin. VI:3:2-4.
Mr. L. A. K. Quashie writes to the Editor. II:18:21-23.
Mr. Mark Cofie: The successful businessman. VI:11:19-20. (ON).
Mr. Quarshie and the Cedi. VI:24:16. (ON).
Misuse of Government dwelling Houses. II:7:11-12. (ON).
MITCHELL, L. E. Education in commercial Art. II:11:7-8.
"Mo ne yo" (Congratulations) Kobina Bucknor. VI:3:8-10. (ON).
Modernising agriculture. R. W. Haines. VI:3:15.
Modernizing agriculture. V. K. Nyanteng. V:26:13-16.
Monkey business. III:22:9-10. (ON).
Moon landing. IV:16:12. (ON).
More about "elephantism." IV:4:28. (ON).
More haste, less speed. VII:19:448-452. (ON).
More price controls in Ghana? J. B. Abban and A. G. Blomqvist.
> VI:2:2-6.
MORTTY, G. ADALI. See Adali-Mortty, G.
Motor accidents. 1) II:11:10. (ON); 2) II:13:12. (ON).
MOZAMBIQUE
> LOBBAN, R. Frelimo and the Struggle in Mozambique.
> VII:7:150-154.

MUANGE, E. A. The Ghanaian intellectual. III:16:22-23.
_____. The land question. III:4:18-20.
_____. A sketch of the growth of the British Commonwealth.
    III:19:18-19.
Much ado about too little. III:15:5-6. (ON).
MUNTU, O. Ingredients of an African ideology. 1) IV:2:2-3; 2)
    IV:3:4-6; 3) IV:4:8-10; 4) IV:7:2-4; 5) IV:8:2-3; 6) IV:10:6-9;
    7) IV:12:3-5; 8) IV:15:6-7.
_____. Ingredients of an African ideology--Beyond the Nation State.
    V:10:10-12.
_____. Ingredients of an African ideology--Can we dispense with
    tribalism? IV:23:6-8.
_____. Ingredients of an African ideology: Perils of the boreal way.
    IV:24:12-14.
_____. Ingredients of an African ideology--The strength of African
    culture. V:6:8-9.
_____. Ingredients of an African ideology--The texture of unity.
    V:2:6-9.
_____. Ingredients of an African ideology--The way of good fellowship.
    V:8:14-16.
MURPHY, G. N. (jt. au.). See Osei-Kwame, P.
Music and drama: the recent offerings. K. A. B. Jones-Quartey.
    IV:6:13-18.
Music and theatre at Legon. J. S. Kennedy. IV:7:24.
My kind of leader. Afum Karikari. IV:5:6.
My new year resolutions. Kontopiaat. V:2:17-18.
N. A. S. S. O. and disqualification. III:16:4-6. (ON).
N. L. C. and the law. K. Afreh. IV:22:11-14.
N. L. C. Committee on the Academy. II:7:11. (ON).
N. L. C. Regime. J. A. Peasah. 1) IV:21:2-4; 2) IV:22:3-6.
N. L. C.--Where are they now? VI:5:3-8.
N. L. C. D. 221 Interim Electoral Commission decree 1968. III:3:16.
N. L. C. D. 222 Constituent Assembly Decree 1968. III:3:16-19.
N. L. C. D. 223 Elections and public offices disqualification Decree
    1968. III:3:19-22.
N. R. C. and a standard rent formula: A comment. A. A. Baa-Nuakoh.
    VIII:8:188-191.
N. R. C. and free expression. Correspondent. II:8:19-20.
N. R. C. and the economy. M. Manu. IX:2:32-36.
N. R. C. and the standard rent. K. Frimpong. VIII:3:57-59.
N. R. C. Budget. K. Manu. VII:19:443-444.
N. R. C. Economic reality versus Political reality. E. Treve.
    VII:8:184-186.
NAIDOO, L. K. Education and sociology--The need for new perspectives.
    VI:2:7-9.
_____. The sociological implications of human rights. IV:1:17-18.
Nailing the coffin of the dead C. P. P. VI:18:15-16. (ON).
Namibia again. VII:24:570-572. (ON).
NANOR, A. T. K. Local government reforms. IV:17:5-7.
_____. The Local Government service in post-coup Ghana. IV:8:4-6.

New University Institute of Journalism. VII:25:598. (ON).
New Year School. VII:1:14-15. (ON).
News from foreign papers. II:5:9. (ON).
NIGERIA
       ADEGOROYE, V. A. Peace prospects in Nigeria. III:4:17-18.
       AKPATA, T. Tragic illusions. III:3:2-4.
       BEDIAKO, K. Biafra--A peoples' right to exist. IV:2:4-6.
       BENTSI-ENCHILL, K. Institution building in Ghana and Nigeria:
          A summary of proceedings. 1) II:13:3-6; 2) II:15:7-8; 3)
          II:17:15-17; 4) II:18:8-10.
       Beyond Biafra. V:2:1-2. (Ed.).
       CHUKWUKERE, B. I. Conflict of idealism and realism: Nigerian-
          Biafran war. II:24:2-5.
       _____. Nigeria--The utopian case in Ghana. III:19:10-12.
       CUKWURAH, A. O. We have no alternative. V:1:3-4.
       EKPEBU, L. B. The minorities and the Nigerian crisis. 1)
          IV:6:2-4; 2) IV:7:4-8; 3) IV:8:8-13.
       ELEGBO, A. Nigeria's dubious friends: Ghana and Gambia.
          II:21:21-22.
       Ending the Nigerian War. III:22:1-2. (Ed.).
       ESEDEBE, P. O. Why international opinion supports Biafra.
          IV:16:9-10.
       Horror in Crescendo. III:17:1-2. (Ed.).
       International jig-saw puzzle in Nigeria. III:9:1-2. (Ed.).
       IRELE, A. The Nigerian civil war and international opinion.
          1) IV:13:2-6; 2) IV:14:11-14.
       _____. The Nigerian situation--A personal view. II:26:5-7.
       JONES-QUARTEY, K. A. B. Nigeria's agony. II:6:6-7.
       MARFO, K. Biafra--A peoples' right to exist--A rejoinder.
          IV:6:4-6.
       Nigeria. II:17:1-2. (Ed.).
       Nigeria: Present, Interim and Future. II:4:5-8. (Culled
          from "Nigerian Opinion.")
       Nigeria: Quo vadis? II:17:18. (ON).
       NWAFOR, S. O. Biafra and Nigeria--Facts on territorial integ-
          rity. IV:23:13-14.
       OFORI-AKYEA, E. Biafra: The politics of relief agencies.
          V:4:8-9.
       OGUM, O. The Ghanaian press and the Nigerian crisis.
          III:7:6-8.
       _____. Nigeria: Africa's problem. II:18:6-7.
       Peace Prospects in Nigeria. III:1:1-2. (Ed.).
       Threatening war clouds in Nigeria. II:12:1-2. (Ed.).
       TICKLE, I. Twelve states in Nigeria. III:10:2-3.
Nigerian crisis. II:10:12. (ON).
Nightmare in Sudan. VIII:6:131-132. (ON).
NII-YARTEY, F. Choreography in traditional dances. VIII:6:126-129.
Nima and the revolution--An open letter to Col. Acheampong. R.
    Gerritsen. VIII:13:299.

59

1969 as seen from Kontopiaatkrom. IV:26:25-26.
1969 elections--A preliminary analysis. J. L. F. Abbey. IV:19:2-4.
1969 in retrospect. IV:26:2-7.
1969/70 Budget. A Correspondent. IV:15:2-4.
1969/70 Budget--A delayed appraisal. A Correspondent. IV:20:5-8.
Ninth Annual Festival of Arts. V:4:17. (ON).
Nixon and the golden fleece. III:17:2. (Ed.).
Nixon as next U. S. President. III:23:6. (ON).
NKANSA-KYEREMATENG, K. Czechoslovakia and world public opinion.
    IV:5:9-10.
NKOUM, R. AKUAMOAH. See Akuamoah-Nkoum, R.
NKRUMAH, K.
        American negroes, western radicals, African students and
            Nkrumah's overthrow. II:22:10. (ON).
        APRONTI, J. Nkrumah and the building of Socialism. VII:9:208.
        ASSIMENG, M. Kwame Nkrumah: the incredible messiah.
            VII:9:205-206.
        British probity, Corruption and the Nkrumah regime.
            II:3:12-13. (ON).
        DORVLO, K. Nkrumah and Busia. VII:4:76-78.
        Legend of Nkrumah's properties. VII:10:238. (ON).
        Nkrumah indicted. II:2:11-12. (ON).
        Nkrumah passes away. VII:9:201-202. (Ed.).
        Nkrumah's friends next door? II:18:10-11. (ON).
NKRUMAH, S. A. The civil service and its masters. VIII:7:150-152.
_____. Some reflections on local government in Ghana. VIII:1:10-11.
_____. Who advises the government? VIII:6:129-131.
No Court. Legal Correspondent. VIII:17:394-397.
No Mau-Mau in Rhodesia--Political Correspondent. 1) II:12:5-7; 2)
    II:13:8-10.
No need for external examiners in West African Universities. K.
    Tuffour. VI:24:15-16.
No Parking in Accra. VII:25:597. (ON).
Nolle prosequi. VII:26:620. (ON).
Non-Aggression jokes. V:21:17-18. (ON).
Non-Returning Ghanaian professional. J. O. M. Pobee. VI:13:13-17.
NORTEY, D. N. A. The Crime problem. V:25:9-13.
"Northern Job 600." III:9:10-11. (ON).
Not by bread alone--A Correspondent. VIII:3:55-57.
Note on Annual Estimates: 1971/72, Part I. VI:19:13-14. (ON).
Note on Ghana's policy of Self-reliance. E. Treve. VII:16:371-372.
Note on Japan, Africa and Apartheid. A. Karikari. V:15:12-14.
Note on land tenure. S. La-Anyane. II:21:10-11.
Note on rehabilitation in Leprosy. D. S. Chaudhury. VI:7:20-21.
Now Labour, now Conservative. V:14:21-22. (ON).
NTIAMOAH-AGYAKWA, Y. Prosposals for education reforms. VII:17:400-404.
NTIM, S. M. Raising minimum wages? V:17:10-14.
NUAKOH, A. A. BAAH. See Baah-Nuakoh, A. A.
Nuisance in the street. V:3:8. (ON).
Nunoo affair. IV:10:11-12. (ON).

Nurses and politeness. V:16:17. (ON).
NWAFOR, S. O. Biafra and Nigeria: facts on territorial integrity.
    IV:23:13-14.
NYAHE, K. S. M. The last days of the giants. V:23:22.
NYANTENG, V. K. Modernizing agriculture. V:26:13-16.
_____. The need for a consumer union in Ghana. VI:13:2-5.
NYARKO, K. The man that was "Che" Guevara. III:23:12-14.
O. F. Y. "Harvest Week" and after. VII:18:429-430. (ON).
OBATALA, J. K. The need for reviving Pan-Africanism. V:3:3-6.
OBESEY-JECTY, K. A. B.Sc. Degree examination results in the University
    College of Cape Coast. IV:17:11.
OBICHERE, B. I. Apartheid in Zimbabwe (Rhodesia). VI:1:12-15.
_____. Collective security in contemporary Africa. VI:6:10-14.
_____. Dr. Francois Duvalier: A political postmortem. VI:11:10-14.
_____. William Vacanarat Schadrach Tubman, President of Liberia,
    1943-1971. VI:18:5-10.
OBITUARIES
        ABABIO, L. N. K. V:10:14-16.
        ACKOM-MENSAH, ISAAC. VII:9:218-219.
        AKROFI, CLEMENT ANDERSON. II:24:22-23.
        AMEDEKEY, E. Y. VII:16:378.
        ATTOH, K. Y. II:1:23.
        BOSSMAN, KOFI ADUMUAH. II:10:20.
        CABRAL, DR. AMILCAR. VIII:2:40-41.
        DAAKU, K. Y. IX:13:320.
        DANQUAH, J. B. II:4:26-29.
        DU SAUTOY, PETER F. de C. III:7:22.
        FIELD, M. J. VII:21:504-505.
        KING, MARTIN LUTHER. III:8:14-15.
        KORSAH, SIR ARKU. II:3:23.
        KOTOKA, GENERAL E. K. II:9:3-5.
        LUTHULI, ALBERT JOHN. II:16:24.
        MBOYA, J. T. IV:15:4-5.
        NKRUMAH, K. VII:9:201-202. (Ed.).
        PREMPEH, OTUMFUO NANA OSFI AGYEMAN (1892-1970). V:12:8-10
        RUSSEL, B. (1872-1970). V:4:10-17.
        SARKODEE-ADDO, JUSTICE JULIUS. VII:4:92-93.
        SEKYI, WILLIAM ESSUMAN-GWIRA. II:24:21-22.
        TUBMAN, W. V. S. VI:18:5-10.
        WORRELL, SIR FRANK. II:8:21.
Obituary: Accra Great Olympics. Soccer Correspondent. IV:3:22.
Obote--the man. 1) R. Neogy. VI:4:4-5; 2) T. A. Kofi. VI:6:20-21.
"Observer" and the Press Conference. II:24:9-10. (ON).
Observer through outside eyes. C. Duodu. VI:14:8-10.
Obstacles to reform in Ghana. L. H. Ofosu-Appiah. IV:9:3-6.
OCRAN, (A. K.). Interviewed. II:4:vii-viii.
OCRAN, M. T. Law and economic development. V:14:8-11.
_____. Oburoni Muntu and African ideology. V:11:4-9.
OCRAN, V. Legon's role in the development of Geological studies in
    Ghana. VIII:9:204-206.

_____. Legon's.... Comments on Dr. Bekoe's rejoinder.
VIII:11:258-259.
ODOOM, S. I. K. Mathematics--Ancient and Modern. VIII:26:615-618.
ODOTEI, E. O. (jt. au.). See Peil, M.
ODURO, K. The need for a "third force." IV:14:7-10.
ODURO, K. K. Berry cure for diabetes--Don't believe it! VI:20:9-10.
_____. Rural development and our economy solvency. VIII:20:478-481.
Official documents. VII:1:13-14. (ON).
OFORI, H. "How to build a dictatorship again." III:2:3-4.
OROFI, I. M. Agriculture and the land problem. IV:1:2-4.
_____. The coming search in Ghana. VII:5:100-102.
_____. The Commission on Land Tenure. II:21:10.
_____. An integrated approach to rural development in Ghana.
V:24:9-10.
_____. The land problem in modernising Ghana's agriculture. 1)
VI:6:2-5; 2) VI:7:8-9.
_____. Reflections on agricultural land reform in Ghana.
VII:10:228-231.
_____. Regional development planning in Ghana. III:8:5-6.
_____. Rural-Urban migration in Ghana. V:25:2-6.
OFORI-AKYEA, E. An African in Latin America. V:12:5-8.
_____. Background to Uganda's politics. V:1:4-7.
_____. Biafra: The politics of relief agencies. V:4:8-9.
_____. Busia and the youth. V:20:4-5.
_____. Guerillas in Latin American Politics. V:16:12-16.
_____. Kenya's political scene. IV:26:7-10.
_____. Organisational instruments of rural development. V:24:4-6.
_____. Problems of rural development. V:19:15-19.
_____. The second world food congress: A report. V:18:6-10.
OFORI-ATTA, J. The Ghana-Abbott Agreement. II:25:15-18.
OFORI-ATTA, W. The Ghana-Abbott Agreement. II:25:9.
OFOSU-AMAAH, G. K. A. and J. E. WIREDU. The future of our public
press: Some Suggestions. III:7:ii-vii.
OFOSU-APPIAH, L. H. African Universities and the Western tradition.
1) II:22:7-9; 2) II:23:11-14.
_____. Authority and the individual in Ghana's educational system.
II:1:4-8.
_____. The case for disfranchisement and disqualification. II:24:7-9.
_____. The crisis in Arts subjects in Ghana. IV:2:10-13.
_____. The Ghanaian establishment. III:26:4-8.
_____. J. B. Danquah--An appreciation. IV:4:i-viii.
_____. Libraries in Ghana's schools and Training Colleges. V:5:13-17.
_____. Obstacles to reform in Ghana. IV:9:3-6.
_____. The report on the University of Science and Technology, Kumasi.
III:5:21-23.
_____. University autonomy and academic freedom in Ghana. 1)
II:6:10-13; 2) II:7:5-8.
OGUM, O. The Ghanaian press and the Nigeria crisis. III:7:6-8.
_____. Nigeria: Africa's problem. II:18:6-7.

Oil crisis--Who pays the ¢120 million oil bill? W. Nelson.
    IX:6:134-136.
Ojukwu goes it alone. II:8:9-10. (ON).
OKAI, O. The government, the Press and the masses. VIII:8:183-184.
Old age discredited. G. Adali-Mortty. VII:4:74-76.
Olympics Appeal Fund. IV:2:16-17. (ON).
OMABOE, E. N. The state of the economy today. II:19:3-8.
Omens are propitious. IV:21:12-13. (ON).
On a future constitution for Ghana. S. O. Gyandoh. IX:11:254-256.
On being educated. E. M. Hartley. II:15:10-11.
On devaluation of the new cedi. G. K. Agama. II:15:3-6.
On getting a passport. V:7:13. (ON).
On having learnt to serve one's masters (A. N. Mensah "Talking about
    Jawa's Poem."). A. Britwum. VII:13:314.
On Party brigandage or the Spoils system--rejoinders. 1) Ansah,
    P. A. V. IX:5:114-116; 2) Adali-Mortty, G. IX:5:116; 3) Manu,
    K. IX:5:118-120.
On point of information, Please. VIII:20:481. (ON).
On Prof. Bentsi-Enchill's idea of "Abusuabo." E. Mends. VI:16:2-5.
On Teachers' Uniforms. J. E. Opoku. V:12:12-14.
On "The Changing views on Sovereignty." G. Adali-Mortty. VII:6:144.
On the Declaration of Assets. VII:5:118. (ON).
On the Declaration of Assets. VII:14:336-338. (ON).
On the implications of the devaluation. G. Chambers. VII:1:2-5.
On the Manipulation of History. VII:5:118. (ON).
Once again: Teachers' Uniform. Ghanapat. V:13:20-22.
One man one wife. III:21:12-14. (ON).
One year after the coup. (Main points). K. A. Busia. II:8:ii-iv.
One-party states and the role of Opposition in Contemporary Africa.
    Jones-Quartey, K. A. B. V:26:4-8.
OPARE-ABETIA, J. The growing overcrowding in our cities. V:25:6-9.
OPEKU, Y. A. The need to understand rural values. 1) VI:10:14-16;
    2) VI:12:13-16.
_____. The rural people and innovations in agriculture. VI:15:4-6.
Open letter to Dr. Busia. P. Gamesu. V:9:22.
Open letter to Maternity Hospital Doctors at Korle-Bu by a disappointed
    father. II:22:15-17.
Open letter to Mr. Harlley. Kontopiaat. II:12:22-23.
Open letter to the members of the Consituent Assembly. K. Kontopiaat.
    1) IV:2:21-22; 2) IV:3:18-20; 3) IV:4:30.
Open letter to party leaders. P. Gamesu. IV:13:8-10.
Open letter to the salaries review Commission. Kontopiaat.
    VI:13:20-22.
Operation Asutsuare. VII:6:139. (ON).
OPOKU, J. E. On Teachers' Uniforms. V:12:12-14.
OPOKU-OWUSU, K. Biafra and international recognition. II:14:20.
OPPONG, E. N. W. Animal health and disease control in Ghana.
    II:22:5-6.
_____. Livestock production under O. F. Y. II. VIII:4:84-86.

OPPONG–AGYARE, J. The case for a press trust again. VII:13:294–297.
_____. The Centre and its critics. III:22:24–26.
_____. Intellectual non-alignment—who wants it? II:26:25–26.
_____. Legal gymnastics. III:17:6–7.
_____. The need for an Opposition paper. V:9:3–4.
_____. South Africa's Apartheid: An invitation to bloodbath.
  V:15:7–10.
_____. Whither Ghana? III:25:3–4.
Opposition Merger. V:22:22–23. (ON).
Opposition walks-out. VI:8:16–17. (ON).
Order of Precedence or of priority? II:5:9. (ON).
ORGANISATION OF AFRICAN UNITY (O. A. U.)
  ASAMOAH, O. Y. The O. A. U. Achievements and failures.
    II:18:4–6.
  ASANTE, S. K. B. The Birth of the O. A. U.: The early years.
    VIII:10:218–223.
  _____. A decade of the O. A. U. Liberation Committee.
    VIII:2:36–38.
  _____. The O. A. U. at 10: Progress and problems.
    VIII:11:242–247.
  _____. Pan-Africanism revisited. VIII:9:194–198.
  _____. The significance of the tenth anniversary Summit
    meeting of the O. A. U. VIII:12:266–269.
  _____. A year of African solidarity: The O. A. U. at eleven.
    IX:12:278–283.
  DAKE, J. M. The road to African Unity. II:22:19–20.
  D'AUROCH, C. O. A. U. Summit Conference 1968. III:20:14–16.
  HESSE, F. The Organization of African Unity: An assessment.
    VI:12:10–13.
  New phase in Biafra—O. A. U. relations. III:11:1–2. (Ed.).
  O. A. U. and African problems. II:18:1–2. (Ed.).
  O. A. U. and the Freedom Fighters. V:14:20–21. (ON).
  O. A. U. "celebrations." VIII:11:241–242. (Ed.).
  O. A. U., Ekangaki and Lonrho. IX:7:156–157. (ON).
  O. A. U. in crisis. VI:12:1–2. (Ed.).
  O. A. U. Liberation Committee. II:16:13. (ON).
  O. A. U. Liberation Committee. VIII:1:17–18. (ON).
  O. A. U. Meeting. III:19:8. (ON).
  O. A. U. Summit. VI:14:10–14. (ON).
  SAWYERR, G. F. A. Recognition and African Unity. VI:16:5–9.
Organisational instruments of rural development. E. Ofori-Akyea.
  V:24:4–6.
Organisational problems facing the Opposition. K. Afreh. V:23:13–18.
Organising Civil Servants. G. Adali-Mortty. VII:12:283–285.
Organising Mass Education. E. S. Aidoo. VIII:6:138.
"Oriental Cow"—Can't it also become the "Cow" of Tropical Africa?
  E. V. Doku and E. F. G. Mante. VIII:15:351–354.
Origins of the Rhodesian Crisis. C. C. K. Dzakpasu. V:9:7–8.
ORLEANS–LINDSAY, J. K. Ghana's policy for economic rehabilitation.
  II:11:5–6.

OSEI, W. E. A. The dangers of tribalism. V:17:8-10.
OSEI-KWAME, P. and G. N. MURPHY. The case for increasing cocoa pro-
    ducer price in Ghana. VIII:20:466-473.
OTCHERE, E. M. Legalisation of Abortion. V:26:19-21.
_____. Who is an ideal ruler in Africa? VI:21:11-12.
Otu episode closed. IV:22:21. (ON).
Our agricultural extension service. E. Bortei-Doku. III:1:2-3.
Our benefactors. II:14:7-8.
Our Christmas wishes. VIII:26:618. (ON).
Our contributors and Correspondents. V:15:14. (ON).
Our economic plight and the non-patriots. IV:25:11-12. (ON).
Our external debts. IV:12:8. (ON).
Our 5th Anniversary number. VI:14:14. (ON).
Our Ghana-bred doctors. IV:21:14. (ON).
Our medical school. IV:14:16-17. (ON).
Our New Year Honours list. K. Kontopiaat. V:3:17-18.
Our New Year resolutions. K. Kontopiaat. VI:1:32-34.
Our present situation and the future. J. E. Wiredu. VIII:2:26-29.
Our stand in the Arab-Israeli Conflict. G. Adali-Mortty.
    VIII:22:530-531.
"Out." II:12:14. (ON).
Out-turn of the first N. L. C. budget. A. Sulitz. III:2:7-8.
Ovambo Revolt. VII:1:12-13. (ON).
Overhead between Bolga and Tamale. II:22:12. (ON).
OWUSU, J. Y. Electoral registration system: Its programme and prin-
    ciples. IV:2:7-9.
OWUSU, (VICTOR) Interviewed. III:14:8-16.
P. I. A. G. C. and the Struggle in Guinea (Bissau). R. Lobban.
    VII:5:111-115.
P. M. and the Judges. V:9:10-12. (ON).
P. M. and the rule of law. V:8:16-17. (ON).
P. M. in London and New York. V:23:18-19. (ON).
P. M.'s fiscal and monetary measures. VII:1:16-17.
P. P. Government so far. R. Kiya-Hinidza. VI:22:14-15.
PADMORE, G.
        KOTEI, S. I. A. George Padmore, black revolutionary.
        II:21:18-21.
PAINTIN, D. M. Comprehending Comprehensive education. VII:13:298-300.
PAKISTAN
        KUMAR, A. Crisis in Pakistan. VI:8:6-9.
        The Pakistani P. O. W.'s--A human problem. A Correspondent.
        VIII:7:147-150.
        QURAISHY, B. B. The economics of the Pakistani prisoners-of-
            war case. VIII:13:290-294.
PAN-AFRICANISM
        ASANTE, S. K. B. The Garveys and the Back-to-Africa movement:
        A restrospective view. VIII:21:506-508.
        _____. Pan-Africanism revisited: The road to Addis Ababa.
            VIII:9:194-198.
        OBATALA, J. K. The need for reviving Pan-Africanism. V:3:3-6.

Parliament of 1970. VI:1:32. (ON).
Parliamentary debate on "Tribe and all its parts of Speech": Extract. P. Gamesu. V:11:2-4.
Parties testaments. M. Assimeng. IV:17:3-5.
Party and the electoral system. Political Correspondent. 1) II:2:3-4; 2) II:3:2-5.
Party Game in Ghana. S. O. Gyandoh. IV:4:4-8.
Pat for Mr. Adomako. III:8:9. (ON).
Pat for Vice-President Humphrey. III:2:11-12. (ON).
Pattern of N. R. C. administration. A Correspondent. VIII:2:30-32.
Peace in Indo-China. VIII:17:406. (ON).
Peace on earth. IV:26:18. (ON).
Peace prospects in Nigeria. V. A. Adegoroye. III:4:17-18.
PEASAH, J. A. Africa 1966. II:14:10-11.
_____. The electoral process. 1) III:7:3-4; 2) III:8:2-4; 3) III:11:6-10.
_____. Institutionalised corruption. II:4:11-13.
_____. The land question. III:3:7.
_____. Military intervention in politics. II:9:6-10.
_____. Ministry of Rural Development. IV:9:12-13.
_____. The N. L. C. Regime. 1) IV:21:2-4; 2) IV:22:3-6.
_____. The Presidency under Ghana's new constitution. IV:19:5-7.
PEIL, M. Ashiaman--Eyesore and opportunity. V:18:4-6.
_____. Many people want to teach. III:9:17-20.
PEIL, M. and E. O. ODOTEI. Return to civilian rule. II:12:7-9.
PEPEE, K. A Stock-exchange for Ghana. VI:6:5-6.
PEPEE, Q. The distribution of the wealth of the nation. VI:4:ix-x.
Permits for demonstrations. VI:3:8. (ON).
Personal Assistants. IV:23:14-16. (ON).
Personality cult. Back to square 1? IV:25:10-11. (ON).
Petrol crisis in Ghana. VIII:25:602-604. (ON).
Phoney Conference? IV:3:10. (ON).
Physical planning in Ghana at the crossroads. N. W. Damptey. VI:13:5-8.
PIPIM, A. Lessons in tolerance for Africa. IV:9:6-7.
Place-seekers and lobbyists. VII:2:38-39. (ON).
Planned Parent-hood. II:6:15-16. (ON).
Planning for rural development in Ghana. C. Kudiabor. V:24:6-9.
Plea for the employee. V:6:12-13. (ON).
Plight of Importers. V:19:19-20. (ON).
Plight of our rural communities. J. Gyinayeh. VI:4:17-18.
Plight of the "Ebi Nte Yie" (Alias Brokemen) Parties. Kontopiaat. IV:16:18.
Plight of the Engineering faculty at Kumasi. V:17:18-20. (ON).
Plight of the Palestinians--Three years after the Six-day-War--Political Correspondent. V:14:14-19.
POBEE, J. O. M. Impressions of a visit to Brong Ahafo: Inside B. A. VII:15:351-354.
_____. Inside the Northern and Upper Regions. IX:4:98-99.

_____.   Inside the Northern and Upper Regions. IX:11:260-262.
_____.   Inside the Western Region. 1) VIII:4:94-95; 2) VIII:5:112-116.
_____.   [Medical education in the U. S. S. R.... reply]. VIII:2:46-47.
_____.   The non-returning Ghanaian professional. VI:13:13-17.
_____.   The Russian-trained Ghanaian Doctors--A Controversy or mis-
understanding. VII:23:544-550.
_____.   World Health Day: Your heart is your health. VII:7:154-158.
POETRY
        ADALI-MORTTY, G. The Spent Scare. II:5:21-22.
        ADDO, J. Memories of an old friend. VI:4:22.
        AIDOO, A. A. On "the fires next time." VII:13:311-312.
        APRONTI, J. The Fires next time. VII:9:220-222.
        BENTSI-ENCHILL, N. K. Attitudes. VII:22:532.
        _____. 3 Revolutions. IX:8:195.
        BRONI. K. Atenteben. V:3:19.
        _____. Ball: Volta Hall--Decennial. V:9:22.
        DEH, S. Y. Poor him. VII:10:246.
        DEI-ANANG, K. K. On the Birth of an unknown God. V:26:22.
        EDUSEI, C. E. Some great little things. II:8:20.
        EDUSEI, E. Contemplation in a forest. IV:22:26.
        _____. Ghana of tomorrow: a vision. IV:16:18.
        _____. To the farmers of Ghana. IV:24:30.
        KENNEDY, S. Ballad for Martin Luther King. IV:8:22.
        KIYA-HINIDZA, R. Robert Kennedy: In Memoriam. IV:11:22.
        KUMAH, O. M. Mr. Briton in Anguilla. IV:9:22.
        KWADU-AMPONSEM, K. A. At war with peace. II:14:11.
        _____. The Child. II:7:22.
        MANN, B. Biriwa. II:1:22.
        _____. Night hunters. II:22:21.
        MENSAH, A. N. Talking about Jawa's Poem. VII:11:268.
        OKAI, J. Ada Thursdawn. VI:27:21-22.
        _____. Modzawe. III:6:21.
        _____. Sunset sonata. III:4:24.
        _____. Taj Mahal. VI:27:22.
        OPIA-MENSAH. Mr. Briton in Anguilla.
        WARD, S. A bush fire. III:26:28.
        _____. Fire and thunder in Ghana. III:26:28.
        _____. I know a land. III:26:28.
        WINFUL, E. A. Fugitive verses. VII:5:122.
        YANKEY, P. On the Nigerian-Biafran war. IV:4:30.
POKU, K. The dilemma of Ghanaian journalists. IX:14:326-330.
Police and security. II:9:17. (ON).
Policies and personalities. J. E. Wiredu. IV:18:8-24.
Policy differences between government and Opposition. O. Y. Asamoah.
    V:23:6-13.
A policy for the fishing industry. G. K. Agama. 1) II:1:2-3; 2)
    II:6:8-9.
Policy of non-alignment in the changing world. S. K. B. Asante.
    VIII:19:447-448.
Political concerts. V:17:18. (ON).

Political consciousness. IV:5:12. (ON).
Political failure of Gbedemah--myths exploded? Y. Twumasi. 1)
    IV:20:3-5; 2) IV:21:8-10.
Political parties. IV:9:14-15. (ON).
Political round-up. Kontopiaat. IV:18:24-26.
POLITICS
    ABBEY, J. L. F. The 1969 election--A preliminary analysis.
       IV:19:2-4.
    ACKOM-MENSAH, I. Chieftaincy in Crisis. II:7:9-10.
    ADALI-MORTTY, G. Change of government to the spoils systems
       again? 1) IX:4:79-80; 2) IX:7:166.
    _____. The changing views on sovereignty. VII:3:49-50.
    _____. Danger signals before and after civilian take-over.
       II:20:17-19.
    _____. Ideologies on sale--whose do we buy? 1) VIII:10:232-234;
       2) VIII:14:332-334.
    _____. Old age discredited? VII:4:74-76.
Administering the bitter pill-or lessons in government. A Cor-
    respondent. IX:13:298-302.
Advance towards democracy. VI:21:2. (Ed.).
Advisory Committee. VII:4:88. (ON).
AFREH, K. The exercise of discretionary powers under the new
    Constitution. IV:25:2-4.
_____. The future of the opposition. V:1:14-18.
_____. Liberty of the press. VIII:8:178-181.
_____. Lt. General Afrifa and the Constitution. V:17:2-8.
_____. Organisational problems facing the Opposition.
    V:23:13-18.
_____. The role of the president under the constitution.
    V:12:2-5.
_____. Some factors which impede progress. VII:9:209-213.
_____. What does the N. R. C. stand for? VII:18:420-428.
After repudiation, What? VII:3:45-46. (Ed.).
Aftermath of disqualification and exemptions. III:24:1-2. (Ed.).
AFUM-KARIKARI. The need for self-reliance. IV:12:5-6.
AIDAM, P. T. K. Are the Abbott criticisms really sincere?
    II:26:10-11.
AMPENE, E. First year anniversary of Legon Observer--The Social
    Scene. II:14:12-13.
AMPONSAH, F. Is there any salvation left. VII:5:102-104.
ANSAH, P. A. V. Instant justice--rough and ready. VIII:4:76-80.
_____. Registration and return to civilian rule. III:21:10-12.
APRONTI, J. Nkrumah and the building of socialism. VII:9:208.
_____. Resistance to apartheid. VI:1:10-12.
ARHIN, K. Institutionalized sycophancy--gains and costs.
    IX:14:330-334.
_____. Mr. Kwesi Lamptey and the P. D. A. threat. VI:3:2-4.
_____. Urgently needed--A genuine revolution. VI:24:4-6.
_____. Why should we let sleeping dogs lie? IV:23:11-12.

Main Index

ASAMOAH, O. Y. Policy differences between government and op-
position. V:23:6-13.
ASSIMENG, M. The Colonel's dispensation. IV:21:4-8.
_____. The electoral panorama. IV:18a:3-6.
_____. Ghana's political "sects"--and their mission.
IV:11:4-6.
_____. The Great experiment. IV:18:4-8.
_____. Is Busia a politician? V:20:5-8.
_____. Kwame Nkrumah, the incredible Messiah. VII:9:205-206.
_____. The parties' testaments. IV:17:3-5.
_____. Politics and ideological portraits. IV:13:6-8.
_____. The prospects of the Parties. IV:16:2-6.
_____. The third force: Dynamics of an ideal. IV:14:4-7.
_____. Tribalism as a syndrome. IV:23:3-6.
ATTA, J. K. Socialist-Capitalist controversy: An economic
appraisal. VII:6:126-130.
Basis of democratic government. VI:17:1-2. (Ed.).
Behave or else.... III:18:8-10. (ON).
BENTSI-ENCHILL, K. Institution-Building in Ghana and Nigeria:
A Summary of proceedings. 1) II:13:3-6; 2) II:15:7-8; 3)
II:17:15-17.
Bentsi-Enchill on the institutional challenges of our time.
A Correspondent. 1) VI:8:4-6; 2) VI:9:2-4; 3) VI:10:2-6.
Between May and September. IV:9:1-2. (Ed.).
BOAHEN, A. A. Afrifa, Busia, "1966 before and after"--comment.
II:8:iv-vii.
BOAHEN, A. The changing views on sovereignty--A rejoinder.
VII:4:70-73.
_____. The new crop of politicians and the military.
IV:18a:6-20.
Brigadier Afrifa's "cabinet." IV:9:13-14. (ON).
British probity, corruption and the Nkrumah regime.
II:3:12-13. (ON).
BUSIA, K. A. One year after the coup (main points).
II:8:ii-iv.
Business in the Constituent Assembly. IV:3:1-2. (Ed.).
Campbell and the N. L. C. IV:9:14. (ON).
Capitalism, Socialism and Ghana--Political Correspondent.
VIII:15:358-362.
Centre for Civic Education. II:14:13-14. (ON).
Civil Commissioners. II:14:13. (ON).
Clause 71. IV:14:3-4. (Ed.).
Code of conduct for Commissioners. IV:15:11-12. (ON).
Conscience on trial. VI:25:19. (ON).
Constituent Assembly. III:26:20-21. (ON).
Coups in Africa and the Ghana coup of the 13th January, 1972.
VII:2:21-26. (Ed.).
Critics and sycophants. VI:21:14. (ON).
Date for a return to civilian rule. II:11:9. (ON).

KONTOPIAAT. What way Dr. Progress Busia? IV:25:18-22.
KUDIABOR, C. What kind of candidates for the next Parliament?
    III:6:6-8.
KWADU, J. The choice of freedom. II:5:15-17.
Kwesi Armah and Britain. II:3:13-15. (ON).
Lessons of history. II:2:13. (ON).
Lifting the ban on May 1st. IV:8:16. (ON).
Management Committees and party politics. IV:15:11. (ON).
MANU, K. Changes in Policies. VII:5:98-100.
_____. The distribution of social facilities: A reply to G.
    Adali-Mortty. IX:5:118-120.
MENDS, E. On Prof. Bentsi-Enchill's idea of "Abusuabo."
    VI:16:2-5.
Military-police Presidential triumvirate. IV:18:1-3. (Ed.).
Minor miracle. III:2:13. (ON).
MUNTU, O. Ingredients of an African ideology. 1) IV:2:2-3;
    2) IV:3:4-6; 3) IV:4:8-10; 4) IV:7:2-4; 5) IV:8:2-3; 6)
    IV:10:6-9; 7) IV:12:3-5; 8) IV:15:6-7.
_____. Ingredients of an African ideology--beyond the Nation
    State. V:10:10-12.
_____. Ingredients of an African ideology--can we dispense
    with tribalism? IV:23:6-8.
_____. Ingredients of an African ideology: perils of the
    boreal way. IV:24:12-14.
_____. Ingredients of an African ideology--the strength of
    African culture. V:6:8-9.
_____. Ingredients of an African ideology--the texture of
    unity. V:2:6-9.
_____. Ingredients of an African ideology--the way of good
    fellowship. V:8:14-16.
N. A. S. O. and disqualification. III:16:4-6. (ON).
N. L. C. Civilian rule and the electoral machinery. III:8:1-2.
    (Ed.).
Nailing of the Coffin of the dead C. P. P. VI:18:15-16. (ON).
NARH, A. K. The role of the Press. VII:8:182-184.
New Political nationalists. VI:2:10-11. (ON).
Nkrumah indicted. II:2:11-12. (ON).
Not by bread alone. A correspondent. VIII:3:55-57.
Nunoo affair. IV:10:11-12. (ON).
OCRAN, M. T. Oburoni Muntu and African Ideology. V:11:4-9.
ODURO, K. The need for a "third force." IV:14:7-10.
OFORI, H. How to build a dictatorship again. III:2:3-4.
OFORI, I. M. The Coming Search in Ghana. VII:5:100-102.
OFORI-AKYEA, E. Busia and the youth. V:20:4-5.
OFOSU-APPIAH, L. H. The case for disfranchisement and dis-
    qualification. II:24:7-9.
_____. The Ghanaian establishment. III:26:4-8.
_____. Obstacles to reform in Ghana. IV:9:3-6.
One year of the N. R. C. VIII:1:1-4. (Ed.).

Towards party politics. IV:4:3-4. (Ed.).

TREBLA, A. Is the top incapacitated? V:19:14-15.

TREVE, E. The availability and non-availability of goods and services--the problem of shortages. 1) VII:25:588-594; 2) VIII:1:7-10.

_____. A note on Ghana's policy of self-reliance. VII:16:371-372.

TWUMASI, Y. The political failure of Gbedemah--myths exploded? 1) IV:20:3-5; 2) IV:21:8-10.

Violence in politics. IV:14:17. (ON).

Warning to the C. P. P. IV:10:12-13. (ON).

What sort of opposition. V:23:2-3. (Ed.).

Why registration is a must. III:21:14. (ON).

WIREDU, J. E. Free speech: A brief comment on an ambiguity. V:6:6-7.

_____. How to build a dictatorship again in Ghana. III:1:4-6.

_____. Our present situation and the future. VIII:2:26-29.

_____. Policies and personalities. IV:18:8-24.

YAWSON, K. Conversation or Confrontation? IV:24:4-6.

POLITICS, INTERNATIONAL

ADALI-MORTTY, G. The incredible prosperity of Lebanon. VI:23:9-12.

_____. Our stand in the Arab-Israeli conflict. VIII:22:530-531.

_____. The significance of President Losconczi's visit. VIII:24:566-568.

APRONTI, J. The fate of non-alignment. V:9:8-10.

ASAMOAH, O. Y. Czechoslovakia raped again. III:18:6-7.

_____. South East Asian trial of strength. III:4:21-22.

ASANTE, S. K. B. The policy of non-alignment in the changing world. VIII:19:447-448.

_____. Politics of racial discrimination: fourteen years after Sharpeville. IX:7:161-164.

ASSIMENG, M. Edward Heath and Africa. V:14:12-14.

The Dilemma of Israel. Political Correspondent. V:15:10-12.

EDJAH, K. Association with the E. E. C. relationship of junior partnership and exploitation. VIII:3:50-55.

JONES-QUARTEY, K. A. B. Economics and human nature. IV:7:11-14.

KARIKARI, A. A note on Japan, Africa and Apartheid. V:15:12-14.

Letter from Britain: January 1972--Special Correspondent. VII:3:51-55.

NKANSA-KYEREMATENG, K. Czechoslovakia and world public opinion. IV:5:9-10.

OFORI-AKYEA, E. An African in Latin-American Politics. V:12:5-8.

_____. Guerillas in Latin American Politics. V:16:12-16.

_____. The Second world food congress: A report. V:18:6-10.

Plight of the Palestinians--Three years after the six day war. Political Correspondent. V:14:14-19.

(POLITICS, INTERNATIONAL)
President Amin, the Asians and Britain--A Political Corre-
spondent. VII:21:490-494.
QURAISHY, B. B. The economics of the Pakistani prisoners-of-
war case. VIII:13:290-294.
Repercussions of China's admissions. VI:23:18-19. (ON).
SIMONDS, R. The Chinese representation question in retrospect
and prospect. VI:23:4-9.
TRUTENAU, H. M. J. A resurgence of intolerance? IV:5:10-11.
Vandalism, anarchy and world order. V:8:1-2. (Ed.).
Politics and religion in the Sudan. R. Greenfield. V:8:2-4.
Politics and sports. VII:17:404-405. (ON).
Politics in the Volta Region. II:11:11-12. (ON).
Politics of confrontation: Background to Africa's break with Israel.
S. K. B. Asante. VIII:24:562-566.
Politics of perfidy. III:22:10-12. (ON).
POLLUTION
MENSAH, K. O. A. The environment: Comment on some pollution
problems in Ghana. IX:12:274-276.
Popular Consultations. VIII:2:38-40. (ON).
Population growth and family planning. D. B. Safo. V:8:8-9.
Portugal and Africa. IX:10:232. (ON).
POSTS AND TELECOMMUNICATION DEPARTMENT
KUMI, E. K. Wake up P. and T. Department. VII:24:568-570.
Posts and telecommunications. IV:5:13. (ON).
Postscript. II:14:30-32.
Prah Committee of Enquiry. V:2:11. (ON).
Preserving our culture--The Adzido Dance Troupe. K. E. Senanu.
II:22:22-23.
Presidency under Ghana's new Constitution. J. A. Peasah. IV:19:5-7.
President and the delegation of power. S. O. Gyandoh. VI:7:2-6.
President Akufo-Addo, the police and the citizen. V:21:16-17. (ON).
President Amin, the Asians and Britain--A Political Correspondent.
VII:21:490-494.
President Kaunda and Ghana. IV:15:10. (ON).
Presidential Election. V:18:12. (ON).
PRESS
ADUAMAH, E. Y. The press after the coup. V:17:14-15.
ANSAH, P. A. V. The press scene since February 1966.
VIII:14:316-320.
BOAFO, S. T. The press, the government and the people.
IX:7:150-156.
Control of the National press. VI:4:1-2. (Ed.).
Debate on a Press Trust. V:25:16. (ON).
Freedom of the Press. VII:2:36-37. (ON).
Freedom of whose Press? VII:14:334-336. (ON).
Future of the independence of the Press. II:19:19-20. (ON).
Future of our public press. IV:11:1-2. (Ed.).
Ghana Press Council takes action. IV:13:12. (ON).
Government and Press. VIII:7:145-146. (Ed.).
Government and the Press. IX:14:325-326. (Ed.).

Projectitis, the incurable disease of Prestige projects. II:11:10-11.
(ON).
Proof of corruption. K. Afreh. IV:11:2-4.
Proposals for education reforms. Y. Ntiamoah-Agyakwa. VII:17:400-404.
Proposed constitution--A riposte to the Republican Constitution?
Y. O. Saffu. III:5:8-12.
Proposed constitution--paradoxes of diagnosis and prescription. S. O.
Gyandoh. III:4:3-5.
Proposed medical school at Kumasi. T. B. B. Sekyi. IX:12:290.
Proposed system of education for Ghana. VII:12:i-iv. (Supplement).
Proposed sytem of education for Ghana: Teacher Training--the need
for more information. E. A. Haizel. VII:12:274-278.
Proscription of the P. P. P. IV:12:18. (ON).
Prospects of the Parties. M. Assimeng. IV:16:2-6.
Public conveniences. II:4:21. (ON).
Public executions--A national disgrace. K. Folson. II:11:21-22.
Public opinion and official attitudes. VII:22:522-524. (ON).
Public opinion pools. III:21:12. (ON).
PUBLIC RELATIONS
DOVLO, M. The nature and purpose of public relations.
VI:25:13-17.
Public servants and presents. IV:8:14-16. (ON).
Public servants or masters? A. Kwamina. II:16:14-15.
Public service. Political Correspondent. II:8:3-5.
Public transportation. II:6:15. (ON).
Public Works Deterioration. VIII:3:296-298. (ON).
Punishing motor traffic offenders. VI:2:12. (ON).
Purpose of University education in Ghana today. VIII:22:523-524. (ON).
QUAIDOO, P. K. K. Ghanaian business today. II:19:15-17.
Quality in local products. VIII:12:272. (ON).
QUARTEY, K. A. B. JONES. See JONES-QUARTEY, K. A. B.
QUASHIE, L. A. K. The Commanding heights of the economy and the
mining industries. VII:16:366-371.
_____. The future of the minerals industry in Ghana. II:10:8-11.
_____. The future of the petroleum industry. VII:17:394-396.
_____. [Mr. Q. writes to the editor]. II:18:21-23.
Question of priorities. III:3:4-5. (ON).
Quick and the damned. III:12:10-12. (ON).
QUIST, M. D. Industrialization and local government. II:21:16-18.
QURAISHY, B. B. The economics of the Pakistani prisoners-of-war case.
VII:13:290-294.
_____. Some thoughts on modernizing agriculture in Ghana. VI:10:9-13.
R. E. N. Y. P./R. A. and the political Scene. Kontopiaat. IV:15:22.
R. E. N. Y. P./R. A. run out. Kontopiaat. IV:17:21-22.
R. I. P. Kaleidescope. V:5:18-20. (ON).
Racial discrimination in America. J. Apronti. V:22:16-18.
Radical "Ebi nte yie" Party. Kontopiaat. 1) III:13:14-16; 2)
III:14:26-27; 3) III:16:21-22.
Radio Ghana. II:1:13-14. (ON).
RADIX, A. The case for disqualification. II:21:3-5.

_____. Foreign participation in State Enterprises: The case of
Abbott Laboratories (Ghana) Ltd. II:23:2-7.
_____. Report of the Commission on the Structure and Remuneration of
the Public Services in Ghana. 1) III:15:20-24; 2) III:16:13-16;
3) III:17:3-6.
_____. The three constitutional decrees. III:4:5-9.
Railway strike. VI:2:10. (ON).
Railway strike. VI:4:18-19.
Rains and the economy. K. Agama. III:19:3-4.
Rains came! VIII:13:298. (ON).
Rains, Ghana and Kontopiaatkrom. Kontopiaat. III:20:20-22.
Raising minimum wages? S. M. Nti. V:17:10-14.
Rallies and demonstrations. V:10:19-20. (ON).
Ratifying the Draft Constitution. B. D. G. Folson. IV:16:6-8.
RAY, M. The coming famine season. III:24:16-18.
Recent Commonwealth Featherweight Title Fight. II:4:30-31.
Recent Commonwealth Featherweight Title Fight--A correction. II:5:19.
Recent rent control legislation. G. Woodman. VIII:9:198-201.
Recognition and African Unity. G. F. A. Sawyerr. VI:16:5-9.
Re:deportation of N. D. Howe. IV:24:2-4. (L. S. N. A. Communication).
"Reflections and refractions" on the election results. Kontopiaat.
IV:18a:21-22.
Reflections on agricultural land reform in Ghana. I. M. Ofori.
VII:10:228-231.
Reflections on higher education in Ghana. B. K. Assuon. VI:9:24-26.
Reflections on higher education, "The Observer" replies. VI:10:20.
Reflections on the exemptions exercise. Kontopiaat. III:26:26.
Reflections on the student revolution. D. Shiman. IV:1:7-8.
Reflective signs for vehicles. IV:16:13-14. (ON).
Reform of the law of succession. J. P. Archer. IX:13:302-308.
Regional Development Corporations. VIII:2:38. (ON).
Regional Development Planning in Ghana. I. M. Ofori. III:8:5-6.
Regional Planning Practice in Ghana. E. S. Atsu. V:21:8-11.
Registration and return to civilian rule. P. A. V. Ansah.
III:21:10-12.
Rehabilitating "wayward" girls. VIII:3:62-64. (ON).
Reinforcing barriers. VII:18:430. (ON).
RELIGION
ASSIMENG, J. M. The dilemma of Christian Missions in Africa
II:5:17-19.
ASSIMENG, M. Catholic laity in search of role. VI:23:15-18.
_____. Confusion among the Saints: The Aladura controversy.
VI:15:13-16.
_____. Dilemma of unfulfilled prophecies. IV:25:9-10.
_____. Jehovah's witnesses and the Millenium. V:2:12-14.
Belief in God--replies. 1) Barker, P. II:1:9-10; 2) Konotey-
Ahulu, F. I. D. II:1:10-13.
GABA, C. R. A Christian thinks aloud at Christmas. IV:26:10-14.
_____. Your God is too small. 1) II:15:16-17; 2) II:18:17.

(RELIGION)
     THROWER, J. Belief in God--reply to my critics. II:3:16-18.
     YEBOAH, S. Is Christmas for Christians? IV:26:14-18.
Religious instruction in Schools. IV:17:14-16. (ON).
Removal of the subsidy and social justice. VIII:3:49-50. (Ed.).
Reorganization of the Ministry of Agriculture: posts, salaries and
    motivation. E. Bortei-Doku. VIII:5:100-102.
Repercussions of China's admission. VI:23:18-19. (ON).
Reply to Kwabena Manu's rejoinders to "Change of Government to the
    Spoils System again?" G. Adali-Mortty. IX:7:166.
Reply to your Editorial date 23 June-6 July, 1967. E. H. Boohene.
    II:14:17-18.
Report from the Regions. K. A. B. Jones-Quartey. 1) VI:19:6-8; 2)
    VI:25:10-13; 3) VI:27:8-12.
Report from the West Coast--Personal account. K. A. B. Jones-Quartey.
    VI:9:14-18.
Report: Ghana Nigeria Cricket. III:9:20.
Report of the Auditor-General: The Character of the Ghanaian elite.
    VI:23:19-20. (ON).
Report of the Commission on the Structure and remuneration of the
    Public Services in Ghana. A. Radix. 1) III:15:21-24; 2)
    III:16:13-16; 3) III:17:3-6.
Report of the Committee on health needs of Ghana (1968). G. A.
    Ashitey. IV:24:16-18.
Report of the Committee on the establishment of a School for Training
    Accountants and other related professionals--A comment. A.
    Ghartey. VIII:20:473-478.
Report of the Education Review Committee. E. A. Haizel. 1)
    III:25:8-12; 2) III:26:16-18.
Report on bribery and corruption. VII:21:498. (ON).
Report on Ghana by the [expert] ugly American. K. B. Koto.
    II:23:20-21.
Report on the University of Science and Technology, Kumasi. A. A.
    Kwapong. III:8:20-22.
Report on the University of Science and Technology, Kumasi. L. H.
    Ofosu-Appiah. III:5:21-23.
Reports of the Educational and Agricultural Committees. II:1:14. (ON).
Research in the Universities. L. K. Idan. 1) VII:5:108-111; 2)
    VII:6:134-138.
Reshuffle. III:6:11. (ON).
Reshuffling of Regional Commissioners. VIII:10:231. (ON).
Resignations, Dismissals and the Information world. II:26:12. (ON).
Resistance to apartheid. J. Apronti. VI:1:10-12.
Rest vs. Volta--A reply to Educat. Ignoramus. 1) IV:24:6-12; 2)
    IV:25:5-8.
Restrictions on travel to Nigeria. IV:19:17-18.
Resurgence of intolerance? H. M. J. Trutenau. IV:5:10-11.
Retirement of N. L. C. members. IV:22:21. (ON).
Return of Kwadwo Kontopiaat. K. Kontopiaat. V:18:20-22.
Return to civilian rule. M. Peil and E. O. Odotei. II:12:7-9.
Return to the barracks. Kontopiaat. III:12:18-19.

Revaluation of the Cedi and Ghana's external debts. I. K. Acheampong.
   VII:3:60-64.
Revised programme for a return to civilian rule. C. Duodu.
   III:24:3-4.
Revolution: Malagasy style. VII:263. (ON).
Rewriting African History? T. K. Cavanagh. V:7:4-6.
RHODESIA (See also ZIMBABWE)
      Anglo-Rhodesian settlement. VI:25:2-4. (Ed.).
      Britain and Smith's referendum. IV:13:13-14. (ON).
      DZAKPASU, C. C. K. Origins of the Rhodesian Crisis. V:9:7-8.
      MANU, Y. The crisis of British policy in Southern Rhodesia.
         VII:4:78-80.
      No Mau-Mau in Rhodesia--Political Correspondent. 1) II:12:5-7;
         2) II:13:8-10.
      O. A. U. and the Rhodesia. VII:1:249-250. (Ed.).
      Rhodesia. VI:21:13-14. (ON).
      Rhodesia again. VII:6:138. (ON).
      Rhodesia: Illegal! illegal! illegal! II:16:12-13. (ON).
      Rhodesia: the gap widens. VIII:8:181-182. (ON).
      Rhodesian executions. III:6:8. (ON).
Richard Nixon Rides Again. VII:23:550-551. (ON).
RICKS, J. C. Liberia's role in Africa. II:26:22-24.
Right about turn, right incline? III:11:12. (ON).
Right to be under-educated. E. A. Haizel. VI:20:6-7.
Right to practise medicine in Ghana: Some implications and a corol-
   lary. F. Hesse. III:5:12-21.
RIZVI, S. W. A. The Advanced Teacher Training College course: A re-
   joinder. IV:5:7-9.
Road safety. VII:20:477-478. (ON).
Road safety campaign. VIII:1:17. (ON).
Road safety: Some facts and figures. S. T. K. Boafo. IX:10:225-226.
Road to African Unity. J. M. Dake. II:22:19-20.
Rogues rendezvous. VIII:12:272. (ON).
Role of direct foreign private investments in Ghana's economic devel-
   opment. A. N. Hakam. II:12:10-12.
Role of history in a developing country. J. K. Fynn. III:2:9-11.
Role of local government in nation building. J. K. Ansere.
   V:3:i-viii.
Role of Middle Easterners in our economy. II:17:23.
Role of the Church in development. C. K. Ashun. VII:7:158-161.
Role of the President under the Constitution. K. Afreh. V:12:2-5.
Role of the Press. A. K. Narh. VII:8:182-184.
Role of the Press. IX:1:6-7. (ON).
Role of Trade Unions in Ghana. K. Afreh. VII:11:258-261.
Roots of dictatorship. VI:9:21. (ON).
ROURKE, B. E. Getting agriculture moving. VIII:16:370-373.
Rule of law and our Regime of Judges? Kontopiaat. III:6:17-20.
RURAL DEVELOPMENT
      AGBOZO, K. Rural development and economic development.
         VII:10:231-233.

(RURAL DEVELOPMENT)
    ANNAN, C. K. Implications of rural water development.
       III:19:4-6.
    DORM-ADZOBU, C. Handicraft industries: A tool for rural
       development in Ghana. VI:12:5-9.
    GYINAYE, J. Plight of our rural communities. VI:4:17-18.
    JONES-QUARTEY, K. A. B. Report from the Regions. 1) VI:19:6-8;
       2) VI:25:10-13; 3) VI:27:8-12.
    KUDIABOR, C. Planning for rural development in Ghana.
       V:24:6-9.
    MANU, O. Rural development and our chiefs. VI:2:16-20.
    Mass literacy and rural development. VII:26:622-623.
    The Mini-budget and rural development. VII:5:97-98. (Ed.).
    ODURO, K. K. Rural development and our economy solvency.
       VIII:20:478-481.
    OFORI, I. M. An integrated approach to rural development in
       Ghana. V:24:9-10.
    OFORI-AKYEA, E. A. Organisational instruments of rural devel-
       opment. V:24:4-6.
    _____. Problems of rural development. V:19:15-19.
    OPEKU, Y. A. The need to understand rural values. 1)
       VI:10:14-16; 2) VI:12:13-16.
    PEASAH, J. Ministry of Rural Development. IV:9:12-13.
    POBEE, J. O. M. Impressions of a visit to Brong-Ahafo: Inside
       B. A. VII:15:351-354.
    Social revolution in our countryside? V:24:1-2. (Ed.).
Rural-Urban migration in Ghana. I. M. Ofori. V:25:2-6.
RUSSIA
    ADALI-MORTTY, G. Industrial productivity: Soviet Style.
       V:13:2-6.
    JONES-QUARTEY, K. A. B. The Russian phenomenon. II:23:10-11.
Russian-trained Ghanaian Doctors--A Controversy or Misunderstanding.
    J. O. M. Pobee. VII:23:544-550.
Russian-trained Ghanaians. IV:16:13. (ON).
SAFFU, Y. Liberia's role in Africa. II:22:3-4.
SAFFU, Y. O. The proposed constitution--A riposte to the Republican
    Constitution? III:5:8-12.
_____. What has changed in Ghano-Ivoirien relations? III:12:4-7.
SAFO, D. B. Department of Post and Telecommunications. IV:11:6-7.
_____. The economic impact of the University on Cape Coast town.
    VIII:16:373-376.
_____. Population growth and family planning. V:8:8-9.
SAFO-ADU, K. Interview with Safo-Adu on the task force. VI:17:17-20.
    (ON).
SAI, F. T. Food, nutrition and agriculture. 1) II:20:5-7; 2)
    II:21:5-7.
Salaries or allowances for M. P.s? IV:12:7-8. (ON).
Salary dispute at Kumasi University. V:9:14-15. (ON).
Sale of, and private participation in, State enterprises. B. D. G.
    Folson. II:25:9-14.
Sale of land in Ashanti. G. Woodman. VI:11:5-8.
Sale of State Farms. II:23:15. (ON).
Sanity at E. C. A. Session. II:5:8-9. (ON).

SANTROFI. And it came to pass. Epistles. 1) VIII:25:606-607; 2) VIII:26:628-630; 3) IX:1:18-21; 4) IX:2:44-48; 5) IX:3:71-73; 6) IX:6:140-143; 7) IX:8:185-188; 8) IX:10:242-243; 9) IX:12:294-295.
_____. And it came to pass.... IX:14:344-347.
SARPONG, K. A. Busia and the new politics. V:20:9-13.
SASU, K. Towards civilian rule. IV:5:5-6.
Savundra, allegations and Commissions of Enquiry. II:25:2. (ON).
SAWYERR, G. F. A. East African Community: Crisis or confidence? VI:9:9-14.

_____. Recognition and African Unity. VI:16:5-9.
Scandal at the Stadium. VIII:5:108. (ON).
Scheck, (Saki). Interviewed. III:20:4-12.
Science degree examination at Cape Coast. V:17:20. (ON).
Scientific manpower crisis in Ghana--A rejoinder. N. Kotey and P. R. C. Williams. VII:4:80-86.
Scientific manpower in Ghana--Crisis in supply and demand. O. A. Y. Jackson. VII:1:6-9.
Scientific medicine--the Ghanaian experience. P. A. Twumasi. VI:27:12-15.
Second language English: Some attitudinal realities in Ghana. M. Kelby. III:17:13-14.
Second World Food Congress: A report. E. Ofori-Akyea. V:18:6-10.
Security Council Meeting in Africa. VII:1:12. (ON).
SEKYI, T. B. B. The proposed medical school at Kumasi. IX:12:290.
Select and annotated chronological history of Legon Society on National Affairs and the "Legon Observer." II:14:6.
Self-reliance all the way. VII:15:355-356. (ON).
Self-reliance and expatriate missionaries. R. A. Ampomah. VIII:20:484-486.
Self-reliance: Some unexplained departures. IX:1:8. (ON).
SENANU, K. E. Preserving our culture--The Adzido Dance Troupe. II:22:22-23.

_____. Thoughts on creating the popular theatre. 1) II:20:25-26; 2) II:21:22-23.
Senghor on Negritude and dialogue--interviewed by K. A. B. Jones-Quartey. VI:10:i-iv.
SERPENTARIUS. Bing on Ghana education. IV:1:4-7.
SETSE, T. K. Utopia and education. VII:14:332-334.
Settlement in the Sudan. VII:6:138-139. (ON).
7 Years later: Work habits in Ghana. VIII:14:327. (ON).
Seven years of history: Highlights from the columns of the "Legon Observer." VIII:14:322-324.
SEWARD, J. N. A comment on the current cocoa price. VI:10:13-14.
_____. Manipulating the budgets. V:7:2-3.
Sewerage works and traffic. VII:15:356. (ON).
SHIMAN, D. Reflections on the student Revolution. IV:1:7-8.
Shortages--What are the causes. W. S. K. Agbemawokla. VIII:5:105-106.
Should Ghana join the E. E. C.? K. Manu. VII:21:494-496.
Should Unions be allowed to strike. K. Adjei. III:20:12-14.
Show business on T. V. II:21:12. (ON).

SIERRA LEONE
    Civilian rule in Sierra Leone. III:10:1-2. (Ed.).
    Interview with the Prime Minister of Sierra Leone, Mr. Siaka
        Stevens. IV:4:i-viii.
    JONES-QUARTEY, K. A. B. Sierra Leone after the "non coups."
        1) II:26:8-10; 2) III:2:2-3.
    _____. Sierra Leone: Explosions in a constitutional crisis.
      II:4:8-9.
    _____. Sierra Leone: Explosions of a constitutional crisis.
      II:5:4-6.
    _____. Sierra Leone: recent changes and present trends. 1)
      III:10:i-vi; 2) III:13:i-viii.
    _____. Sierra Leone: Return to turmoil. V:21:11-16.
    _____. Sierra Leone--The role of the Press. V:25:i-viii.
    _____. Sierra Leone: tensions of a constitutional crisis.
      II:3:5-8.
    _____. Sierra Leone's turn. II:7:3-4.
    N. R. C. and free expression. Correspondent. II:8:19-20.
    Sierra Leone. II:25:6-7. (ON).
    Sierra Leone musical chairs. III:9:11-12. (ON).
    Sierra Leone situation. V:22:23-24. (ON).
    Sierra Leone: Soldiers and politicians. II:7:1-2. (Ed.).
    Sierra Leone: The dons reaffairm their faith in freedom
      (Memorandum). II:12:3-4.
    Sierra Leone: The lawyers review the position (Memorandum).
      II:9:18-19.
    Sierra Leone's new Republic--A Correspondent. 1) VI:13:8-12;
      2) VI:15:6-10.
Sight and Sound comes to Ghana. III:1:13. (ON).
Significance of income tax in developing countries. C. Lawson-Anson.
    IV:13:10-11.
Significance of President Losconczi's visit. G. Adali-Mortty.
    VIII:24:566-568.
Significance of the tenth anniversary Summit Meeting of the O. A. U.
    S. K. B. Asante. VIII:12:266-269.
SIMMONDS, R. The Chinese representation question in retrospect and
    prospect. VI:23:4-9.
Sincerity and poetry. (A reply to A. Britwum and A. A. Aidoo).
    A. N. Mensah. VII:13:314-315.
Sketch of the growth of the British Commonwealth. E. A. Muange.
    III:19:18-19.
Slow justice: An introduction to a problem. E. S. Aidoo. V:5:4-12.
So the scapegoat is dead. II:20:16. (ON).
So-called Joloff Rice. IV:1:10. (ON).
Soccer: Ghana bows to Morocco. Soccer Correspondent. III:14:31-32.
Soccer league system needs recasting. C. Boye. VIII:13:304-305.
SOCIAL PROBLEMS
    ADAM, B. Capital punishment--time to abolish it? V:3:7-8.
    ADOMAKO-BONSU. Some aspects of population growth and economic
      development in Ghana. VI:26:12-16.
    ANSAH, P. A. V. The case for identity cards. VII:10:236-238.

ASHUN, C. K. The role of the church in development.
VII:7:158-161.
BAAH-NUAKOH, A. A. The N. R. C. and a standard rent formula:
A Comment. VIII:8:188-191.
BAFI-YEBOAH, V. Educating the mentally retarded. IX:11:246-250.
BLACKIE, N. The youth and the national revolution.
VII:8:190-192.
BLANKSON, T. Development from the grass roots. VII:22:520-522.
BOAFO, S. T. The press, the government and the people.
IX:7:150-156.
BOAFO, S. T. K. Road safety: Some facts and figures.
IX:10:225-226.
BROOKS, R. G. Financing health services. VIII:25:596-601.
_____. The Hospital fees report. VIII:23:538-544.
GERRITSEN, R. Nima and the revolution--An open letter to Col.
Acheampong. VIII:13:299.
KPAKPOE-GLOVER, J. N. Government rent control policy.
VIII:5:102-105.
FISCIAN, C. E. The uses and abuses of drugs. 1) VI:7:11-14;
2) VI:8:9-15; 3) VI:9:19-20.
LAING, W. N. Medical laboratory technologists--A case for
recognition. VIII:24:571-574.
LAWSON-ANSONG, C. The struggle of youth for emancipation.
IV:11:11-14.
LOCK, J. M. Bush fires in Ghana. IX:12:270-274.
MENDS, E. Traditional values and bribery and corruption.
V:25:13-14.
Nation and language. A correspondent. VI:15:10-13.
NORTEY, D. N. A. The crime problem. V:25:9-13.
OFORI, I. M. Rural-Urban migration in Ghana. V:25:2-6.
OPARE-ABETIA, J. The growing overcrowding in our cities.
V:25:6-9.
OTCHERE, E. M. Legalisation of abortion. V:26:19-21.
PEIL, M. Ashiaman: Eyesore and opportunity. V:18:4-6.
POBEE, J. O. M. Impressions of a visit to Brong Ahafo--Inside
B. A. VII:15:351-354.
_____. The non-returning Ghanaian professional. VI:13:13-17.
Time for an enquiry into crime. VI:11:1-2. (Ed.).
TWUMASI, P. A. Scientific medical--The Ghanaian experience.
VI:27:12-15.
_____. Underdevelopment as a Social problem. VI:24:12-14.
Unemployment has become a major national problem. VI:15:1.
(Ed.).
Wanted: A new approach to social problems. V:25:1-2. (Ed.).
SOCIAL RESEARCH
DATE-BAH, E. The need for sociological research in Ghanaian
industries. VI:3:4-6.
Socialism in Africa. A. Lewis. III:12:7-10.
Socialist-Capitalist controversy: An economic appraisal. J. K. Atta.
VII:6:126-130.

Sociological implications of human rights. L. V. Naidoo. IV:1:17-18.
Solving the transport problem in Accra. E. K. Vorkeh. 1)
    VIII:13:294-296; 2) VIII:15:348-351; 3) VIII:16:378-382.
SOMALI
       GREENFIELD, R. Some impressions of Mogadishu--June 1974.
          IX:13:308-316.
Some aspects of population growth and economic development in Ghana.
    Adomako-Bonsu. VI:26:12-16.
Some factors in the growth in agricultural output. S. Kyemfe.
    VI:15:2-4.
Some factors which impede progress. K. Afreh. VII:9:209-213.
Some impressions of Mogadishu--June 1974. R. Greenfield.
    IX:13:308-316.
Some legal trends since the coup. K. Afreh. VI:5:16-21.
Some misgivings about the present state of the accountancy profession
    in Ghana. A. Ghartey. VIII:26:618-624.
Some misgivings about the present state of the accountancy profession
    in Ghana--A rejoinder. P. T. K. Aidam. IX:1:14-16.
Some misgivings about the present state of the accountancy profession
    in Ghana--Reply to a rejoinder. A. Ghartey. IX:3:70-71.
Some reflections on local government in Ghana. S. A. Nkrumah.
    VIII:1:10-11.
Some reflections on the performance of the economy since the coup.
    A Correspondent. VI:5:8-10.
Some thoughts on modernising agriculture in Ghana. B. B. Quraishy.
    VI:10:9-13.
Some trends in criminal legislation since independence. K. Afreh.
    1) VIII:17:397-403; 2) VIII:18:427-435; 3) VIII:19:448-454.
Some unfinished business. IV:22:22. (ON).
SOUTH AFRICA, REPUBLIC OF
       BUSIA, K. A. Statement on South Africa...in the National As-
          sembly.... VI:1:20-23.
       Inside the apartheid Kingdom--Letter to a friend. V:11:10-18.
       KARIKARI, K. A. The South African Problem. V:9:6.
       KITOSH. South Africa--Background to recent Political trends.
          1) V:15:4-7; 2) V:16:10-12.
       MGXASHE, M. South Africa. VI:7:15-16.
       OPPON-AGYARE, J. South Africa's Apartheid: An invitation to
          bloodbath. VI:5:7-10.
       Politics and economics in Southern Africa. II:21:1. (Ed.).
       President Banda's gamble. VI:18:1-2. (Ed.).
       The South Africa arms affairs. V:23:19. (ON).
       Vorster's Trojan horse. VI:7:1-2. (Ed.).
South East Asian trial of Strength. O. Y. Asamoah. III:4:21-22.
South West Africa and the U. N. II:8:9. (ON).
South West Africa and the U. N. III:7:10. (ON).
Southern Africa again. VIII:13:296. (ON).
Soviet trained Ghanaian doctors. III:2:4-22.
SOYINKA, W.
       Wole Soyinka: his talent and the mystery of his fate. C.
          Duodu. III:16:17-18.

Speaking for myself, I am not impressed.... II:14:14-15. (ON).
Special statement on Legon Observer (Special Issue) October 3, 1974.
SPORTS
>   BOYE, C. Soccer league system needs recasting. VIII:13:304-305.
>   Football slump. Sports Correspondent. (I) II:5:19-21.
>   Ghana and inter-African Soccer. IV:20:14-16. (ON).
>   Ghana and the Games. V:11:24. (ON).
>   Ghana vs. Nigeria. Soccer Correspondent. II:4:29-30.
>   Gift of Brazilian Football. Correspondent. V:14:24-26.
>   NYAHE, K. S. M. The last days of the giants. IV:23:22.
>   Obituary: Accra Great Olympics. Soccer Correspondent.
>   IV:2:22.
>   Recent Commonwealth Featherweight title fight. II:4:30-31.
>   Recent Commonwealth Featherweight title fight--A correction.
>   II:5:19.
>   Report: Ghana-Nigeria Cricket. III:9:20.
>   Soccer: Ghana bows to Morocco. Soccer Correspondent.
>   III:14:31-32.
Springs of fascism. V:2:11. (ON).
Standardization of vehicle imports and the economy. R. A. Kotey.
   VII:24:562-566.
Standing room only? VI:26:17. (ON).
State and religion. IV:21:13-14. (ON).
STATE ENTERPRISES
>   AGAMA, G. K. Foundations of economic policy: The State
>   Enterprises. II:10:5-8.
>   Profit and loss in State Enterprises. IX:12:284. (ON).
>   RADIX, A. Foreign participation in State Enterprises....
>   II:23:2-7.
>   Sale of, and private participation in State Enterprises.
>   Symposium and comment. II:25:9-28.
>   Sale of State Farms. II:23:15. (ON).
>   State Electronics Corporation. II:10:13-14. (ON).
>   State Enterprise in Ghana. The S. E. P. C. II:7:11. (ON).
>   State Enterprises. VII:2:37. (ON).
State Hotels and foreign participation. III:24:8-10. (ON).
State of the economy today. E. N. Omaboe. II:19:3-8.
State Protocol. IV:21:13. (ON).
State Transport Buses. III:24:11. (ON).
State visit and traffic. IV:17:16. (ON).
Statement by Public Officers and Politicians. VII:1:14. (ON).
Statement on South Africa by the Rt. Hon. Prime Minister at the Na-
   tional Assembly on Thursday, 10th December, 1970. IV:1:20-23.
Steps towards a disciplined policy--A Citizen. III:7:16-18.
STEUR, M. D. The devaluation debate. VIII:12:273-274.
_____. The growing data shortage. IX:3:58-59.
_____. Why the economy is not growing and what can be done about it.
   VIII:8:170-173.
STEVENS (S.). Interviewed. IV:4:i-viii.

Stock-exchange for Ghana. K. Pepee. VI:6:5-6.
Strategy for economic recovery: The 1967/68 budget. J. A. Dadson.
 II:17:13-15.
Strategy for inducing cocoa processing factories to locate in Ghana.
 A. N. Hakam. IX:9:198-201.
Stratification in Secondary Schools. VIII:16:382. (ON).
STREEK, B. Ghana: A visitor's view. VI:14:16-22.
Street markings and the rush hours. III:13:10. (ON).
Strikes and industrial harmony. S. Twum. V:16:2-8.
Structure of Education in rural areas. R. K. A. Gardiner. V:13:6-14.
Struggle of youth for emancipation--C. Lawson-Ansong. IV:11:11-14.
Student contribution to national affairs in 1973. A. Koi-Larbi.
 VIII:26:611-615.
Student demonstrations. VI:7:16-17. (ON).
Student power and the closure of the University of Ghana--Special
 reporter. III:23:2-4.
Student power of sorts. III:22:14. (ON).
Student's death at Sarbah Hall. V:4:16-17. (ON).
Students in politics. VI:10:16. (ON).
Students' Loan Scheme. J. Kambu. VI:17:12-16.
Students, Teachers and Student power. VII:24:572. (ON).
Successes in Guinea Bissau. VIII:8:181. (ON).
SUDAN
 Politics and religion in the Sudan. R. Greenfield. V:8:2-4.
Sugar industry in Ghana. A. Koranteng. VI:3:6-7.
Sugar Problem. J. C. W. Ahiakpor. VII:9:202-205.
Suggested amendments to the Draft Constitution. III:26:8-16.
Suggested local government reforms for Post-coup Ghana--A. T. K.
 Nanor. IV:15:8-10.
SULITZ, A. The out-turn of the first N. L. C. budget. III:2:7-8.
Supervision and accountability. VII:3:56. (ON).
Supreme Court and the Ghana Bar Association. VII:9:213-214. (ON).
T. V. tax. II:2:10-11. (ON).
Taking higher justice to the Regions. VIII:5:106-107. (ON).
Taking over haulage Companies. III:2:12. (ON).
TANSLEY, E. World Cocoa prices and underdevelopment in Ghana--A re-
 joinder. VII:24:578-580.
Task ahead. K. Achampon-Manu. IV:10:10-11.
Task force. VI:12:19-20. (ON).
Tasteless anti-climax. IV:23:18. (ON).
Taxi and "Tro-Tro" fares. II:4:22. (ON).
Taxi rates: a bad case of capitulation. J. Apronti. VIII:9:208-210.
Teacher and Ghanaian education: In search of an orientation.
 K. A. B. Jones-Quartey. VII:16:374-377.
Teachers and the Secondary Schools. A. Dickson. II:15:8-10.
Teachers and unionism. IV:23:16-18. (ON).
Teachers' salaries. II:7:15.
TEKYI, J. R. [et al]. The Mills-Odoi report and pharmacists.
 III:13:16.
That "Man of the Month" film. IV:19:8-9. (ON).

That statement. II:25:2-3. (ON).
These charter flights. N. Blackie. VIII:6:141-142.
These postponements. VI:21:14-16. (ON).
These Prime Minister's Motorcades. V:19:20. (ON).
Thinking about our future constitution. IX:9:205. (ON).
Third force: Dynamics of an ideal. M. Assimeng. IV:14:4-7.
Third U. N. E. S. C. O. international conference on Adult Education--
    Tokyo--July 25 to 7th August 1972. K. Ampene. VII:19:455-456.
Third Woman. M. F. Castagno. IV:4:iii-vii.
THOM, T. K. D. The Vea tragedy. III:19:17-18.
Those afternoon Jumps. V:13:25-26. (ON).
Those jaunts in the United States. V:22:24-25. (ON).
Thoughts from the North. II:22:11-12. (ON).
Thoughts on creating the popular Theatre. K. E. Senanu. 1)
    II:20:25-26; 2) II:21:22-23.
Three constitutional decrees. A. Radix. III:4:5-9.
365 days of the rule of law. II:4:19-20. (ON).
Three leading issues in agricultural policy. S. La-Anyane. II:20:3-5.
"Three women." II:24:10-11. (ON).
THROWER, J. Belief in God--reply to my critics. II:3:16-18.
TICKLE, I. Twelve states in Nigeria. III:10:2-3.
To our detractors. VII:14:318-322.
To those who have.... VIII:17:406-407. (ON).
To Uli and back. J. Apronti. VII:22:530-532.
Tourism and Ghana. A. N. Hakam. II:3:10-12.
Tourism in Ghana. III:21:16. (ON).
Tourists and foreign exchange. VII:17:405. (ON).
Towards civilian rule. K. A. Sasu. IV:5:5-6.
Towards civilian rule. S. O. Gyandoh. II:8:6-8.
Towards happier regions. III:3:5. (ON).
Towards the dignity of blackness. O. Y. Asamoah. II:20:8-9.
Trade Fair and Ghana's prospects for trade and investments. A. N.
    Hakam. II:5:14-15.
Trade Fair and the economy. G. K. Agama. II:3:9-10.
Trade Fair preparations. II:2:10. (ON).
Trade surpluses and shortages. VII:26:619. (ON).
TRADE UNIONS
        AFREH, K. The role of Trade Unions in Ghana. VII:11:258-261.
        The Government and T. U. C. VI:19:1. (Ed.).
TRADITION AND CULTURE
        ACKOM-MENSAH, I. Chieftaincy in crisis. II:7:9-10.
        ARHIN, K. Behind the Asantehene's majesty. V:21:5-8.
        Chieftaincy. VIII:1:16. (ON).
        Chieftaincy on trial. V:12:1-2. (Ed.).
        Courts for chiefs. VI:22:2. (Ed.).
        GYANDOH, S. O. Chieftaincy in crisis. II:2:6-8.
        KUMASI, B. L. J. Chieftaincy disputes in Bolgatanga.
            VI:3:16-17.
        Nation and its culture. VII:18:413-414. (Ed.).
        Preserving our culture--The Adzido Dance Troupe. II:22:22-23.
        Traditional courts. IV:14:16-17. (ON).

Traditional values and bribery and corruption. E. Mends. V:25:13-14.
Tragic illusions. T. Akpata. III:3:2-4.
Training mining engineers. VIII:3:59-62. (ON).
Training of local council staff in Ghana. A. T. K. Nanor. V:16:9-10.
Transport authority for Accra-Tema. II:20:14-15. (ON).
Transport problem reconsidered. K. Ewusi. VI:9:5-8.
Travelling Salesman of Evil. V:12:10. (ON).
TREBLA, A. Is the top incapacitated? V:19:14-15.
Trends in the cocoa trade. W. R. Koranteng. II:19:10-12.
TREVE, E. The availability and non-availability of goods and services--
    the problem of shortages. 1) VII:25:588-594; 2) VIII:1:7-10.
_____. Economic measures for 1973-74: Strengths and Weaknesses. 1)
    VIII:18:418-422; 2) VIII:19:442-447; 3) VIII:21:493-496.
_____. The management of the Ghanaian economy--The reliance on
    controls. IX:6:130-134.
_____. The N. R. C.: Economic reality vs. Political reality.
    VII:8:184-186.
_____. A note on Ghana's policy of Self-reliance. VII:16:371-372.
Tribalism as a syndrome. M. Assimeng. IV:23:3-6.
Tribalism in Ghana? M. Bossman. II:15:20-21.
Tributes to Lieutenant General E. K. Kotoka. II:9:3-5.
Trip to Ho. D. Hereward. VII:26:630-631.
Troops on exercises. III:21:16. (ON).
Truces in Nigeria. IV:1:9. (ON).
TRUTENAU, H. M. J. A resurgence of intolerance? IV:5:10-11.
Tubman, W. V. S. President of Liberia 1943-1971. B. I. Obichere.
    VI:18:5-10.
TUFFUOR, K. No need for external examiners in West African Universities.
    VI:24:15-16.
Twelve States in Nigeria. I. Tickle. III:10:2-3.
Twenty-five years of the United Nations and human rights: An African
    Viewpoint. S. K. B. Asante. VIII:25:591-596.
Two decades of growth. A. Lewis. III:9:3-4.
Two great men. VI:15:18-19. (ON).
TWUM, S. Industrial relations and the high court. VI:24:6-10.
_____. Strikes and industrial harmony. V:16:2-8.
TWUM-BARIMA, V. O. D. The tragic death of a national hero, Lt. Gen.
    E. K. Kotoka, as seen from the occult point of view. II:13:16-17.
TWUMASI, P. A. Scientific medicine--the Ghanaian experience.
    VI:27:12-15.
_____. Underdevelopment as a social problem. VI:24:12-14.
TWUMASI, Y. (jt. au.) See IRELE, A.
TWUMASI, Y. The political failure of Gbedemah--myths exploded. 1)
    IV:20:3-5; 2) IV:21:8-10.
U. N. C. T. A. D. VI:11:262. (ON).
U Thant of the U. N. V:2:9-10. (ON).
UGANDA
        EL AMIN, R. N. The Asians in Uganda. VII:17:392-394.
        Coup d'etat in Uganda. VI:3:1-2. (Ed.).
        General Amin and the Asians. VII:17:389-390. (Ed.).

IRELE, A. and Y. TWUMASI. Press Freedom on Trial in Uganda.
   IV:4:25-26.
KOFI, T. A. Obote-the man. VI:6:20-21.
NEOGY, R. Obote-the man. VI:4:4-5.
OFORI-AKYEA, E. Background to Ugandan politics. V:1:4-7.
Under-And Over-Invoicing. VII:11:261-262. (ON).
Underdevelopment as a social problem. P. A. Twumasi. VI:24:12-14.
Unemployment in Ghana. K. N. Afful. 1) VII:11:254-258; 2)
   VII:12:279-282.
Unemployment problem. J. L. S. Abbey and K. Brew. V:26:11-13.
UNITED NATIONS
   ASANTE, S. K. B. Africa in the United Nations. VII:22:514-519.
   _____. Twenty-five years of the United Nations and human
   rights: An African Viewpoint. VIII:25:591-596.
   _____. The United Nations: Twenty-eight years of trial.
   VIII:22:514-518.
   Dilemma of the United Nations. V:14:3-4. (Ed.).
   The future of the U. N. V:22:1-2. (Ed.).
   KARIKARI, K. A. The United Nations: Crisis of Confidence and
   Will. II:20:11-13.
   KWAKU, K. The United Nations as an instrument of peace--An
   African viewpoint. VII:24:566-568.
   U Thant of the U. N. V:2:9-10. (ON).
   United Nations. VI:21:13. (ON).
UNITED STATES OF AMERICA
   America at the Cross-roads. Political Correspondent.
   III:9:4-10.
   APRONTI, J. Racial discrimination in America. V:22:16-18.
   ASAMOAH, O. Y. America in Agony. III:8:6-8.
   BRUCHAC, J. Assassination--An American Art. III:13:6-8.
   GYANDOH, S. O. Watergate, law and commonsense. VIII:22:518-520.
   JONES-QUARTEY, K. A. B. The view from Washington.
   VIII:18:424-427.
   KUMAR, A. The dollar crisis. VI:18:12-15.
   MACDONALD, A. D. The U. S. foreign aid debate. VI:25:8-10.
   U. S. Presidency. III:24:7-8. (ON).
UNIVERSITIES
   Background to the University close-down. IX:4:82-84. (ON).
   Closing down the Universities. IX:4:77-78. (Ed.).
   Duplication in our Universities. IX:10:221-222. (Ed.).
   Extravagance at Congregations. IV:6:1-2. (Ed.).
   Purpose of University education in Ghana today. VIII:22:523-524.
University autonomy and academic freedom in Ghana. L. H. Ofosu-Appiah.
   1) II:6:10-13; 2) II:7:5-8.
University College of Cape Coast: A unique experiment. K. A. Karikari.
   V:8:9-11.
University Congregations. V:6:10-12. (ON).
University entrance and guidance in Schools. A. K. Bulley.
   VIII:23:544-546.
University grades and standards. VI:4:13-14. (ON).
University Loan Scheme. P. T. K. Aidam. VI:16:9-10.

UNIVERSITY OF GHANA
    ASSIMENG, M. Legon: The frustrated tribe. V:7:8-10.
    ATOBRA, K. Legon's role in the development of geological
        studies in Ghana--The discussion so far. VIII:11:257-258.
    The Auditor-General and the University of Ghana   II:6:1-2.
        (Ed.).
    AYETEY, J. K. Geological training at Legon.... VIII:11:259.
    BEKOE, D. A. Legon's role in the development of geological
        studies in Ghana--A rejoinder. VIII:9:206-208.
    DODOO, E. O. The accusation of extravagance at Legon.
        IV:8:16-18.
    KWASHIE, A. P. Geological training.... VIII:11:259.
    OCRAN, V. Legon's role in the development of geological studies
        in Ghana. 1) VIII:9:204-206; 2) VIII:11:258-259.
UNIVERSITY OF SCIENCE AND TECHNOLOGY
    Report of the University of Science and Technology, Kumasi.
        1) A. A. Kwapong. III:8:20-22; 2) L. H. Ofosu-Appiah.
        III:5:21-23.
UPHOFF, N. An element of repetition in Ghanaian elections: 1956 and
    1969. V:1:19.
UPPER REGION
    POBEE, J. O. M. Inside the Northern and Upper Regions. 1)
        IX:4:98-99; 2) IX:11:260-262.
    RAY. M. The coming famine season. III:24:16-18.
Urban planning; towards better city centres. C. C. T. Blankson.
    VIII:12:269-271.
Urgently needed--A genuine revolution. K. Arhin. VI:24:4-6.
Urgently needed--Responsible Journalism. VII:5:115-116. (ON).
Uses and abuses of drugs. C. E. Fiscian. 1) VI:7:11-14; 2)
    VI:8:9-15; 3) VI:9:19-21.
Utilization of executive talents in a developing Ghana. K. Adjei.
    II:16:10-12.
Utopia and education. T. K. Setse. VII:14:332-334.
Vandalism in International football. IX:12:286. (ON).
VAN DANTZIG, A. See Dantzig, A. Van.
VARTARIAN, G. A. Medical education in the U. S. S. R.--A rejoinder.
    VIII:2:43-46.
Vea tragedy. T. K. D. Thom. III:19:17-18.
Vice-Chancellor S. O. Biobaku of University of Lagos, Interviewed by
    K. A. B. Jones-Quartey. V:12:i-vii.
Vietnam--A glimpse of hope. III:23:6. (ON).
Viet-Nam, the President and the people. IV:22:22. (ON).
View from Washington. K. A. B. Jones-Quartey. VIII:18:424-427.
Violence in politics. IV:14:17. (ON).
Visions and compromises: thoughts on the budget speech. A Corre-
    spondent. VI:17:2-8.
Visit of the Surinam chiefs. V:24:18. (ON).
Voluntary sterilisation as a component of a family planning programme.
    C. E. Fiscian. VIII:11:247-251.
"Volunteers to America" and the Ministry of Education. II:10:12-13.
    (ON).

VORKEH, K. Ghana's declining poultry industry. IX:8:174-178.
_____. Solving the transport problem in Accra. 1) VIII:13:294-296;
      2) VIII:15:348-351; 3) VIII:16:378-382.
Vultures are flying. IV:26:21-22. (ON).
Wage and salary increases--Are they necessary? (and our economy)
      K. Adjei. III:14:16-17.
Wake up P. and T. Department. E. K. Kumi. VII:24:568-570.
Wanted--A national health policy. A Ghanaian. III:17:18-20.
War and economics in Nigeria. III:1:11-12. (ON).
Warning to the C. P. P. IV:10:12-13. (ON).
Wasting talent. III:1:10-11. (ON).
Watergate, law and commonsense. S. O. Gyandoh. VIII:22:518-520.
We have no alternative. A. O. Cukwurah. V:1:3-4.
We too can do! IV:24:21. (ON).
Wealth of the nation. J. H. Mensah. VI:14:i-ix.
Welcome Transition! V:24:18. (ON).
West African drought. VIII:18:435-436. (ON).
WESTERN REGION
      POBEE, J. O. M. Inside the Western Region. 1) VIII:4:94-95;
            2) VIII:5:112-116.
What does the N. R. C. stand for? K. Afreh. VII:18:420-428.
What has changed in Ghano-Ivorien relations? Y. O. Saffu. III:12:4-7.
What I think. G. A. Ashitey. III:21:18-19.
What is left of Non-alignment? V:19:20-21. (ON).
What is respect? E. F. G. Mante. VI:7:18-19.
What John Fynn said. VI:11:18-19. (ON).
What kind of candidates for the next Parliament? C. Kudiabor.
      III:6:6-8.
What next on the VC-10 affair? IV:3:10. (ON).
What price "Culture?" VI:17:20. (ON).
What price import substitution? J. C. W. Ahiakpor. VI:26:2-9.
What the public should know about rabies. P. A. K. Addy.
      VII:26:615-618.
What type of teacher? E. K. Asamoah. II:22:17-18.
What will go wrong. K. Kontopiaat. VII:4:93-94.
What's in a Name? VII:11:263-264. (ON).
When Lonhro comes rolling in. Kontopiaat. III:24:14-16.
When the Abbott came marching in. Kontopiaat. II:23:21-23.
When women congregate. III:25:16-18. (ON).
When ye Abbott went marching on. Kontopiaat. III:1:21-22.
Which way Dr. Progress Busia? Kontopiaat. IV:25:18-22.
Whither Ghana? J. Oppong-Agyare. III:25:3-4.
Who advises the government? S. A. Nkrumah. VIII:6:129-131.
Who gets what job? VI:13:18-19. (ON).
Who is a Ghanaian? K. Kontopiaat. V:3:16-19.
Who is an alien? VI:27:16-17. (ON).
Who is an ideal ruler in Africa? E. M. Otchere. VI:21:11-12.
Who pays the ¢120 million oil bill? W. Nelson. IX:6:134-136.
Whose freedom of the Press? VIII:17:407-408. (ON).
Whose responsibilities are priorities? VIII:7:160. (ON).

Why international opinion supports Biafra. P. O. Esedebe.
    IV:16:9-10.
Why registration is a must. III:21:14. (ON).
Why should we let sleeping dogs lie. K. Arhin. IV:23:11-12.
Why the economy is not growing and what can be done about it. M. D.
    Steur. VIII:8:170-173.
Why we study the Classics. L. Gyesi-Appiah. IV:15:12-14.
Why we study or not study the Classics. Educat. IV:17:10-11.
WILLIAMS, D. The horse's mouth: Adzido. III:1:22-23.
WILLIAMS, P. R. C. (jt. au.). See Kotey, N.
WIREDU, J. E. 'Dialogue' as a problem. VI:1:23-29.
_____. Free speech: a brief comment on an ambiguity. V:6:6-7.
_____. How to build a dictatorship again in Ghana. III:1:4-6.
_____. Our present situation and the future. VIII:2:26-29.
_____. Policies and personalities. IV:18:8-24.
WIREDU, J. E. (jt. au.). See Ofosu-Amaah, G. K. A.
Withdrawal of scholarships. K. Arhin. II:7:20-21.
Wole Soyinka: his talent and the mystery of his fate. C. Duodu.
    III:16:17-18.
WOODE, A. The Ghana-Abbott Agreement. II:25:14-15.
WOODE, S. N. District and local councils. VI:6:8-10.
_____. Leadership in local government. V:26:i-viii.
WOODMAN, G. How can rents be controlled? VII:20:466-470.
_____. Land law reform: reducing insecurity of title. 1)
    III:22:6-9; 2) III:23:7-11.
_____. Making land available for agricultural development.
    VII:14:i-viii.
_____. The recent rent control legislation. VIII:9:198-201.
_____. Sale of land in Ashanti. VI:11:5-8.
Working hours. III:22:12-14. (ON).
World and America. II:4:20. (ON).
World cocoa prices and Underdevelopment in Ghana. T. A. Kofi. 1)
    VII:18:414-420; 2) VII:19:438-443; 3) E. Tansely. VII:24:578-580.
World Health day: Your heart is your health. J. O. M. Pobee.
    VII:7:154-158.
Women and the nation. C. O. Kisiedu. V:7:17-18.
Women's nightmare at security check-point. II:4:20-21.
Women's Society for Public Affairs. III:13:8-10. (ON).
YAKUBU (B. A.). Interviewed. III:14:4-8.
YARTEY, F. NII. See Nii-Yartey, F.
YAWSON, K. Conversation or Confrontation. IV:24:4-6.
Year in retrospect. Editorial Staff Writer. III:14:28-31.
Year of African solidarity: The O. A. U. at eleven. S. K. B. Asante.
    IX:12:278-283.
Year's economic review. K. Manu. VIII:1:4-6.
YEBOAH, S. Is Christmas for Christians? IV:26:14-18.
YEBOAH, V. BAFI. See Bafi-Yeboah, V.
Yendi crisis. IV:19:8. (ON).
Yet another team of Experts! IV:2:16. (ON).
Your God is too small. C. R. Gaba. 1) II:15:16-17; 2) II:18:17.
Youth and the national revolution. N. Blackie. VII:8:190-192.

YOUTH ORGANISATIONS
      A caution on the creation of a national youth organization.
         A. Koí-Larbi. VIII:24:580-583.
ZAMBIA
      ASSIMENG, M. Zambia's Sectarian problems. IV:7:8-11.
Zambia vs. Rhodesia and Co. Deeds, not words. VIII:1:18. (ON).
Zambian delegation and that flag. V:21:18. (ON).
ZIMBABWE
      GREENFIELD, R. Lord Pearce and Zimbabwe: The report of the
         Commission on Rhodesian opinion. VII:11:250-254.
      Kicking Zimbabweans around. VII:16:379-380. (ON).
      OBICHERE, B. I. Apartheid in Zimbabwe. VI:1:12-15.
ZUOLO, C. T. Civil servants and pay increase. III:11:251-253.

Correspondence

A. K. M. Administrative arrogance. II:23:17.
ABAIDOO, R. M. Apples. VII:24:575-576.
ABAKAH, K. National government for Ghana. VII:15:358.
_____. Reward for N. L. C. II:24:16.
ABAKAH, N. Compliance order exercise--A failure. V:24:22.
ABANYIE, P. B. University admission requirements. IX:7:160.
Abbott-Ghana Controversy. 1) I. K. Minta; 2) Korle-Bu Doctor.
    II:24:11; 3) An Expatriate.
Abbott-Ghana Ltd. K. Agbeli. II:26:14.
Abbott marches off. Y. Assah-Sam. III:2:16-17.
"Abe Fortas affair"--A reply. B. Osakwe. IV:13:14-16.
ABIRI, J. Omnibus politics. II:22:14.
ABIRI, K. Was this necessary--or just big? VIII:10:237.
Aboabo Day Nursery. K. N. Hanson. IV:26:25.
ABOAGYE, F. S. Jehovah's witnesses and the millennium. V:6:15.
ABOAGYE-AKYEA, N. "Black is beautiful."--A reply. IV:13:14.
_____. Not one better than another. IV:23:19.
Abolition of Cocoa spraying scheme. K. Akwabi-Ameyaw. VIII:6:137.
ABRADU, K. KWABERE. See Kwabere-Abradu, K.
ABROKWAH, K. C. P. P. and blows. II:3:15.
ABROKWAH, K. Y. Disqualification and exemption. III:14:22.
ABRUQUAH, J. W. Church and education in Ghana. III:23:18-19.
_____. Turmoil in Ghana Schools and Colleges. II:18:16.
"Abuse of Freedom." J. M. Asante-Yeboah. V:8:18.
Academy of Sciences. L. W. Hesse. II:8:14-16.
Accidents--Macchi jet aircraft. M. A. Otu. II:6:16.
Accra-Tema City Council. 1) A. Barney, 2) K. A. Sasu. II:14:27.
Accra-Tema City Transport. E. K. Ofori. II:24:17.
Accusations of tribalism. M. Charles. V:14:23.
ACHAMPONG, A. P. Organising Mass Education. VII:23:552.
ACHEAMPONG, A. K. "Nkrumah passes away"--Rejoinder. VII:11:264.
ACHEAMPONG, K. MANU. See Manu-Acheampong, K.
ACHEAMPONG, P. K. Nkrumah and the building of Socialism. VII:11:267.
ACHEAMPONG, P. S. Low local production: Its remedy. III:20:22-24.
ACHEAW, W. OWUSU. See Owusu-Acheaw, W.
ACHINA, P. C. K. Personality cult again? IV:16:16.

Correspondence

ACHINA, P. C. T. Mills-Odoi and P. and T. technicians. V:11:26-28.
ACKAH, F. Scholarships. II:4:12.
ACKAH-MENSAH, A. The Middle-East crisis. VIII:26:626.
_____. [Santrofi]. IX:1:10.
ACKOM, P. E. Price of foodstuff. IX:4:87.
_____. Re-establish the G. C. E. VIII:21:504-506.
ACKOM-MENSAH, I. Development of Saturday Expectation. II:15:19.
ACKON, A. Who will go to heaven? VII:23:555.
ACQUAH, S. N. Family rearing at public expense? V:21:18.
ACQUAYE, J. A. Gilbey's gin. II:20:22.
ACQUAYE, S. K. Of grammatical rules and literary habits. IV:19:12.
Action not words. L. Blay-Amihere. VIII:12:285.
ADARKWA, J. K. Give us some more. VIII:16:384.
_____. The police and the public. IV:19:10.
_____. Scrap this project. VIII:14:336.
ADDAE, C. Cape Coast University College. V:11:26.
_____. Personal Assistants. IV:26:24.
_____. Trade with South Africa? III:11:14.
ADDAE, F. The beaver aircraft accident. V:14:22.
ADDAE, F. F. Disgruntled politicians and all that--rejoinder.
    VIII:20:482.
_____. Street names in Ghana--rejoinder. VIII:15:364.
ADDAE, K. Where is Kontopiaat? IV:15:16.
ADDAE-MENSAH. Nkrumah passes away--rejoinder. VII:10:240-241.
ADDAE-MENSAH, I. Safety on our roads--A rejoinder. IX:10:232-234.
ADDAE-MENSAH, K. Trade with South Africa. VI:11:21.
ADDAI, F. The concept of service. IX:3:67-68.
ADDEI, K. Car maintenance allowance. VI:17:22.
ADDO, A. Nkrumah passes away--Rejoinder. VII:10:241-242.
ADDO, AMOAKO. See Amoako-Addo.
ADDO, J. "Nkrumah passes away."--Rejoinder. VII:11:264.
ADDO, K. A. Recognition of chiefs. III:1:17.
ADDO, N. T. Impartiality for sale. VII:26:629-630.
ADDY, C. Student Loan Scheme. VI:16:21.
ADDY, E. Dishonesty in public life. VI:18:18.
_____. The need for press council. V:26:18-19.
ADEI, C. K. Ghana Airways to serve Ghanaian food? VII:19:453.
ADETI, E. K. Kwame Nkrumah and Ghana. VI:13:20.
ADIBI, S. Q. The Observer Standard. V:7:16.
ADIELE, A. C. Truth about Biafra. III:8:10.
ADINKRAH, K. O. Students and Self-interest. IX:1:10.
ADINKRAH, S. W. Keep it up, Observer. VII:10:242.
ADJEI, A. O. Military training in the Universities. VIII:12:284-285.
ADJEI, B. Coup d'etat in Uganda. VI:7:18.
_____. 'The Ghanaian establishment.' IV:4:29.
_____. Observer's stand. VI:10:18-19.
_____. One can apportion blame. VIII:16:383-384.
ADJEI, M. Giving unto God and unto Caesar. VIII:8:185.
ADJEI, P. K. Mini-Beer in state Hotels. VII:21:500.

ADJEI-BRENYA, D. Biafra and Nigeria. IV:25:17-18.
_____. Christianity and maternal inheritance. VIII:26:626-627.
_____. Disgruntled politicians and all that. VIII:19:458.
_____. Hutchful's confrontation. V:24:21.
_____. No Sir, Sir Alec! IX:4:90.
_____. Stop this drilling. VIII:3:64-65.
_____. The tragedy in Burundi. VII:12:288.
_____. The University Loan Scheme. VI:2:15.
ADJEI-FAH, M. Keep right in 1794? VIII:23:558.
Administering the bitter pill or lessons in government--A rejoinder.
     G. M. Afeti. IX:14:342.
Administration of the Bawku district. S. Dahamani. II:20:20.
Administration of the Kusasi district. A. A. Yakubu. II:18:15-16.
Administrative arrogance. 1) K. M. A. II:23:17; 2) F. T. Sai.
     II:25:8.
ADOMAKO, Y. O. Ghana's unemployment problems. V:14:23-24.
ADOTEY, S. The cement situation. VIII:6:137.
_____. Choosing trading partners. VIII:7:163.
_____. Compound surnames for our wives. VII:7:172.
_____. Fire fighting in Ghana. IX:3:67.
_____. Ghana Sports must be reviewed. VIII:3:68.
_____. Good quality products are needed. VIII:26:626.
_____. Granulated sugar and foreign exchange. VIII:22:529.
_____. High costs and price control. VI:15:20.
_____. Quality control and made-in-Ghana goods. VII:17:406.
ADU, J. Oil and the economy. V:16:22.
ADU, J. E. B. The significance of Guru Nanak. V:3:14-16.
ADU, K. Violation of Territorial Waters. III:24:12.
ADU, M. A. Asutsuare sugar underweight? VIII:8:187.
_____. We must examine ourselves. VIII:14:336.
ADUGU, G. H. K. AMEHIA. See Amehia-Adugu, G. H. K.
ADU-GYAMFI, P. Disqualification Decree. IV:5:14-16.
_____. Education in Ghana. III:22:20-21.
_____. Ghana Airways V. C. 10. IV:3:16.
_____. How non-aligned are we? III:4:12.
_____. The Nigerian War. V:3:12.
_____. Political detainees and National reconciliation. VII:25:602.
_____. Return to civilian rule. 1) III:12:16; 2) VII:22:525.
_____. What next, Mr. Wilson. IV:14:20.
_____. Youth Associations. IV:1:12.
ADU-SARKODIE, A. "Operation Feed Yourself." VII:13:307.
_____. Osofo Dadzie and the Graduate. VIII:7:163.
ADUONUM, L. E. D. Slow justice in Ghana. V:9:18-20.
ADUONUM-DARKO. What is more worthy--the car or the road? VIII:8:187.
Adverts in the Legon Observer. 1) E. Hinson. IX:11:254; 2) K. Agbley.
     IX:13:318.
Advisory opinion and draft constitution. 1) K. Baah. III:17:12; 2)
     E. S. Aidoo. III:18:18.
AFARI-GYAN. The case for identity cards--A rejoinder. VII:12:287.
_____. Welfare state in Ghana? V:25:19.

Correspondence

AFATSIAWO, S. F. The Ghana Airways conflict. III:9:14.
AFEIDZI, K. Slot machines and all that. VII:26:628.
AFETI, G. M. Administering the bitter pill or lessons in Government--
    A rejoinder. IX:14:342.
AFFUL, R. A. Southern Rhodesia--Case of British hypocrisy. III:7:11.
_____. Whither Ghana? II:25:30.
AFFUL, S. K. Who was in contempt? VII:26:629.
AFRANE, O. The Press. VII:9:217.
AFREH-KASAAM, J. Ghanaians in Nigeria today. II:21:13.
Africa and the E. E. C. G. Asiama-Ansong. VIII:12:285.
Africa and western values. D. Hereward. V:6:15.
African deal. K. O. Tetteh. IX:13:318.
African in Latin America. H. M. J. Trutenau. V:13:27.
African intellectuals and western tradition. K. Archampong.
    II:24:13-16.
African scene. J. Markham. II:1:15-16.
African Scholarships Programme for American Universities. III:3:12.
African viewpoint on human rights. P. A. V. Ansah. VIII:26:624-625.
Africans on African affairs. F. Amoakohene. IX:1:12-13.
Africa's unstable governments? 1) M. Charles. V:4:18; 2) V.
    Balakrishrian. V:6:13.
Afro-Americans and Africa. Amoako-Addo. V:5:21.
Afro-Arab solidarity? J. A. Owusu-Yaw. IX:14:344.
After the fires next time. C. Hayford. VII:15:360.
AGBELENGOR, C. K. Redeployment of Ex-C. C. E. officers. VII:18:432.
AGBELI, K. Abott-Ghana Ltd. II:26:14.
AGBENGU, G. K. Rice in financial crisis. V:8:20.
AGBEL, G. M. Keep the standards high. IV:20:18-19.
AGBLE, J. M. These multiple taxes. V:11:28.
AGBLE, Y. Protecting the consumer. VII:25:603.
AGBLE, Y. M. Kotoka, Freedom and Justice. II:16:17.
_____. Postmen and mosquitoes. II:7:19.
_____. The Rhodesian Independence issue. VI:25:21.
_____. Talking Point. VII:18:432.
_____. West Indians and British services. VIII:9:214.
AGBLEY, K. Adverts in the Legon Observer--A rejoinder. IX:13:318.
AGBOKLU, F. W. Y. The case for disqualification. II:24:12.
AGBOSU, M. The barometer of public opinion. III:23:16.
_____. Foreign Government Scholarships. IV:6:23.
AGBOSU, M. Y. The big cars and our economy. III:16:20.
_____. These military promotions! V:18:14.
AGBOZO, K. Around the world on the nation's business. II:23:16-17.
AGEZO, C. N. L. C. and future politics. III:18:20.
Agricultural and other research papers. J. O. Gordon. III:1:17.
Agricultural Loans. P. Manso. VI:19:15.
Agricultural research papers. 1) Lawson and Innes. II:24:16; 2)
    G. M. K. Kpedekpo. II:25:30.
Agricultural 'revolution' in Northern Ghana. B. E. Rourke. VII:1:15.
AGYARE, J. A. These pot-holes. III:14:24.
AGYARE, J. OPPONG. See Oppong-Agyare, J.

Correspondence

AGYARE, K. The "Legon Observer's" defeat. II:25:29.
AGYARKO-APPEA, Y. Let us be realistic. VIII:4:93.
AGYEI, B. Apology of a report. IV:9:18-20.
AGYEKUM, A. Duplication in our Universities--rejoinder. IX:11:250-251.
AGYEMAN, K. The Czech issue. III:19:16.
AGYEMAN, K. B. Cover charge in State Hotels. VII:21:501.
AGYEMANG. O. Legon Observer's shattering defeat. II:24:17.
AHIA, K. Milk more valuable than blood. VIII:6:137.
AHIABOR, C. The plight of poverty. V:19:21-22.
AHULU, F. D. KONOTEY. See Konotey-Ahulu, F. D.
AIDOO, E. S. Advisory opinion and the Draft Constitution. III:18:18.
_____. Articles in the "Legon Observer." VII:21:502.
_____. Kontopiaat and the Judicial Service. II:16:16.
_____. Legal aid in Ghana. V:6:14.
_____. National honours. IX:4:87.
_____. Onward with the revolution--A rejoinder. IX:11:252.
_____. Self-reliance and expatriate missionaries--rejoinder.
     VIII:23:556.
_____. Sewerage works and traffic. VII:16:380.
_____. The subversion decree. VII:16:380.
AIDOO, K. EDRISAH. See Edrisah-Aidoo, K.
AIDOO, W. Y. Salary increases for the lower income group. III:11:16.
_____. Unemployment. III:5:26.
Air pollution. D. Hereward. III:21:18.
Airport parking toll. E. Daniel. VIII:7:161-162.
AKAINYAH, L. B. Encouraging immorality. V:8:21.
_____. Opinion polls. III:3:8.
Akainyah in retrospect. R. S. Blay. II:1:17-18.
AKIDA, S. Opinion polls. III:26:23.
AKIWUMI, A. A. Discrimination in our own country. II:4:23.
AKOM K. Sekou Toure and Nkrumah's body. VII:11:264-265.
Akosombo Power. K. A. Sasu. II:9:21.
AKPANYA, J. K. S. Split in the Volta Region. V:26:19.
AKUETTEH, D. Financing National Service Corps. V:4:18.
AKUETTEH, D. N. General Afrifa and the Constitution. V:18:14.
AKUETTEH, N. K. Declaration of Assets. VI:2:14.
AKUFFO, G. B. Stop this bullying now--A rejoinder. VII:6:141.
AKUFFO, H. K. Delays at the licensing offices. V:13:26-27.
_____. Where is Kontopiaat? V:7:14-16.
AKUFFO, S. B. "Capitalism, Socialism and Ghana."--A rejoinder.
     VIII:17:410.
_____. The critics are wrong. VIII:14:336.
_____. The L. O. and its detractors. VII:15:360.
_____. "The "L. O." and its detractors." VII:16:380.
AKUFFO-BOAFO, S. Decline in Ghana Sports. III:13:12.
AKUOKO, E. A. K. Power from Akosombo. II:11:13-14.
AKUTTEH, B. Transfer fees in Soccer. V:12:16.
AKWABI-AMEYAW, K. Abolition of cocoa spraying scheme. VIII:6:137.
_____. Foreign experts and self-reliance. VIII:13:308.
_____. Nigeria and Biafra. IV:3:16-17.

Correspondence

_____. Overburdened Commissioner. VIII:20:484.
_____. Rent cuts. VII:17:407.
AKWABOAH, S. The new order. V:11:25.
AKWAYENA, S. W. K. Prime Minister's New Year Message. VI:3:10.
AKYEA, N. ABOAGYE. See Aboagye-Akyea, N.
AKYEAMPONG, H. K. Occult significance of Kotoka's death. II:15:19-20.
AKYEAMPONG, M. A. Ghana's stock of advice by experts. III:10:10.
ALARAH, J. Ambiguities in the Road Traffic Regulations. VI:8:18-20.
_____. Comment on Dr. Ephson's Shadow Commissioners. III:5:25.
_____. Democracy must begin at home. III:14:23.
_____. First aid on Ghana Airways plane. VIII:19:460-461.
_____. The General Legal Council and Lawyers. III:10:10.
_____. Neutrality run riot. III:16:20.
_____. Students and politics. III:4:15.
A-LASHIE. From Ministerial to Military peregrination. VII:13:305-306.
_____. The Price of arrogance and complacency. VII:3:58-59.
_____. A report of Auditor-General: Character of Ghanaian elite. VI:24:19.
_____. The youth and the aged. VII:4:89.
ALAWAH, A. R. EL. See El-Alawah, A. R.
ALBERT, N. K. Amendment to the Constitution. VI:2:15.
ALHASSAN, A. I. L. Wanted: African Self-help. VI:4:16.
Aliens order. K. E. Senanu. IV:26:24.
ALLOTEY, E. A. "Film shows must be frequent." V:24:23.
Allowance for Commissioners. Y. Opong. VIII:5:111.
AMANEY, K. Citizenship and the draft Constitution. III:5:26.
AMANKWA, J. A nation of hypocrites--Rejoinder. VII:13:307.
AMANKWA, P. A. F. Working hours. II:19:22.
AMANKWA-MENSAH, J. P. The case for Biafra. III:23:18.
AMANQUAH, S. N. Control of enterprises. III:2:17.
AMARFIO, N. The Czech Issue. III:19:16.
AMARFIO, W. Legon Observer Editor again! VII:10:242-243.
AMARTEY, S. Happy birthday. III:15:29.
Ambassador and Continental Hotels. K. A. Sasu. IV:7:20-21.
Ambiguities in the road traffic regulation 1970. J. Alarah. VI:8:18-20.
AMEHIA-ADUGU, G. H. K. How democratic is G. N. A. T.? V:20:28.
_____. Teachers and the Ministry. VIII:11:261-262.
Amendment to the Constitution. N. K. Albert. VI:2:15.
AMENYA, E. M. K. The Pito Brewery at Tamale. IV:19:12-14.
"American intervention." H. A. Lynch-Robinson. II:23:18.
American reaction to "Import Licensing." H. J. Smith. II:8:12.
Americans in Ghana. O. Obetsebi-Lamptey. II:7:17-18.
AMETOWOBLA, A. P. Atomic Energy Commission: Losses. VI:27:18-19.
AMEVOR, A. S. University of Ghana Examinations. II:21:14.
AMEYAW, K. AKWABI. See Akwabi-Ameyaw, K.
AMEYIBOR, K. T. U. C.--Rise up or Pack up! VI:17:22.
AMIHERE, L. BLAY. See Blay-Amihere, L.
AMINA, S. No more "Adanko" business. IV:1:11.
AMISSAH, J. The logistic fiasco. VIII:17:410.

Correspondence

AMOA-ANTWI, Y. Civilians in the administration. IX:2:40.
AMOAFO, J. B. Wanted: quality teachers. VI:20:14.
AMOAH, S. K. Sly corner. VII:24:574-575.
AMOAKO, T. K. No need to change Ghana flag. IV:6:23.
_____. Training of Certificate 'B' teachers. IV:17:20.
AMOAKO-ADDO. Afro-Americans and Africa. V:5:21.
AMOAKO-ADDO, J. Centre to train Evangelist. IV:1:12.
_____. Congrats, Legon Observer. IV:16:16.
_____. Does Ghana need the Atomic Reactor. II:24:17.
_____. Plea to future Politicians! III:23:17-18.
_____. The strength of African culture. V:8:18-20.
AMOAKO-ADDO, Y. General declaration of Assets? VII:17:408.
AMOAKO-ATTAH, B. G. A. E. C. must act--A rejoinder. VII:10:243-244.
AMOAKO-CRENTSIL, K. Who's telling the truth? IX:1:10.
AMOAKOH, K. Mr. Abedi's explanation. VI:6:19.
AMOAKOHENE, F. Africans on African affairs. IX:1:12-13.
_____. Obscene revolution. IX:3:67.
AMPADU-MARI, Making the observer "lively." V:15:17.
AMPAH, J. K. The Development levy and workers. VI:22:16-17.
_____. Ten seconds of English please--A rejoinder. VIII:22:529.
AMPOFO, D. A. Population and planning. II:2:17.
AMPONSAH, F. Dr. Busia's Odorkor house. IX:10:236.
AMPONSAH, R. A. Self-reliance and expatriate missionaries--rejoinder.
     VIII:23:555-556.
AMPONSAH, V. The purpose of University education. VIII:24:580.
AMUZU-KPEGLO, A. Bid to improve our roads. VI:4:16.
_____. Letters to the Editor. II:15:19.
ANAGLATE, A. Ovambo revolt. VII:2:41.
ANAMAN, P. K. The Constituent Assembly. IV:3:14-16.
ANAMZOYA, M. M. Ghana Airways let down in Abidjan--A reply.
     VIII:19:460.
_____. Hand baggage surcharge--A rejoinder. IX:6:137.
Ancient and modern. D. Hereward. IV:5:17.
ANDERSON, C. K. Insurance for funerals. VII:22:528.
ANDO, K. B. BRESI. See Bresi-Ando, K. B.
ANDOH, E. N. Another coup in Africa. IX:8:184-185.
ANDOH, F. A. The case of the aliens. V:2:16-17.
ANDOH, F. A. A. The free text-book scheme. VII:21:504.
ANHWERE, P. K. Strong need for an Opposition Press. VI:7:18.
ANKOMAH, K. "Barbara Castle as Elizabeth II!" IV:10:15.
_____. More "Banned" books? IV:5:16.
ANNAN, A. K. Unidentified accident victims. VII:22:524-525.
ANNOBIL, G. The public executions. II:11:16-17.
ANOKYE, H. Genocide in Biafra. III:22:22.
_____. An unacceptable substitute. IV:24:25-26.
ANOKYE, K. B. Real progress? VII:11:266.
Another coup in Africa. E. N. Andoh. IX:8:184-185.
Another earthquake in 1969? K. A. Attobrah. III:6:14.
"Another electronics industry?" A. Moubarak. II:16:18.
Another electronic industry for Ghana. P. Weiden. II:13:13.

Correspondence

Another kind of revolution. Obeng-Manu. IV:6:18.
ANSAH, G. J. A. OWUSU. See Owusu-Ansah, G. J. A.
ANSAH, P. "Non-farming" Saltpondites. VI:27:19.
ANSAH, P. A. V. An African viewpoint on human rights. VIII:26:624-625.
_____. The Anti-intellectual syndrome. VII:7:168-169.
_____. Beer, beer, beer, everywhere. VII:23:552-554.
_____. The Cape Coast-Sekondi road. IX:10:234.
_____. Cattle Development Board. VIII:17:411.
_____. Face-lift for Accra, Ho, Cape Coast, etc. VIII:3:66.
_____. Judges and the proposed Constitution. III:6:12.
_____. Leave Israel alone. IV:1:12-13.
_____. New mathematics and the generation gap. VII:26:626-628.
_____. Price of newspapers. VIII:13:305.
_____. The purge in the Public Service. V:6:13.
_____. Roadworthy cars and car worthy roads. VIII:7:161.
_____. Self-reliance and expatriate missionaries--rejoinder.
VIII:23:556.
_____. Stop this bullying now. 1) VII:5:120; 2) VII:8:194-195.
_____. That Black Star. VII:2:40-41.
_____. U. C. C. C. Science results. IV:16:14.
_____. University Cafeteria. III:22:22.
_____. The "What-went-wrong" lectures. IV:17:20.
_____. Whatever happened to "Talking Point." VII:3:60.
_____. Who will escape the hanging? VII:13:307.
_____. Women and the nation. V:8:20-21.
ANSAH, W. K. The denizens of the street. 1) VII:3:59-60; 2)
VII:4:89-90.
_____. "Down with the Legon Observer." VI:7:17.
_____. The lost opportunity of the Hutchful incident. V:26:18.
_____. "Who will escape the hanging?"--A rejoinder. VII:15:358-359.
ANSERE, K. The East African Asian. III:5:23.
ANSO, K. Reconciliation and future politics. II:1:18.
ANSONG, G. ASIAMA. See Asiama-Ansong, G.
ANSU-KYEREMEH, K. Duplication in our Universities--Another rejoinder.
IX:12:288.
ANTEPIM, K. Political Assassinations. IV:15:16.
ANTHONY, P. K. Civil Service appointments and promotions. IV:24:24.
_____. Easy access to Accra Airport. V:9:21.
Anti-Apartheid movement. 1) D. R. Mobbs. II:14:28; 2) I. Eshun.
II:15:17-18.
Anti-Apartheid movement in Ghana. 1) D. R. Mobbs. II:12:15-16; 2)
I. Eshun. II:13:14; 3) P. W. C. Maxwell. II:13:14-15.
The Anti-intellectual syndrome. P. A. V. Ansah. VII:7:168-169.
ANTI-TAYLOR, W. Moscow diary. III:6:13.
ANTWI, A. KYEREME. See Kyereme-Antwi, Y.
ANTWI, Y. AMOA. See Amoa-Antwi, Y.
ANTWI-BADU, S. Who authorized higher rates? VIII:13:309.
ANTWI-BOADI. Students at Customs. III:12:17.
ANTWI-YEBOAH, K. E. Business students need help. VIII:21:504.
APALOO, M. K. Detention in Angloga. II:11:13.
Apartheid and dialogue. S. A. R. Asiamah. VI:3:11.
APEAGYEI, K. White paper and Apaloo Commission. II:3:16.

Correspondence

Apology of a report. B. Agyei. IV:9:18-20.
APPAW, L. K. Report from Brong Ahafo. VII:17:408.
APPEA, M. ONYINA. See Onyina-Appea, M.
APPEA, Y. AGYARKO. See Agyarko-Appea, Y.
APPIAH, E. Tax on Rest houses. VII:21:501.
APPIAH, E. G. ATTA. See Atta-Appiah, E. G.
APPIAH, L. H. OFOSU. See Ofosu-Appiah, L. H.
Apples. R. M. Abaidoo. VII:24:575-576.
APREKU, N. K. Interviews. III:20:24.
APRONTI, J. Drama and theatre in Ghana. IV:21:17.
_____. Ideological conflict. VI:15:20.
_____. Improving Ghana Airways Services. VIII:22:528-529.
_____. Mensah and Odumase farms. VI:25:20.
_____. Nixon said it! VII:6:141.
_____. On opting out. VI:2:15-16.
_____. State Enterprise and the G. C. B. VII:24:575.
_____. What boring stuff. VIII:26:625.
Archaeology and African history. 1) M. Posnansky. V:12:14-15; 2)
    A. A. Ayisi. V:12:23; 3) K. Osafo. V:12:5.
ARCHAMPONG, K. African intellectuals and Western tradition.
    II:24:13-16.
_____. Registration of voters. III:21:17.
Are Ghanaians different or just indifferent? I. M. Ofori. VI:26:20.
Aren't politicians adults? M. K. Effah. IV:19:10.
ARHIN, K. Training our intellectuals. V:3:10.
_____. The withdrawal of scholarships. II:13:13.
ARMAH, J. E. Why the hurry? III:24:11.
ARMAH, J. E. C. The Ghanaian Press and public speakers. III:9:14.
Armed Forces military parade. K. E. Senanu. IX:2:40-42.
Around the world on the nation's business. K. Agbozo. II:23:16-17.
Arrest Ian Smith. A. C. Coleman. III:23:14-16.
ARTHIABAH, P. B. Comment on Observer Notebook entry. VIII:13:305.
_____. Criticise at the right time. VII:15:357.
_____. Expatriate civil servants. VIII:24:578.
_____. Justice and peace. IX:7:160.
_____. L. O. Critic writes. VIII:13:305.
_____. National Service. VIII:17:410.
_____. "Party brigandage and the spoils system."--Rejoinder.
    IX:6:138-139.
_____. 25 years of Adult Education. IX:2:40.
ARTHUR, H. D. Neo-Colonialism and the future of Ghana. II:26:14.
Articles in the "Legon Observer." E. S. Aidoo. VII:21:502.
ARYE, K. The withdrawn ¢30 million subsidy--A rejoinder. VIII:4:90-92.
ASAMANI, K. O. Southern Rhodesia--A case of British hypocrisy.
    III:7:11-12.
ASAMOAH, Y. 'Educating children abroad'--A rejoinder. VII:23:552.
ASANTE, E. D. How to deal with burglars. III:11:18.
ASANTE, G. K. Obstacles to reform in Ghana. IV:15:14.
ASANTE, J. A. Fair treatment for all teachers. II:12:16.
ASANTE, K. Who is an intellectual? VII:7:168.

ASANTE, OWUSU. See Owusu-Asante.
ASANTE, S. K. B. Black Africa. II:26:17.
ASANTE-OFFEI, J. D. Self-reliance and trade surplus. VIII:1:20-22.
ASANTE-YEBOAH, J. M. The "Abuse of Freedom." V:8:18.
ASARE, de BECK A. The Compliance Order. V:5:22.
_____. Colonial hang-overs. VI:9:24.
_____. Teachers and incentives. VI:6:20.
ASARE, E. The trouble with Ghanaians. VIII:9:213-214.
ASARE, G. The new cedi. II:8:14.
ASEMPA, K. Whither is the Bus Service drifting? II:22:13.
ASEMPANAYE, K. Diplomatic arrogance or sabotage? III:25:18.
ASENSO, K. Hawkers and the University. II:1:19.
Ashanti Goldfields Lonrho deal. J. A. Peasah. III:23:14.
"Ashanti Goldfields 1967." T. H. Foden. III:11:12.
ASHITEY, G. A. Medical education. III:8:13.
_____. Open letter to Maternity Hospital Doctors at Korle-Bu.
    III:1:17-18.
_____. The task ahead for the youth. IV:1:11-12.
ASHLE, Y. M. This foreign exchange. IV:8:20.
ASHU, M. N. F. What's wrong with Africa? III:26:22.
ASHUN, C. K. Budget and taxation. VII:22:529-530.
ASIAMAH, S. A. R. Apartheid and dialogue. VI:3:11.
ASIAMA-ANSONG, G. Africa and the E. E. C. VIII:12:285.
Asians deserve their fate. A. R. El-Alawah. III:6:12-13.
ASIEDU, F. Brigadier Afrifa and the disqualification decree.
    III:24:11.
ASIEDU, F. A. Background promoter of the war. IV:23:19.
_____. The Commonwealth and Members' "Common Weal." IV:3:16.
_____. N. L. C. rulers and imminent retirement. III:26:22.
_____. The N. R. C. and rural development. VII:6:140.
_____. The Nigerian civil war. IV:2:18-20.
_____. "The old order changeth...." IV:19:10.
_____. On the extinction of the "Biafra Republic." V:3:10-12.
_____. Please, Mr. Electoral Commissioner. IV:17:18.
_____. The Rhoesian issue. III:26:24-25.
_____. Some problems for the next Civilian Government. IV:15:14-16.
_____. Tribalism and the new politics. IV:12:10.
ASMAH, K. The Trade Union Congress. III:12:16.
ASSAH-SAM, Y. Abbott marches off. III:2:16-17.
_____. Good photographs for calendars. II:24:16.
ASSANI, J. B. New police order. VIII:13:309.
ASSASIE-GYIMAH, B. Give it another thought, N. R. C. VIII:22:529.
Assets Commission. Q. K. K. Bruce. II:26:13.
ASSIMENG, M. Electoral panorama revisited. IV:21:14-16.
_____. Legon New Year School. V:2:16.
_____. Release of political detainees. VII:11:266-267.
Assisting Independent Schools. D. Hereward. VII:12:287-288.
ASUAH, K. Mini-budget unfair to rural folks? VII:6:140.
Asutsuare sugar underweight? M. A. Adu. VIII:8:187.
ATEDECHIRA, B. S. Ghanaians and family planning. V:20:28.

Correspondence

ATEGEDEWEH, A. Courts for the chiefs. VI:24:19.
ATIAPA, E. A. Training of Certificate 'B' Teachers. IV:20:16.
ATOBRAH, K. The future of our mines--Another rejoinder. VIII:3:65-66.
_____. Let us protect our constitution. VI:27:19.
Atomic Energy Commission losses. A. P. Ametowobla. VI:27:18-19.
ATSIOGBE, F. Redeployment of C. C. E. Staff. VII:19:454-456.
ATTA, B. AMOAKO. See Amoako-Attah, B.
ATTA, E. E. B. OFORI. See Ofori-Atta, E. E. B.
ATTA, J. K. The proposed ¢3 million palace. VIII:13:306-309.
ATTA-APPIAH, E. G. Should Nkrumah be pardoned? V:11:25.
ATTA-QUAYSON, J. Who deserves scholarships? IX:6:137.
ATTAKU, E. Uncontrolled pricing. II:10:15-16.
ATTIEKU, H. S. M. The Observer language. V:9:21.
ATTOBRAH, K. A. K. Legon and the Legon Observer. VII:15:359.
_____. Another earthquake in 1969? III:6:14.
_____. Houses at one cedi each? III:9:13-14.
ATTOBRA, K. A. K. (jt. au.). See Frempong, J. E.
ATTOBRAH, KUMI K. A. and FRIMPONG, J. E. Underground railway for
    Accra. III:1:16.
ATTOPLEY, M. Urgently needed--a genuine revolution. VI:25:20.
ATTOPLEY, M. A. Socialist revolution due in Ghana? VI:6:18-19.
ATTRAMS, O. Sale of land in Ashanti. VI:15:20.
ATTUMBU, B. Electoral process. III:13:10.
_____. The malefactors in our society. III:19:14.
AUGUSTO, H. B. A nation of hypocrites--Rejoinder. VII:13:306.
Austerity patterns: Somalia and Ghana. K. Frimpong. V:15:16.
Average Ghanaian. K. Frimpong. VII:17:408.
AWADZIE, K. A. The future of our liberators. II:6:17.
Award for Policemen. K. B. Kwansah. VII:18:432-433.
AWUAH, K. BAAFUOR. See Baafuor-Awuah, K.
AWUA-KYERETWIE, B. Street names in Ghana--Rejoinder. VIII:15:362-364.
AWUDIE, E. W. Reckless driving of motor cars at Christmas. III:24:14.
_____. Sanitation in Accra. III:11:14.
AWUKU, F. Observer unfair to G. B. C.? VI:3:10.
AWUKU, O. The liberty of the majority. IV:14:19.
AYISI, A. A. Archaeology and African history. V:14:23.
AZUWIKE, A. N. Call a spade a spade. III:18:17-18.
B. Hughes and Salary increase. 1) P. T. Yiadu. II:5:10; 2) J. Spio.
    II:6:18-19.
B. K. Kontopiaat on Judicial Secretary. II:22:14.
BAAFUOR-AWUAH, K. Kwame Nkrumah--hero or villain? VIII:8:186.
BAAH, K. Advisory opinion and draft Constitution. III:17:12.
_____. On drafting for the public. III:9:12.
Background promoter of the war. F. A. Asiedu. IV:23:19.
Bad roads and the tax-payer. F. C. Essandoh. III:15:29.
BADDOO, C. Return to the barracks. III:14:24.
BADU, E. M. The land question. III:5:24.
BADU, S. ANTWI. See Antwi-Badu, S.
BADU-NKANSAH, A. "The Public Executions--A national disgrace?"--A
    rejoinder. II:12:15.

Correspondence

BADU-YEBOAH. National Service and Salary increases. IX:7:160-161.
BAETA, C. G. What went wrong.... II:1:16-17.
BAH, S. K. DATE. See Date-Bah, S. K.
BALAKRISHNAN, V. Africa's unstable government. V:6:13.
BAME, K. N. Ghanaian Times and Busia's speech. II:8:13-14.
_____. We should cater for their children too. II:12:16.
Ban, politics and leaders. O. Kantanka. IV:10:14-15.
Banda betrays Africa. F. N. Nwigwe. II:9:21.
BANIN, S. K. O. The devaluation of the cedi. II:21:14-15.
_____. Higher salaries for members of the Judiciary. II:10:16.
BANNERMAN, N. K. Oil drilling in Ghana. II:14:27.
Banning Echo and Pioneer. C. E. Mensah. VII:15:359.
"Barbara Castle as Elizabeth II"! K. Ankomah. IV:10:15.
BARNEY, A. Accra-Tema City Council. II:14:27.
BARNWELL, F. R. Seamy side of industrial civilization. V:24:23.
Barometer of public opinion. M. Agbosu. III:23:16.
Basic attitude--Legon Varsity unrest. E. Vorkeh. III:24:13.
BASILIDE, K. S. Military training in our varsities. VIII:8:185.
BATSA, K. Did Batsa belong to the United Party? V:21:22.
Bawku (Kusasi) District. A. Dinko. II:23:19.
Beaver aircraft accident. 1) O. Yaw. V:12:14; 2) F. F. Addae.
   V:14:22.
BEDANE, B. Shopping: S. C. O. A. Technoa--A reply. VII:526.
BEDIAKO, Y. Waste of public funds on drugs. VI:17:20-22.
Beef sales at G. I. H. O. C. meat cottage, Osu. E. Dadzie.
   VII:24:575.
Beer, Beer, Beer, everywhere. P. A. V. Ansah. VII:23:552-554.
BEKOE, D. A. Nigeria. II:23:17.
BEKOE, Y. Where is Kontopiaat? VI:26:21.
BEKOE-DAWSON, R. Military training in the Universities. VIII:12:284.
BEMPAH, K. Repudiation and Washington. VII:7:168.
BENSON, G. K. Withdrawal of scholarships. II:11:14-15.
BERALE, P. C. G. British justice and Kwesi Armah. II:5:10.
_____. Please Take a Ghanaian Child. IV:22:24-26.
Better manners. K. A. B. Jones-Quartey. II:1:19.
Beware of such women. E. K. Kumi. VIII:20:482-483.
Biafra: a second Katanga? T. N. Ward-Brew. III:18:18.
Biafra and Nigeria. D. Adjei-Brenyah. IV:25:17-18.
Biafra has come to stay. S. Lotsu. IV:12:12.
BIBBY, J. "Dekwamefication" and anti-myths. II:8:16.
Bid to improve our roads. A. Amuzu-Kpeglo. VI:4:16.
Big cars and our economy. M. Y. Agbosu. III:16:20.
Big Dada's histrionics--A rejoinder. W. Nelson. VIII:25:606.
"Big Talk" and unemployment. Obeng-Manu. IV:14:29.
BIRNIE, J. R. Remittances to students abroad. IV:14:19.
Black Africa. S. K. B. Asante. II:26:17.
Black is beautiful. L. Gough. IV:12:14. Reply: 1) N. Aboagye-Akyea.
   IV:13:14; 2) O. Kantanka. IV:13:14.
Black Star. D. W. Ewer. IV:7:22.
Black Star? J. K. Brako. VII:20:480.
Blame magazines and books too. N. N. Kofi. III:21:18.

Correspondence

BLANKSON, C. The Post Office Sorting Division. VIII:3:67.
BLANKSON, C. C. T. Developing the rural areas. V:8:17.
_____. The Hackman case. IV:24:25.
_____. Made in Ghana goods. II:2:15-16.
_____. These promises! V:5:21.
BLANKSON, K. Casinos in State Hotels? VII:19:453.
_____. Let us now praise humourous men. IX:8:185.
_____. Santrofi and the professors of literature. IX:11:254.
_____. Working in mysterious ways. IX:9:208.
BLANKSON, V. N. On family planning. VI:23:21.
BLAY, K. Debating tricks. V:1:20.
BLAY, R. S. Akainyah in retrospect. II:1:17-18.
BLAY-AMIHERE, L. Action not words. VIII:12:285.
_____. The withdrawn ¢30 million subsidy--Rejoinder. VIII:4:90.
BOADI, ANTWI. See Antwi-Boadi.
BOAFO, S. AKUFFO. See Akuffo-Boafo, S.
BOAFO, S. T. Paradoxes and contradictions. IX:2:42.
_____. The press and students' demonstration. IX:4:87.
BOAFO, Y. "Nkrumah passes away."--Rejoinder. VII:11:264.
BOAKYE, G. DUA. See Dua-Boakye, G.
BOAKYE, K. The laws of apartheid. V:25:19.
BOAL, G. A. Revive the Ghana Consumers Association. VI:18:18-19.
BOATENG, A. Posh Cars. VII:4:91.
_____. University of Ghana External Degrees. VII:26:628.
BOATENG, E. New method of spelling words. VII:11:266.
_____. The Observer standard. V:7:16.
_____. The study of Ghanaian languages. II:26:16.
_____. The study of the classics. IV:17:20.
BOATENG, E. A. Traffic and Ghana V. I. Ps. II:18:15.
BOATENG, G. L. Civilian rule--Let us hasten slowly. II:14:26.
BOATENG, J. K. Exaggerated claims of O. F. Y.--Rejoinder. VII:24:578.
_____. Ghana's external debts. VII:2:39.
_____. Korle-Bu and its surroundings. VII:15:358.
_____. Observer Notebook--A rejoinder. VI:25:22.
BOATENG, J. W. A. Roadworthiness: Prosecute the authorities too!
     VIII:9:214.
BOATENG, K. Russian trained doctors. II:20:21-22.
BOMBANDE, M. The United Nations has defeated its aims. IV:2:18.
BONNAH-KOOMSON, K. The purpose of University education--A rejoinder.
     VIII:26:625-626.
BONNIE, M. Meddling with mass media? V:4:18.
BONSU, MENSAH. See Mensah-Bonsu.
BORQUAYE, A. Spirit of tolerance. VII:25:602-603.
BOSOMPEM, K. Return to civilian rule. IX:3:67.
BOSQUE, K. Miss Hereward and Western liberalism. V:5:22.
BOSSMAN, M. Registered mail. II:14:27.
_____. War clouds in Nigeria. II:13:15.
Bouncing cheques. V. M. Ocloo. V:24:22.
BOYE, CHARLIE. See Charlie-Boye.
BRAIMAH, M. S. "Intellectual M..." and all that--rejoinder.
     VIII:21:503.
_____. Jeafan/Guardian publications. IV:11:18.

Correspondence

_____. Political parties and Centre for Civic Education. III:18:18-20.
_____. Soviet-trained Ghanaian Doctors. VIII:3:66.
Brain crisis in the teaching profession. K. Fiafor. III:8:12.
Brain drain. K. B. Haizel. III:25:20.
BRAKO, J. K. Black Star? VII:20:480.
"Bravo! Mr. Secretary." E. King. VI:19:15.
Breach of contract by "Legon Observer"? D. Obeng-Sasu. VIII:7:164.
BRENYA, D. ADJEI. See Adjei-Brenya, D.
BRENYA, Y. Postponing the inevitable. IX:8:184.
BRESI-ANDO, K. B. Reform of Ghana Constitution. II:6:18.
BRETTON, H. L. Rise and fall of Nkrumah. III:4:12.
BRETUO, B. Whose freedom of the Press?--A rejoinder. VIII:19:458-460.
BRETUO, K. "The Pioneer." VII:20:480.
BREW, T. N. WARD. See Ward-Brew, T. N.
Brigadier Afrifa and the disqualification Decree. F. Asiedu.
    III:24:11.
Britain and Kwesi Armah. J. K. Sebuava. II:4:23.
Britain and Rhodesia. A. C. Coleman. III:18:20.
Britain, Nigeria and Rhodesia. E. Tandoh. III:8:10.
Britain's aid to Ghana. J. Lamptey. IV:25:14-16.
British arms sales. O. Yaw. VI:9:23-24.
British justice and Kwesi Armah. 1) P. C. G. Berale. II:5:10; 2)
    C. N. Wadia. II:5:10.
British not to be blamed. D. Hereward. IV:6:22.
BROBE-MENSAH, E. Y. Duplication in our Universities. IX:11:251.
BROMLEY, S. Campaigning for better service in Ghana. II:2:16.
BROOKES, S. Moral corruption in Ghana. V:17:21.
BROWN, D. A. Volunteers to America and the Ministry of Education.
    II:11:15-16.
BROWN, M. Radio Ghana, Brazil and Africa. VII:24:573-574.
BRUCE, K. Nationalised babies? IV:6:22.
BRUCE, Q. K. K. Assets Commission. II:26:13.
BRUKU, S. Specialist Teachers' salaries. VI:6:19-20.
_____. Teachers' uniforms. V:12:16.
BRUKU-SAMUELS, E. Mr. Ollenu and Kotoka's statue. IV:24:24-25.
BUADU, K. Reconciliation and not revival. VIII:10:236.
BUCKLEY, A. Occult significance of Kotoka's death. II:14:29.
Budget and public morality. 1) K. M. Sape. VI:22:16; 2) A reader.
    VI:22:16.
Budget and Rest Houses. E. Hinson. VII:20:480.
Budget and taxation. C. K. Ashun. VII:22:529-530.
Budget and the elite. K. Kanawu. VI:22:16.
BUDU, K. Impartiality of the State Press? III:25:19-20.
Building the new national soccer team. G. N. Tetteh. III:19:16.
BUKARI, S. A. Education Ministry and A. T. T. C. VIII:6:133.
_____. Let's mind our own problems. VIII:2:42.
Bungalow syndrome. K. T. Mensah. VII:7:170.
BUOR, F. K. World prices of exportable goods. IX:14:342.
Burnt-out marriage. D. Hereward. III:14:23-24.
Bus service report. A. Serwah. II:22:13-14.

Busia's effigies. K. Enu. IV:17:18.
Business students need help. K. E. Antwi-Yeboah. VIII:21:504.
BUSUMAFI. The new changes. II:15:17.
BYSTANDER. The mental hospital. III:15:28.
C. O. S. and Mfum. P. A. Ray. III:17:12-13.
C. P. P. and blows. K. Abrokwah. II:3:15. Reply--K. Semordzi.
    II:4:23-24.
Calculated public deception? Y. Twumasi. IV:14:20.
Call a spade a spade. A. N. Azuwike. III:18:17-18.
Campaigning for better service in Ghana. S. Bromley. II:2:16.
Cape Coast-Sekondi road. P. A. V. Ansah. IX:10:234.
Cape Coast University. C. Addae. V:11:26.
Cape Coast University and town. A. Cole. VIII:18:438.
"Capitalism, Socialism and Ghana."--A rejoinder. S. B. Akuffo.
    VIII:17:410.
Car maintenance allowance. K. Addei. VI:17:22.
Cars in Ghana's economy. E. D. Kemevor. III:10:8-10.
Case for Biafra. J. P. Amankwa-Mensah. III:23:18.
Case for disqualification. F. W. Y. Agboklu. II:24:12.
Case for identity cards.--A rejoinder. Afari-Gyan. VII:12:287.
Case of the aliens. F. A. Andoh. V:2:16-17.
Casinos in State Hotels? K. Blankson. VII:19:453.
Cattle Development Board. P. A. V. Ansah. VIII:17:411.
CATWRIGHT, J. B. Report of the Auditor-General. VI:25:21-22.
Cause for alarm. R. A. Kotey. IV:5:16.
Cecil Rhodes and Rhodesia. 1) Minta, I. V:11:25; 2) Okorley, R.
    V:11:25-26.
Cedi and entertainment. E. Daniel. II:6:17.
Cement situation. S. Adotey. VIII:6:137.
Centre to train Evangelists? J. Amoako-Addo. IV:1:12.
Chairman of the Constitutional Commission and the critics. K. Nyarko.
    III:8:10-11.
CHANDLER, M. Reviving Pan-Africanism. V:10:21.
Changes in the educational system. J. S. Djangmah. IV:15:17-18.
Changing of the Guard. A. Iddrisu. VIII:5:109.
Charity begins at home. K. N. Hanson. IV:15:14.
CHARLES, M. Accusations of tribalism. V:14:23.
_____. Africa's unstable governments. V:4:18.
_____. The effects of the surcharge. V:23:21.
_____. On the "Illustrated Weekly of India." VII:23:554.
_____. P. M. and the Sallah case. V:10:20.
_____. Roadworthiness. VIII:9:214.
_____. This changing of sides. V:17:22.
CHARLES, M. C. A good programme for the government. VI:13:20.
_____. Who or what incites the workers to strike. VI:10:19.
CHARLIE, B. Onward with the revolution--Rejoinder. IX:12:286.
CHARLIE-BOYE. Whose freedom of the Press?--A rejoinder. VIII:20:483.
Check off system. G. Obeng-Yeboah. VI:18:18.
Check these traders. E. M. Kumaga. II:17:19-20.
Checking smuggling. III:24:12.

CHENERY, P. J. Dictatorship of Judges. III:8:10.
CHEVALLEY, P. Discrimination. II:6:16-17.
CHICANOT, D. Education and indigenous culture. VIII:8:185-186.
Chiefs and Ghana's "corpse culture." K. A. B. Jones-Quartey.
    VI:26:20.
Chieftaincy affairs in the Upper Region. B. J. L. Kumasi. VI:25:21.
China and the United Nations. K. Osafo. V:22:25.
CHIRA, K. Disqualification and exemption. III:14:22.
Choosing trading partners. S. Adotey. VIII:7:163.
CHRISTIAN, E. Dilemma of a patriot. IV:2:17-18.
_____. The Nigeria-Biafra war and capitalist interests. IV:13:16.
_____. Religious discrimination in Ulster. V:21:20-24.
_____. Repeating our forebearers' mistakes? IV:5:16.
Christianity and material inheritance. D. Adjei-Brenya.
    VIII:26:626-627.
Christmas spirit. K. Osafo. IV:26:22.
CHUKWUKERE, B. I. Nigeria. II:23:17-18.
Church and education in Ghana. J. W. Abruquah. III:23:18-19.
Churches and society. P. K. Kumankama. V:21:20.
Citizen and the police. K. Marfo. IV:7:22.
Citizenship and the draft constitution. K. Amaney. III:5:26.
Civil servants under Nkrumah's rule. Obeng-Manu. IV:26:24.
Civil Service appointments and promotions. P. K. Anthony. IV:24:24.
Civilian rule.--Let us hasten slowly. G. L. Boateng. II:14:26.
Civilians in the administration. Y. Amoa-Antwi. IX:2:40.
Classical, Western and Free! Y. Dodoo. IV:19:10-11.
Classics. 1) A. A. Hammond. IV:19:11; 2) C. M. Mills. IV:19:11; 3)
    D. Hereward. IV:19:11; 4) P. E. Dean. IV:19:11-12.
Classless society. A. Van Dantzig. VIII:10:237.
COCKRA, A. The Pope and birth control. III:21:17.
Cocoa prices and underdevelopment in Ghana--A rejoinder. T. A. Kofi.
    VII:26:624.
COLE, A. Cape Coast University and Town. VIII:18:438.
COLEMAN, A. C. Arrest Ian Smith. III:23:14-16.
_____. Britain and Rhodesia. III:18:20.
_____. Parents should advise students. III:23:17.
Col. Afrifa's speech. B. D. G. Folson. II:7:16.
Col. Bernasko and the O. F. Y. Programme. Obeng-Manu. IX:4:87-90.
Colonial hang-overs. A. de Beck Asare. VI:9:24.
Colonial Mentality. K. Haizel. IV:5:17.
Commemorative gold coin. E. O. Quarcoo. III:9:14.
Comment on Dr. Ephson's Shadow Commissioners. J. Alarah. III:5:25.
Commentary on Observer Notebook entry. P. B. Arthiabah. VIII:13:305.
Commonwealth and members' "Common Weal." F. A. Asiedu. IV:3:16.
Community Centre in Bawku town. A. Dinko. II:26:18.
Compensation for N. L. C. members. G. N. Tetteh. IV:16:17.
Competitive Examination--What about syllabuses? A. K. Narh.
    II:22:21.
Compliance Order. A. de Beck Asare. T. G. Kumi. V:5:22.
Compliance Order Exercise--A Failure. N. Abakah. V:24:22.
Compound surnames for our wives. S. Adotey. VII:7:172.

Correspondence

Compromise plan for Nigeria. P. D. Dzilah. IV:13:16.
Concept of service. F. Addai. IX:3:67-68.
CONDUA-HARLEY, J. E. Danquah Memorial Library. III:2:17.
Conflict of idealism and realism. H. Von Stuckrad. III:1:16.
Congrats Legon Observer. J. Amoako-Addo. V:16:16.
Congrats Observer. 1) P. Gamesu. VII:14:338; 2) J. K. Opoku. VII:15:360.
Consider us first. W. K. Johnson. III:23:17.
Constituent Assembly. P. K. Anaman. IV:3:14-16.
Constitutional Commission. J. C. Quaye. II:3:16.
Constructive criticism. A. Kyereme-Antwi. VIII:6:137.
Contracts for the S. C. C. J. A. A. Niboi. IV:2:18.
Control of Enterprise. S. N. Amanquah. III:2:17.
Corruption among the Clergy. E. Osei. V:18:17.
Corruption and economic Progress. 1) Obeng-Manu. V:9:21-22; 2) K. Osafo. V:9:22.
Cost of living: Ghana and Sierra Leone. K. A. B. Jones-Quartey. V:18:13.
Counter-coup attempt. K. A. Sasu. II:10:15.
Coup d'etat in Uganda. B. Adjei. VI:7:18.
Courts for the chiefs. A. Ategedeweh. VI:24:19.
Cover charge in state hotels. K. B. Agyeman. VII:21:501.
CRENTSIL, K. AMOAKO. See Amoako-Crentsil, K.
Crime in Ghana. K. Marfo. III:14:24.
Crime wave, the drowsy cops and public safety. J. D. Croffie. II:10:15.
Critics are wrong. S. B. Akuffo. VIII:14:336.
Critics, Counter-critics and the future of Ghana. I. K. Minta. III:1:15.
Criticise at the right time. P. B. Arthiabah. VII:15:357.
Criticising the government. K. K. Oduro. IX:2:42.
Criticism as criticism. P. Gamesu. III:2:14.
Criticism: constructive and destructive. A. Kyereme-Antwi. VIII:10:234.
Criticism of private schools. D. Hereward. III:19:16.
CROFFIE, A. The devaluation and economic recovery. II:16:16.
CROFFIE, J. K. The crime wave, the drowsy cops and public safety. II:10:15.
Crop production in Ghana. 1) J. B. Wills. II:23:18-19; 2) E. V. Doku. II:25:29-30.
Culture, tradition and obscurantism. VII:18:432.
Current unemployment and future politics. K. Ewool. III:26:22-23.
Czech invasion by Russians. 1) K. A. Darkwah. III:20:24; 2) T. N. Ward-Brew. III:20:24; 3) K. A. Taylor. II:20:25.
Czech issue. K. Agyeman. N. Amarfio. III:19:16.
DADZIE, E. Beef sales at G. I. H. O. C. Meat Cottage, Osu. VII:24:575.
DAHAMANI, S. Administration of the Bawku district. II:20:20.
DAKE, K. Nkrumah's role in history. V:8:17.
_____. The price of Newspapers--rejoinder. VIII:15:364.

_____. Somersault in logic. IV:12:11-12.
DANIEL, E. Airport parking toll. VIII:7:161-162.
_____. The Cedi and entertainment. II:6:17.
_____. "Intellectual M..." and all that--rejoinder. VIII:21:503.
_____. Unedifying newspaper attacks. V:5:22.
DANIEL, G. F. Entertainment. II:7:18.
DANIEL, H. C. Let Nigeria leave Biafra alone. IV:3:16.
_____. Who is a rebel in Nigeria? III:6:12.
DANIEL, H. N. Shortcomings of intellectuals. V:6:14.
DANIELS, H. "That Pele Match." IV:5:18.
DANKWA, A. Theatre at Legon. IV:8:20.
DANKWA, B. K. Who is to do what? IX:8:184.
DANQUAH, P. Gilbey's gin. II:21:13.
Danquah Memorial Library. J. E. Condua-Harley. III:2:17.
DANSO, A. Society wives. III:11:14.
DANSO, G. Uncritical Ghanaians. VI:19:14.
DANTZIG, A. Van. A Classless society. VIII:237.
_____. For whose benefit? IX:6:138.
_____. 4,750 disappointments. III:3:10.
_____. On the treatment of "Benzosis." VII:5:119-120.
_____. A public transport: Another prestige project? II:6:17-18.
_____. Safety on our roads.--A subsequent rejoinder. IX:11:251-252.
_____. Students loans scheme. VI:18:18.
DAPAAH, B. The police and the public. II:17:19.
DARKO, A. Made in Ghana products. IV:13:17.
_____. No certificates from S. I. C.? V:11:28.
DARKO, ADUONUM. See Aduonum-Darko.
DARKO, E. To Kontopiaat. III:4:14-15.
DARKWAH, K. A. Czech invasion by Russians. III:20:24.
DATE-BAH, S. K. Ghana Airway's let down in Abidjan. VIII:18:436-438.
D'AUROCH, C. The execution of Pierre Mulele. III:22:19-20.
DAVIES, M. B. On the Soyinka night. IV:7:22-24.
_____. There are revolts--and revolts. III:26:23-24.
DAVIS, R. A. "Oh Dunia." IX:12:288.
DAWSON, J. K. Declaration of Assets. VI:2:14-15.
DAWSON, R. BEKOE. See Bekoe-Dawson, R.
DAY, G. K. OWENS. See Owens-Day, G. K.
DE BECK, A. ASARE. See Asare, A. de Beck.
DEAN, P. E. Classics (on). IV:19:11-12.
Death penalty for robbers? A. Lanquaye. VII:3:59.
Debate on the return to civilian rule. T. O. A. Onifade. II:10:15.
Debating tricks. K. Blay. V:1:20.
DEBRAH, K. KISSI. See Kissi-Debrah, K.
Declaration of Assets. 1) N. K. Akuetteh, VI:2:14; 2) J. K. Dawson,
    VI:2:14-15; 3) A. Tsikata. VII:9:214.
Decline in Ghana Sports. S. Akuffo-Boafo. III:13:12.
Decline in Ghana Sports. The Writer. III:14:23.
Decrees 230 and 233. J. A. Peasah. III:7:12.
Deep seated conspiracy? K. Yankah. IX:4:87.
DEFOE, R. T. What price tribalism? IV:20:19.

Correspondence

DEFOE, R. Y. T. Kotoka's Statue. IV:25:16.
_____. Scramble for Africa--Twentieth Century. III:26:24.
"Dekwamefication and anti-myths." J. Bibby. II:8:16.
Delays at licensing offices. H. K. Akuffo. V:13:26-27.
Democracy must begin at home. J. Alarah. III:14:23.
Denizens of the street. 1) W. K. Ansah, VII:3:59-60; 2) W. K.
    Ansah, VII:4:89-90; 3) A. N. Mensah. VII:3:60.
DENKYI, S. K. O. Forty pesewas to the policeman. IV:25:16-17.
_____. On party discipline. V:18:17.
_____. Politicians and their pronouncements. IV:16:17.
_____. "Provocation" indeed. VI:22:17.
_____. Where is the editor of the Graphic. VI:3:15.
_____. Why this soccer fanaticism. V:2:17.
DESEWU, P. M. Wanted: Ghana's social history. VIII:10:236.
Detention in Angloga. M. K. Apaloo. II:11:13.
Devaluation and economic recovery. A. Croffie. S. K. Zormelo.
    II:16:16.
Devaluation--how far? F. C. Essandoh. III:20:24.
Devaluation of the cedi. S. K. O. Banin. II:21:14-15.
Developing the North. S. M. Sibidow. V:15:17.
Development levy and workers. J. K. Ampah. VI:22:16-17.
Development of "Saturday, Expectation." I. Ackom-Mensah. II:15:19.
Devouring the Revolution? F. K. Prah. IV:17:18-20.
DEY, T. OWENS. See Owens-Dey, T.
DICKSON, K. B. Our secondary schools revisited. II:20:20.
_____. Repairing cars at R. T. Briscoe. V:4:19.
Dictatorship of judges. P. S. Chenery. III:8:10.
Did Batsa belong to the United Party? K. Batsa. V:21:22.
Dignity of the worker. VIII:20:484.
Dilemma of a patriot. 1) R. Maverick, III:25:18; 2) E. Christian,
    IV:2:17-18.
DINKO, A. The Bawku (Kusasi) District. II:23:19.
_____. Community Centre in Bawku town. II:26:18.
Diplomatic arrogance or sabotage? K. Asempanaye. III:25:18.
Discrimination. P. Chevalley. II:6:16-17.
Discrimination in our own country. A. A. Akiwumi. II:4:23.
Discrimination in our own country? J. L. Zwennes. II:2:14-15.
Discussing the proposed constitution. J. M. D. Kwapong. III:9:12.
Disgruntled politicians and all that. D. Adjei-Brenya, VIII:19:458;
    and Rejoinder. F. F. Addae. VIII:20:482.
Dishonesty in public life. E. Addy. VI:18:18.
Disqualification and exemption. K. Y. Abrokwah. K. Chira. III:14:22.
Disqualification Decree. P. Adu-Gyamfi. IV:5:14-16.
Disqualification of C. P. P. officials. S. B. Mfodwo. II:20:19.
DITTO, S. "Out of bounds to civilians!" VII:20:480.
_____. Spirit of tolerance--A rejoinder. VIII:2:42.
Division of labour. A. P. Lamptey. VII:20:480.
DJANGMAH, J. S. Changes in the educational system. IV:15:17-18.
DJARBENG, E. DOUGLAS. See Douglas-Djarbeng, E.
DJOLETO, S. A. A. On asking for help. III:3:10.
Dr. Blaiberg and that heart. A. Fiadjoe. III:2:16.

Correspondence

Dr. Busia and the judges. A. Ntim. V:9:18.
Dr. Busia's Odorkor House. F. Amponsah. IX:10:236.
Dr. Gardiner and Abbott. J. A. Peasah. III:3:8.
Doctors' prescription. K. Kuttin. VIII:21:504.
Doctors' salaries. S. Lotsu. III:26:25-26.
Doctors to be sacked? A. N. Mensah. VII:20:480.
DODOO, J. A. Fan Milk Co. III:12:17.
DODOO, Y. Classical, Western and Free! IV:19:10-11.
DODOO, Y. A. Ghanaian Doctors overseas. II:16:16-17.
_____. Scholarships for University students. III:22:21-22.
Does Ghana need the Atomic Reactor. J. Amoako-Addo. II:24:17.
Does it make sense? C. N. Wadia IV:6:20; G. M. K. Kpedekpo.
    IV:7:22.
DOGBE, B. K. A few rules for politicians. VII:7:169.
DOKU, E. V. Crop production in Ghana. II:25:29-30.
DOLPHYNE, F. Ghanaian Association of University Women. III:23:19.
DOMFEH, J. E. Observer's language. V:26:19.
_____. Organisational problems of Opposition. VI:3:10-11.
DOMPREH, C. Tribute to Mr. E. Y. Amedekey. VII:18:433.
DONYUO, L. Specialist teachers salary. VI:3:14-15.
Double-edged weapon. K. Kuttin. IX:1:13.
DOUGLAS-DJARBENG, E. The watch tower prophecies. V:3:14.
"Down with the Legon Observer." W. K. Ansah. VI:7:17.
Drama and Theatre in Ghana. J. Apronti. IV:21:17.
DREVICI, U. Food storage facilities. IV:26:22-24.
Drill-happy soldiers in Cape Coast (By a Citizen). VIII:4:92-93.
Drivers and overloading. N. N. Kofie. IV:17:21.
DROULERS, D. The Nigerian Civil War. III:12:14.
DUA-BOAKYE, G. University students and military discipline.
    VIII:13:308-309.
DUKU, K. External Affairs annex and dissipation of funds. II:22:13.
DUMMETT, M. (jt. au.). See TULLOCH, D.
DUMOR, E. Undercurrents and Abbott. II:26:13-14.
Duplication in our Universities--Rejoinder. 1) A. Agyekum.
    IX:11:250-251; 2) E. Y. Brobe-Mensah. IX:11:251; 3) K. Ansu-Kyere-
    meh. IX:12:288.
DWAMENA, O. Public holidays. IX:5:112.
DZILAH, P. D. A compromise plan for Nigeria. IV:13:16.
DZIMA, E. A. O. A. U. Liberation Committee. II:18:16.
DZODANU, B. Ghanaian doctors. II:15:20.
DZORKPE, S. K. The need for a Press Trust--A rejoinder. VII:15:356-357.
Earthquake at Kumasi--essentially a paradox. A. N. Mensah. VIII:3:66.
East African Asian. K. Ansere. III:5:23.
Eastern Region Project--Akim-Wenchi. Owusu-Asante. VI:15:22.
Easy access to Accra Airport. P. K. Anthony. V:9:21.
EBEGARE, M. O. The recognition of Biafra. II:15:19.
EBERGBARE, S. Ghana, Nigeria and Kaunda. IV:15:17.
Economic development and the training of scientists. K. A. Longman.
    II:2:15.
Economic independence in the Congo. A. K. Kattah. II:3:15.
Economics of the aliens' order. M. K. Gbordzoe. V:8:17-18.

Correspondence

EDITOR. "Servitude?" Has Dr. Busia said that? V:24:21.
EDRISAH-AIDOO, K. The environment: Comment on some pollution problems in Ghana. IX:14:344.
Educating Children abroad--A rejoinder. Y. Asamoah. VII:23:552.
Education and indigenous Culture. D. Chicanot. VIII:8:185-186.
Education in Ghana. P. Adu-Gyamfi. III:22:20-21.
Education Ministry and A. T. T. C. S. A. Bukari. VIII:6:133.
Educational reforms in Ghana. Reader. VII:22:526-528.
EDUSEI, E. National Government. VII:17:406.
_____. "Party brigandage and the spoils system."--Rejoinder. IX:6:138.
EFFAH, M. K. Aren't politicians adults? IV:19:10.
Effects of the surcharge. 1) M. Charles. V:23:21; 2) E. E. B. Ofori-Atta. V:26:17-18.
EGHAN, J. A. The U. A. C. and Guinea Bissau. VIII:25:606.
Ekangaki--Lonrho connection. K. Enu. IX:7:157-158.
EL-ALAWAH, A. R. Asians deserve their fate. III:6:12-13.
_____. The end of Secession. V:3:10.
_____. Nigeria, Biafra and the relief problem. V:4:19.
Electoral panorama revisited. M. Assimeng. IV:21:14-16.
Electoral process. B. Attumbu. III:13:10.
Electorate consultation. F. C. Essandoh. V:1:21.
Elmina and Cape Coast Castles. A. A. Ntiri. III:14:24.
Encouraging immorality. L. B. Akainyah. V:8:21.
End of a war. E. Y. Frempong-Mensah. V:2:16.
End of Secession. A. R. El-Alawah. V:3:10.
Engineer and the Mills-Odoi Report. Osafo-Kantanka. IV:9:16-18.
English and Latin. D. Hereward. IV:7:22.
English vs. Local languages. D. O. Kwapong. IV:22:26.
English woman's view of Christmas. L. Gough. V:3:14.
ENNINFUL, A. A. Reply to Abiri Kwabena. VIII:12:284.
Entertainment. G. F. Daniel. II:7:18.
ENTI, A. A. Is discipline lost in the Police Service? III:7:14.
ENU, K. Busia's effigies. IV:17:18.
_____. The Ekangaki--Lonrho connection. IX:7:157-158.
_____. "Essential Commodities." VII:20:478.
_____. Let there be light. VIII:21:504.
_____. Price differentials. VII:2:40.
_____. Was it a reward or a punishment. VIII:4:93.
Environment: Comment on some pollution problems in Ghana. K. Edirisah-Aidoo. IX:14:344.
"Epilogue" on G. B. C. television. O. A. Lawal. VII:21:502.
Equatorial Guinea. J. Tavira. III:23:17.
ESHUN, I. Anti-Apartheid movement. II:15:17-18.
ESHUN, I. Anti-Apartheid movement in Ghana. II:13:14.
ESHUN, J. K. The Sergeant and the Sales girl. VII:24:575.
ESHUN, P. A volunteer is a volunteer. VIII:14:336.
ESHUN, T. A new status symbol? VIII:19:461.
ESSANDOH, F. C. Bad roads and the tax-payer. III:15:29.
_____. Devaluation--how far? III:20:24.

_____. Electorate Consultation. V:1:21.
_____. Essential Commodities. III:23:17.
_____. Ghana Transport System. III:22:20.
_____. Housing the workers. III:16:19-20.
_____. Implementing Commissions of Enquiry Reports. V:3:12.
_____. Low-Cost Housing Projects. VII:7:169.
_____. Low-wage earners housing Scheme. VII:16:380.
_____. N. L. C. should inform the public. IV:1:10.
_____. Personal attack? III:4:14.
_____. Polygamy in Ghana. III:21:18.
_____. Retrenchment and political exercise? IV:6:20.
_____. Salary review and the budget. III:6:14.
_____. Selection of the National Soccer Team. VII:26:629.
_____. Smuggling at the Borders. V:7:14.
_____. What's our reserve position now? IV:10:15.
ESSANDOH, J. B. Who really needs help? VIII:17:410.
ESSELL, K. A. General Ankrah's reception in London. II:22:13.
Essential Commodities. 1) F. C. Essandoh. III:23:17; 2) K. Enu.
    VII:20:478; 3) G. K. Essien. VII:21:504.
ESSIAR, K. Foreign Commodities for farmers. VIII:17:411.
ESSIEN, G. K. "Essential Commodities." Again. VII:21:504.
EWER, D. W. The Black Star. IV:7:22.
_____. Time and energy wasted. VIII:19:461.
EWOOL, K. Current unemployment and future politics. III:26:22-23.
EWUSI, K. Incentives and Ghana's economy. V:16:22.
Exaggerated claims of O. F. Y. Obeng-Manu. VII:23:554-555.
Exaggerated claims of O. F. Y.--Rejoinder. 1) G. J. A. Owusu-Ansah.
    VII:24:576; 2) D. S. Payida. VII:24:576; 3) A. Phillips.
    VII:24:576-578; 4) J. K. Boateng. VII:24:578.
Exams Council and the G. C. E. fees. I. Minta. IV:5:16-17.
Exchange control decree. IX:1:12.
Execution of Pierre Mulele. C. D'Auroch. III:22:19-20.
Exemptions Commission. I. Minta. III:12:16.
Expatriate. The Abbott-Ghana Controversy. II:24:11.
Expatriate civil servants. P. B. Arthiabah. VIII:24:578.
Expatriates in the Civil Service. VII:20:480.
"Expert" on Ghana. G. R. Farmer. II:24:11-12.
Explaining government policies. K. Ngyeduam. V:5:21.
Explanation please, N. L. C! K. Yankah. IV:20:18.
Exploitation of the youth? D. Hereward. V:20:28.
Exploited and lowly headteacher. 1) F. K. Tanyegbe. VIII:5:111; 2)
    VIII:9:212-213.
External Affairs Annex and dissipation of funds. K. Duku. II:22:13.
External degree courses. II:17:20.
EYIAH, D. M. Manufacturing and servicing of electric equipment.
    IX:1:13.
EZENWINYINYA, V. Support for the Federal Government. IV:1:13.
F. C. Kontopiaat Muzzled. VI:26:21.
Face-lift for Accra, Ho, Cape Coast etc. P. A. V. Ansah. VIII:3:66.
Facts about Kaleidescope. K. Ngyeduam. V:7:14.

Correspondence

FAGBEMI, E. A. Ghana and the Nigerian crisis. II:19:22-23.
FAH, M. ADJEI. See Adjei-Fah, M.
Fair treatment for all teachers. J. A. Asante. II:12:16.
Fairer distribution of teachers. K. Opare. VII:21:500.
Family rearing at public expense? S. N. Acquah. V:21:18.
Fan Milk. L. E. Mitchell. III:7:14-16.
Fan Milk Co. J. A. Dodoo. III:12:17.
FARMER, G. R. The "Expert" on Ghana. II:24:11-12.
Farmers money: What for? H. Trutenau. II:15:18.
Farms or social centre? W. Nattey. IV:3:17-18.
FERGUSON, J. D. Is Christmas for Christians? V:3:14.
Few rules for politicians. B. K. Dogbe. VII:7:169.
FIADJOE, A. Dr. Blaiberg and that heart. III:2:16.
_____. O. A. U. and the mercenaries. II:26:15.
FIADJOE, A. K. "The O. A. U. and the Mercenaries." III:2:18.
FIAFOR, J. H. Success at what price? VI:25:21.
FIAFOR, J. H. K. On teachers' uniforms. V:14:24.
_____. Our leaders and wealth. VII:7:169.
_____. The quality of teachers. V:18:16-17.
_____. Split in the Volta Region. V:17:22.
FIAFOR, K. The brain crisis in the teaching profession. III:8:12.
FIE, M. A. Students and the salary review. IX:3:68.
FIELD, M. J. George Padmore. II:24:12-13.
Film shows must be frequent. 1) J. Gyinayeh. V:18:17; 2) E. A.
    Allotey. V:24:23.
Financing National Service Corps. D. Akutteh. V:4:18.
Financing political parties. B. D. G. Folson. IV:9:16.
Fire fighting in Ghana. S. Adotey. IX:3:67.
Fire outbreak in factories. W. Tamakloe. VIII:7:164.
"Fires next time?" K. Ofori. VIII:2:43.
Firestone Agreement. E. A. Mahama. III:16:18-19.
First aid on Ghana Airways plane. J. Alarah. VIII:19:460-461.
FISCIAN, C. E. Howe's deportation. IV:25:14.
Flagstaff House Zoo. J. B. Hall. IV:9:18.
FLEISCHER VON, A. R. C. See Von Fleischer, A. R. C.
Flood our markets with matchets. Y. Gyasehene-Yeboah. IX:9:206-208.
FODEN, T. H. "Ashanti Goldfields 1967." III:11:12.
FOLI, V. Revolution with a human face. IX:1:13.
FOLSON, B. D. G. Col. Afrifa's speech. II:7:16.
_____. Financing political parties. IV:9:16.
_____. The Minerals Industry. II:18:15.
_____. Newspapers and public speakers. III:8:12.
_____. Ratifying the Constitution. IV:19:9-10.
Food for our neighbours. R. A. Kobina. VIII:20:484.
Food storage facilities. U. Drevici. IV:26:22-24.
Foodstuff allowances. G. S. Molah. VIII:5:11.
Football. J. K. Tawiah. II:14:28-29.
For whose benefit? A. Van Dantzig. IX:6:138.
Foreign banks and their employees. K. Safo. V:4:18-19.
Foreign commodities for farmers. K. Essian. VIII:17:411.
Foreign exchange indulgence. O. Kantanka. IV:16:17.

Foreign experts and local talents. E. Y. Frempong-Mensah. V:12:15.
Foreign experts and self-reliance. K. Akwabi-Ameyaw. VIII:13:308.
Foreign foods in the bush. K. Nokware. VIII:7:164.
Foreign government scholarships. M. Agbosu. IV:6:23.
FORGE, K. Secondary Day-schools. IV:13:17.
_____. Towards a common Ghanaian language. IV:6:22.
FORGE, K. B. Oburoni Muntu and African ideology. V:3:12.
_____. Preserving Ghana's Monuments. V:12:15.
Forgotten Axim-Half Assini Road. A. J. Kwofie. VIII:26:627.
FORSON, A. The Services of Accra-Tema City Council. II:21:15.
FORSON, B. Save Six from "free" text-book trap. VII:22:524.
_____. Soccer incentives. IX:3:69.
Forty pesewas to the policeman. S. K. O. Denkyi. IV:25:16-17.
4,750 disappointments. A. Van Dantzig. III:3:10.
Frantz Fanon. T. C. McCaskie. III:10:11-12.
Free education. D. Y. A. Okraku. III:20:27.
Free text-book scheme. F. A. A. Andoh. VII:21:504.
Freedom and the State press. K. Mbrah. VII:13:306.
FREMPONG, G. A. Is that all? III:13:12.
_____. A tasteless crisis. IV:26:25.
_____. That expensive day. II:26:17.
FREMPONG, J. E. and ATOBRA, K. A. K. One way traffic highway for Accra.
    III:4:14.
FREMPONG-MANSO. Going back to the land. IV:25:16.
FREMPONG-MENSAH. Tro-tro fares. V:2:17.
FREMPONG-MENSAH, E. Y. The end of a war. V:2:16.
_____. Foreign experts and local talents. V:12:15.
_____. The Kumasi resignations. V:10:20.
_____. "Operation Feed Yourself" Campaign. VII:9:216-217.
_____. Opposition--Blessing or Curse? IV:21:16.
_____. University appeal funds. V:7:14.
_____. Whither Red China? IV:25:17.
FREMPONG, OWUSU. See Owusu-Frempong.
FRIMPONG, J. E. (jt. au.). See Attobrah, K. A. F.
FRIMPONG, J. K. Why the Mission Schools? IV:25:18.
FRIMPONG, K. Austerity patterns: Somalia and Ghana. V:15:16.
_____. "The average Ghanaian." VII:17:408.
_____. Kente industry dying. VIII:5:112.
_____. The National House of Chiefs. VIII:1:22.
_____. Open letter to F. G. Mante. VI:2:13.
From Ministerial to Military peregrination? A-Lashie. VII:13:305-306.
Fuel policy of Ghana. S. Ocansey. III:3:11.
Future of our liberators. K. A. Awadzie. II:6:17.
Future of our mines. Rejoinder. 1) A. F. J. Smit. VIII:1:19; 2)
    K. Atobrah. VIII:3:65-66.
G. A. E. C. must act. R. Thomas. VII:9:217; Rejoinder--B. Amoako-
    Attah. VII:10:243-244.
G. N. T. C. and crash helmets. B. L. J. Kumasi. VIII:25:528.
G. N. T. C. selling Portuguese goods? I. N. Nympha. IX:1:12.
GADZEKPO, C. K. The Nigerian War: Chance for a solution? III:14:22.

Correspondence

Games politics play. K. A. B. Jones-Quartey. V:14:22.
GAMESU, P. Congrats Observer. VII:14:338.
_____. Criticism as criticism. III:2:14.
_____. Intellectuals. VII:21:501-502.
_____. No bridge-crossing, this time. III:24:11-12.
_____. Nominations. IV:17:17-18.
_____. Senator Kennedy and "Caesar's Wife." IV:16:14-16.
GANAWAY, M. Ghanaian doctors. II:14:27-28.
"Gaping Sycophants" again? Obeng-Manu. IV:22:24.
GARBRAH, E. S. Onward with the revolution--Rejoinder. IX:12:288.
Gardiner on intellectuals in politics. E. Vorkeh. VIII:1:20.
GBOBI, R. The Nigerian Civil War. III:10:10.
GBODZOE, M. K. Economics of the aliens order. V:8:17-18.
General Afrifa and the Constitution. D. N. Akuetteh. V:18:14; T.
    Owens-Dey. V:18:14.
General Ankrah's reception in London. K. A. Essell. II:22:13.
General declaration of assets? Y. Amoako-Addo. VII:17:408.
The General Legal Council and Lawyers. J. Alarah. III:10:10.
Genocide in Biafra. H. Anokye. III:22:22.
GEORGE, B. Socialist re-emergence? VI:16:20-21.
George Padmore. M. J. Field. II:24:12-13.
Ghana Airforce accidents. M. F. Owusu. II:2:16.
Ghana Airways conflict. S. F. Afatsiawo. III:9:14.
Ghana Airways let down in Abidjan. S. K. Date-Bah. VIII:18:436-438--
    Reply. M. M. Anamzoya. VIII:19:460.
Ghana Airways mess! J. V. Quaye. VII:6:141.
Ghana Airways to serve Ghanaian food? C. K. Adei. VII:19:453.
Ghana Airways V. C. 10. P. Adu-Gyamfi. IV:3:16.
Ghana and the N. L. C. A. Osei. II:9:21.
Ghana and the new cedi. E. D. Kemevor. II:2:15.
Ghana and Nigeria crisis. 1) J. B. Mensah. II:16:17; 2) E. A.
    Fabgemi. II:19:22-23; 3) K. Okum. II:19:22; 4) D. Koleoso.
    II:20:21.
Ghana Ayikoo! A. Jarry. IV:20:18.
Ghana, Nigeria and Kaunda. S. Ebegare. IV:15:17.
Ghana privileged few. E. Sibundvski. V:18:13-14.
Ghana Sports. I. A. Mensah. III:16:21.
Ghana Sports must be reviewed. S. Adotey. VIII:3:68.
Ghana Transport System. F. C. Essandoh. III:22:20.
Ghanaian and the West. B. J. K. Kumasi. VIII:9:213.
Ghanaian architects and the housing problem. L. Koi-Larbi.
    VIII:12:286.
Ghanaian Association of University Women. F. Dolphyne. III:23:19.
Ghanaian culture retrieved. I. Minta. V:7:14.
Ghanaian doctors. 1) M. Ganaway. II:14:27-28; 2) B. Dzodanu.
    II:15:20.
Ghanaian Doctors Overseas. Y. A. Dodoo. II:16:16-17.
Ghanaian Economic Enterprise. K. Tekyi. III:12:16.
Ghanaian establishment. B. Adjei. IV:4:29.
Ghanaian Press and Public Speakers. J. E. C. Armah. III:9:14.

119

Correspondence

Ghanaian Times and Busia's Speech. J. K. Mensah. II:8:13; K. N.
Bame. II:8:13-14.
Ghanaians and family planning. B. S. Atedechira. V:20:28.
Ghanaians and writing. D. Hereward. VII:22:528.
Ghanaians in Nigeria today. 1) J. Afreh-Kassam. II:21:13; 2) K.
Kwabere-Abradu. II:21:13-14.
Ghana's Art Treasures. H. M. J. Trutenau. V:19:22.
Ghana's destiny. K. Kissi-Debrah. V:1:20.
Ghana's external debts. J. K. Boateng. VII:2:39.
Ghana's external relations. 1) M. N. Nyamikeh. II:6:18; 2) K. A.
Karikari. II:7:18-19.
Ghana's housing problems. K. Osafo. V:8:18.
Ghana's lost culture is retrieved. J. Gyinayeh. V:6:14.
Ghana's Passports? V:17:22.
Ghana's privileged few. 1) E. Sbundvski. V:18:13-14; 2) K. Osafo-
Atta. V:21:18.
Ghana's rural roads. J. Gyinayeh. V:18:16.
Ghana's stock of advice by experts. M. A. Akyeampong. III:10:10.
Ghana's tax structure. K. Osafo. V:18:13.
Ghana's unemployment problems. 1) J. Gyinayeh. V:12:15; 2) I. Tano.
V:13:28; 3) Y. O. Adomako. V:14:23-24.
Ghost of the "Lincolnite." S. K. Opoku. II:21:15.
Gibbs review--Another rejoinder. B. Marshall. IV:13:17.
Gilbey's gin. 1) J. A. Acquaye. II:20:22; 2) P. Danquah. II:21:13.
Give it another thought, N. R. C. B. Assasie-Gyimah. VIII:22:529.
Give us some more. J. K. Adarkwa. VIII:16:384.
Giving and accepting gifts. M. N. Nyamikeh. II:24:16.
Giving Unto God and Unto Caesar. M. Adjei. VIII:8:185.
God and the Coup--A rejoinder. VII:4:90.
GODI, G. K. Tribal names and surnames. VI:22:17-18.
GOGO, B. A. On military training. VIII:16:387.
GOGO, G. A. Recent changes--Regional Commissioners. VIII:10:234.
Going back to the land. Frempong-Manso. IV:25:16.
GOKA, G. Lip-service to press freedom? VI:4:15-16.
Good photographs for calendars. Y. Assah-Sam. II:24:16.
Good programme for the government. M. C. Charles. VI:13:20.
Good quality products are needed. S. Adotey. VIII:26:625.
GORDON, J. The new farmer. III:4:12-13.
GORDON, J. O. Agricultural and other research papers. III:1:17.
GOUGH, L. Black is beautiful. IV:12:14.
_____. An English woman's view of Christmas. V:3:14.
Government White paper on Cargo Handling Co. J. B. Spio. III:21:17.
Graduate employment. G. Twum. VIII:5:111.
Granulated sugar and foreign exchange. S. Adotey. VIII:22:529.
GRAVES, A. Nigeria-Biafra crisis. IV:8:21.
Great Men. K. A. Taylor. III:2:18.
GREENFIELD, R. Libraries and dancers. V:7:14.
_____. An Oxford first for Ghana's President? VI:11:21.
Gulder bottles. S. K. Oduro-Denkyi. VIII:5:112.
GYAMFI, ADU. See Adu-Gyamfi.
GYAN, AFARI. See Afari-Gyan.

Correspondence

GYANDOH, S. O. Mr. Gyandoh writes. VII:6:142.
GYASEHENE-YEBOAH, Y. Flood our markets with matchets. IX:9:206-208.
_____. Restore the subsidy on examination fees. IX:7:158.
GYASI, I. K. That shocking editorial. II:25:8.
GYEFUOR, K. Prices of petrol and kerosene. IX:7:161.
GYIMAH, B. ASSASIE. See Assasie-Gyimah, B.
GYINAYEH, J. Film shows must be frequent. V:18:17.
_____. Ghana's lost culture is retrieved. V:6:14.
_____. Ghana's rural roads. V:18:16.
_____. Ghana's unemployment problems. V:12:15.
_____. Is payment of special levy justified? VI:6:19.
_____. Oburoni Muntu--Congrats! V:9:21.
_____. Tourism in Ghana. VI:2:16.
_____. What is wrong with Ghanaian Agriculturists? VII:6:141.
Hackman case. C. C. T. Blankson. IV:24:25.
Hail Kontopiaat. G. N. Tetteh. V:1:21.
HAIZEL, K. Colonial mentality. IV:5:17.
HAIZEL, K. B. The brain drain. III:25:20.
HALIGAH, K. What kind of candidates for the next Parliament?
    III:7:12-13.
"Hall" fees--A rejoinder. J. Kofi. VIII:20:482.
HALL, J. B. Flagstaff House Zoo. IV:9:18.
HAMMOND, A. A. "The Classics." IV:19:11.
_____. The Opposition in the Second Republic. IV:14:18.
HAMMOND, G. The honest man. II:14:26.
Hand baggage surcharge--A rejoinder. M. M. Anamzoya. IX:6:137.
HANSON, K. N. Aboabo Day Nursery. IV:26:25.
_____. Charity begins at home. IV:15:14.
_____. Madjitey and the dialogue question. VI:2:13-14.
_____. Military training for students. VII:25:603-604.
_____. Politicians' promises. IV:14:18.
_____. Salaries for N. R. C. men. VII:12:286-287.
Happy Birthday. 1) S. Amartey. III:15:29; 2) J. Okai. III:15:29.
HARLEY, J. E. CONDUA. See Condua-Harley, J. E.
Hats off to the "Observer." I. M. Josselson. VI:14:22.
Hawkers and the University. K. Asenso. II:1:19.
HAYFORD, C. After the fires next time. VII:15:360.
HAYFORD, K. A second medical school. IX:7:158-160.
Help! E. K. Senahe. V:1:20.
Help me! I am in a dilemma. S. A. Yirenkyi. III:24:14.
HEMANG, K. Mr. Kontopiaat. III:2:15.
HEREWARD, D. Africa and Western values. V:6:15.
_____. Air pollution. III:21:18.
_____. Ancient and modern. IV:5:17.
_____. Assisting Independent Schools. VII:12:287-288.
_____. The British not to be blamed. IV:6:22.
_____. The burnt-out marriage. III:14:23-24.
_____. Classics. IV:19:11.
_____. Criticism of private schools. III:19:16.
_____. English and Latin. IV:7:22.

_____. Exploitation of the Youth? V:20:28.
_____. Ghanaians and writing. VII:22:528.
_____. Is it contempt? III:7:14.
_____. The Legon probe. II:12:17.
_____. Missionary Schools and liberalism. V:3:12.
_____. "Non-education" for Africans? V:13:27.
_____. On students. V:21:22.
_____. On "Utopia and education." VII:17:407.
_____. Our educational system. VIII:12:285.
_____. Private schools. IV:26:25.
_____. Relevance of Ancient History. VIII:5:112.
_____. Self-reliance and expatriate missionaries--rejoinder.
VIII:22:527.
_____. Teaching of Classics. III:15:29.
_____. Translate and be read! IV:23:19.
_____. Underpriviledged Schools. VIII:6:133-134.
_____. The University and Society--A rejoinder. VIII:1:18-19.
_____. The University Loan Scheme. VI:6:18.
_____. Why we study Classics. IV:16:16.
HESSE, F. National Committee on Apartheid. V:2:15.
HESSE, L. W. Academy of Sciences. II:8:14-16.
High cost and price control. S. Adotey. VI:15:20.
High cost of living. K. Obinim. VI:11:21.
Higher salaries for members of the judiciary. S. K. O. Banin.
II:10:16.
HINIDZA, R. KIYA. See Kiya-Hinidza, R.
HINSON, E. Adverts in the Legon Observer. IX:11:254.
_____. The budget and Rest Houses. VII:20:480.
_____. "Intellectual M..." and all that--rejoinder. VIII:21:503.
Holland aids Togo School. IV:2:26.
Honest man. G. Hammond. II:14:26.
HORE, A. Opinion polls. III:5:25.
Horror in Crescendo. O. Ogum. III:18:17.
Hospital fees report. F. D. Konotey-Ahulu. VIII:26:625.
Houses at one cedi each? K. A. K. Attobrah (et al). III:9:13-14.
Housing the people. I. B. Phillips. II:8:16.
Housing the workers. F. C. Essandoh. III:16:19-20.
How democratic is G. N. A. T.? G. H. K. Amehia-Adugu. V:20:28.
How many political parties? IV:6:22-23.
How non-aligned are we? P. Adu-Gyamfi. III:4:12.
How to deal with burglars. E. D. Asante. III:11:18.
How to revive the one party system in Ghana. J. E. Wiredu.
VII:6:139-140.
Howe's deportation. C. E. Fiscian. IV:25:14.
HUGHES, B. Salary increases. II:1:18-19.
HUNTUMA, K. The L. O. and its critics. VII:14:338.
Hutchful's confrontation. D. Adjei-Brenya. V:24:21; E. M. Kumaga.
VI:3:11.
IDDRISU, A. Changing of the Guard. VII:5:109.
_____. O. F. Y. and the bush fires. VIII:4:92.

Correspondence

Ideal ruler in Africa. A. Seyire. VI:24:19.
Identity of writers. E. O. Okeem. VI:9:24.
Ideological conflict. J. Apronti. VI:15:20.
Ideologies on sale--Another rejoinder. S. Kusi-Yeboah. VIII:13:308.
IFEZULIKE. The Nigerian War: Chance for a solution? III:14:22.
Impartiality for sale. N. T. Addo. VII:26:629-630.
Impartiality of the State press? K. Budu. III:25:19-20.
Implementing Commissions of Enquiry Reports. F. C. Essandoh. V:3:12.
Import Licensing and St. John. S. K. Manu. II:10:16.
IMPRAIM, T. K. The lady can't be serious. VIII:13:306.
Improving Ghana Airways Services. J. Apronti. VIII:22:528-529.
Incentives and Ghana's economy. K. Ewusi. V:16:22.
Incentives for teachers? J. Nukafo. VI:21:16.
Independence for the Inspection Division please. R. A. Kotey.
    VII:20:478.
INNES, R. and LAWSON, R. Agricultural Research Papers. II:24:16.
Installation of Chiefs. B. J. L. Kumasi. VI:12:23.
Insurance for funerals. C. K. Anderson. VII:22:528.
"Intellectual M..." and all that--Rejoinder. 1) M. S. Braimah.
    VIII:21:503; 2) E. Daniel. VIII:21:503; 3) E. Hinson. VIII:21:503;
    4) W. Nelson. VIII:23:556.
Intellectuals. P. Gamesu. VII:21:501-502.
Interplay of reasoning. G. O. Yeboah. VII:2:40.
Interviews. N. K. Apreku. III:20:24.
Is Christmas for Christians? J. D. Ferguson. V:3:14.
Is discipline lost in the Police Service? A. A. Anti. III:7:14.
Is it contempt? D. Hereward. III.7.14. Legonite. III:7:14.
Is payment of special levy justified? J. Gyinayeh. VI:6:19.
Is that all? G. A. Frempong. III:13:12.
Is the closure necessary. M. D. Nii Addy. VIII:11:261.
Is the Otumfuo's N¢3 million palace really necessary? J. C. Quansah.
    VI:12:22-23.
Is the problem salaries or high cost of living? C. E. Quist. II:12:17.
Is the 2 year D-plan necessary? M. N. Karikari. III:17:10-11.
JAMES, K. Wives. III:10:10.
JARRY, A. Ghana Ayikoo! IV:20:18.
Jeafan/Guardian Publications. M. S. Braimah. IV:11:18.
Jehovah's Witnesses and the millennium. F. S. Aboagye. V:6:15.
JOHNSON, M. T. V. Tortures. III:2:18.
JOHNSON, P. H. K. Operation Asutsuare--A rejoinder. VII:9:216.
_____. Stop this bullying now--A rejoinder. VII:8:194.
JOHNSON, W. K. Consider us first. III:23:17.
JONES-QUARTEY, K. A. B. Better manners. II:1:19.
_____. The chiefs and Ghana's "corpse culture." VI:26:20.
_____. Cost of living: Ghana and Sierra Leone. V:18:13.
_____. The games politics play. V:14:22.
_____. Nigerian crisis. II:7:16-17.
_____. Parliament and the N. U. G. S. VI:11:20-21.
_____. Peace with cultural honour. VIII:10:238.
_____. Powerful but not gods. VII:25:600.
_____. "Rubbish Trash!" VIII:13:310.

Correspondence

JOSSELSON, M. Hats off to the "Observer!" VI:14:22.
Judges and the proposed Constitution. P. A. V. Ansah. III:6:12.
Just what is provocation? K. Obinim. VI:21:16.
Justice and peace. P. B. Arthiabah. IX:7:160.
Justice, man's fallibility and the people. K. Opare. III:14:23.
K. A. The National Executive Council. II:14:26.
KAKRABAH-QUARSHIE, R. The N. R. C. and rural development. VII:8:193.
KANAWU, K. The Budget and the elite. VI:22:16.
KANTANKA, O. The ban, politics and leaders. IV:10:14-15.
_____. "Black is beautiful"--A reply. IV:13:14.
_____. Foreign exchange indulgence. IV:16:17.
_____. Let sureties produce their picture. VIII:15:362.
_____. Plight of the low-paid worker. VIII:11:260.
_____. Tribalism and the new politics. IV:11:16.
KARIKARI, K. Recording Nkrumah's ideas. VII:25:602.
KARIKARI, K. A. Ghana's external relations. II:7:18-19.
KARIKARI, M. N. Is the 2-year D-Plan necessary? III:17:10-11.
KASAAM, J. AFREH. See Afreh-Kasaam, J.
KATTAH, A. K. Economic independence in the Congo. II:3:15.
Keep it up, Observer. S. W. Adinkrah. VII:10:242.
Keep right in 1794? M. Adjei-Fah. VIII:23:558.
Keep the Standards high. G. M. Agble. IV:20:18-19.
KEMEVOR, E. D. Cars in Ghana's economy. III:10:8-10.
_____. Ghana and the new Cedi. II:2:15.
_____. Quo Vadis Ghana? IV:1:12.
_____. To what extent can a man sacrifice? III:14:24.
KENT, K. Thanks for rescue. VIII:8:186.
Kente industry dying? K. Frimpong. VIII:5:112.
KEPLER, A. Unemployment and crime. III:3:8-10.
Kete-Krachi Hospital. C. Y. Khra. IX:4:90.
KHEMCHARD, N. Radicalism. VII:4:91.
KHRA, C. Y. The Kete-Krachi Hospital. IX:4:90.
_____. Split in the Volta Region. V:23:22.
Killing of Karume. G. F. A. Sawyerr. VII:10:244.
KING, E. "Bravo! Mr. Secretary." VI:19:15.
_____. Salary increases. V:11:26.
KISSI-DEBRAH, K. Ghana's destiny. V:1:20.
KISSIEDU, C. O. Women and the Nation. V:12:15-16.
KIYA-HINIDZA, R. National anthem turning commonplace? VII:13:307.
KOBINA, R. A. Food for our neighbours. VIII:20:484.
KODZO, J. Nkrumah passes away--Rejoinder. VII:10:241.
KOFI, A. B. B. "St. John's International" import licensing.
    II:9:20-21.
KOFI, J. "Hall" fees--A rejoinder. VIII:20:482.
KOFI, N. N. Blame magazines and books too. III:21:18.
KOFI, T. A. Cocoa prices and under-development in Ghana--A rejoinder.
    VII:26:624.
_____. World Cocoa prices and under-development in Ghana. A note.
    VII:22:528.
KOFIE, N. N. Drivers and overloading. IV:17:21.
KOFISON, D. Stop these unnecessary arrests. II:22:14.

Correspondence

KOI-LARBI, L. Ghanaian architects and the housing problem.
VIII:12:286.
_____. The N. R. C. and temporary solutions. VIII:5:109.
_____. Save us from Makola women. VIII:7:163.
KOLEOSO, D. Ghana and the Nigeria crisis. II:20:21.
KONOTEY-AHULU, F. D. The Hospital fees report. VIII:26:625.
KONTOPIAAT. Mr. Judicial Secretary, action not threats please.
II:19:21.
KONTOPIAAT, K. Kontopiaat and Oguaa gods. V:23:22.
Kontopiaat and Oguaa gods. 1) J. Pobee. V:21:20; 2) K. Kontopiaat.
V:23:22.
Kontopiaat and the Judicial Service. E. S. Aidoo. II:16:16.
Kontopiaat muzzled. C. F. VI:26:21.
Kontopiaat on Judicial Secretary. K. B. II:22:14.
Kontopiaat: the Party. I. Minta. III:15:29.
KONUAH, K. G. Political parties in Ghana. IV:9:18.
_____. Taxation and the Ghanaian tax-payer. IV:7:20.
_____. Tribalism in its true perspective. IV:3:17.
KOOMSON, K. BONNAH. See Bonnah-Koomson, K.
KORANTENG, O. Personality cult--true or false? IV:20:19-20.
Korle-Bu and its surroundings. J. K. Boateng. VII:15:358.
Korle-Bu Maternity Hospital. IV:2:17.
KOTEY, R. A. Cause for alarm. IV:5:16.
_____. Independence for the inspection division, please. VII:20:478.
KOTO, K. G. The recognition of Biafra. III:10:10-11.
Kotoka, Freedom and Justice. Y. M. Agble. II:16:17.
Kotoka Trust Fund. K. Semanya. II:23:19.
Kotoka's Statue. R. Y. T. Defoe. IV:25:16.
KPABITEY, E. B. What's wrong with Manya-Krobo local council?
IV:11:18.
KPEDEKPO, G. M. K. Agricultural research papers. II:25:30.
_____. Does it make sense? IV:7:22.
_____. The land question. III:5:23-24.
_____. The Legon Observer warned us. IV:8:18.
_____. Mentally retarded children. III:11:16-18.
_____. Opinion polls. III:1:14.
_____. This foreign exchange. IV:9:20.
KPEGLO, A. AMUZU. See Amuzu-Kpeglo, A.
KRAHENE, C. That Black Star again. VII:4:89.
KUENYEHIA, N. The uncertainty of future politics. III:13:10.
KUMAGA, E. M. Check these traders. II:17:19-20.
_____. Hutchful's confrontation. VI:3:11.
_____. The long vacation period should change. VI:15:20-22.
_____. Ministers' salaries. IV:26:24.
_____. Top civil servants and politicians. IV:24:24.
KUMANKAMA, P. K. The churches and society. V:21:20.
KUMASI, B. J. L. Chieftaincy affairs in the Upper Region. VI:25:21.
_____. G. N. T. C. and crash helmets. VIII:22:528.
_____. The Ghanaian and the West. VIII:9:213.
_____. Installation of chiefs. VI:12:23.

_____. Mass transfer of teachers. VI:23:20.
_____. Recent changes.... A rejoinder. VIII:12:284.
_____. School holidays. VIII:16:387-388.
_____. The Teaching Service Decree. IX:3:68.
KUMASI, K. J. L. Tribal names and surnames. VI:20:14.
Kumasi resignations. E. Y. Frempong-Mensah. V:10:20.
KUMI, E. K. Beware of such women. VIII:20:482-483.
KUMI, T. G. The Compliance Order. V:5:22.
_____. "On drafting for the public." III:10:12-13.
KUSI-YEBOAH, S. Ideologies on sale--Another rejoinder. VIII:13:308.
KUTTIN, K. Doctors' prescription. VIII:21:504.
_____. A double-edged weapon. IX:1:13.
_____. The press, the people and the Government--A rejoinder. IX:8:184.
_____. The problem of shortages--A personal note. VIII:26:628.
KUTTIN-MENSAH, K. Road safety and word games. VIII:1:23.
KWABERE-ABRADU, K. Ghanaians in Nigeria today. II:21:13-14.
KWAKU-SAFO. Overhauling the passport office. IV:22:26.
KWAKUTSE, K. What kind of candidates for the next Parliament? III:9:13.
KWAKWA, R. S. Reflective number plates. III:5:27.
KWAME, A. The Nunoo Affair. IV:12:11.
Kwame Nkrumah and Ghana. E. K. Adeti. VI:13:20.
Kwame Nkrumah as we knew him: Genoveva and Ofosu-Appiah. G. Marais. VII:26:626.
Kwame Nkrumah: hero or villain? 1) G. Osei. VIII:6:136; 2) K. Baafuor-Awuah. T. G. K. Owens-Dey. VIII:8:186.
Kwame Nkrumah revisited. T. P. Omari. V:17:21.
KWAME, P. OSEI. See Osei-Kwame, P.
KWAMENA, A. Walls: Architectural craze or fortresses? III:2:17-18.
KWAMI, V. Working hours. II:17:20.
KWANSAH, K. B. Award for policemen. VII:18:432-433.
KWANSIMA, A. Operation Feed Youself gone awry? VII:21:501.
KWAPONG, D. O. English vs. local languages. IV:22:26.
KWAPONG, J. M. D. Discussing the proposed constitution. III:9:12.
KWARTELAI-QUARTEY, J. Let's forget about Nkrumah. VI:15:19-20.
KWEI, E. A. Tribute to Mr. B. A. Yakubu. VI:14:22.
KWENUAH, E. Making profits or doing charity? IX:8:185.
Kwesi Armah's extradition. 1) P. W. C. Maxwell. II:3:15; 2) T. P. Odoi. II:4:22-23.
KWOFIE, A. J. The forgotten Axim-Half Assini Road. VIII:26:627.
_____. Limestone deposits at Nawule. VIII:16:384-385.
KYEI, K. OWUSU. See Owusu-Kyei, K.
KYERE, K. The new working hours. VII:7:170.
_____. The N. R. C. must not fail. VII:9:214-216.
KYEREME-ANTWI, A. Constructive criticism. VIII:6:137.
_____. Criticism: Constructive and destructive. VIII:10:234.
KYEREMEH, K. ANSU. See Ansu-Kyeremeh, K.
KYERETWIE, B. AWUA. See Awua-Kyeretwie, B.
L. O. and its critics. K. Huntuma. VII:14:338.

Correspondence

L. O. and its detractors. S. B. Akuffo. 1) VII:15:260; 2) VII:16:380.
L. O. critic writes. P. B. Arthiabah. VIII:13:305.
L. O. Editor again! W. Amarfio. VII:10:242-243. Rejoinders: 1)
    Obeng-Manu. VII:11:265; 2) I. Minta. VII:12:287.
Lack of courtesy in a public officer. H. Limann. II:26:17.
Lady can't be serious. T. K. Impraim. VIII:13:306.
LAMPTEY, A. P. Division of labour. VII:20:480.
LAMPTEY, J. Britain's aid to Ghana. IV:25:14-16.
LAMPTEY, O. OBETSEBI. See Obetsebi-Lamptey, O.
LAMPTEY, V. E. O. PORTUPHY. See Portuphy-Lamptey, V. E. O.
Land question. G. M. K. Kpedekpo. III:5:23-24; E. M. Badu. III:5:24.
LANE, H. C. Protecting the consumer--A rejoinder. VIII:1:19.
Language question in school. J. M. Stewart. IV:6:22.
LANQUAYE, A. Death penalty for robbers. VII:3:59.
LARBI, A. The Sallah judgement. V:10:20.
LARBI, L. KOI. See Koi-Larbi, L.
LARBI, S. G. What price, sycophancy--A rejoinder. VII:11:266.
LARTEY, J. Love-hate psychosis and the rest. VIII:11:262.
LARVERH, E. S. What are the facts? VIII:6:137.
LARYEA, A. The rural development programme and the economy.
    VII:4:90-91.
LARYEA, B. Wake up A. T. C. C. IX:3:67.
LARYEA, B. O. The Leyland buses and Apartheid. VIII:8:187.
_____. P. P. P. still going strong? VIII:3:67.
_____. The withdrawn ¢30 million subsidy. A rejoinder. VIII:4:90.
LARYEA, O. Stealing at the ports. VIII:16:387.
_____. Stealing at the Ports--A correction. VIII:21:504.
LAWAL, O. A. "Epilogue" on G. B. C. Television. VII:21:502.
Laws of Apartheid. K. Boakye. V:25:19.
LAWSON, R. and INNES, R. Agricultural Research papers. II:24:16.
Leadership in rural development. N. Parker. V:26:18.
Learn to respect. S. Owusu. VI:3:11-14.
Leave Israel alone. P. A. V. Ansah. IV:1:12-13.
Leave the Artiste fee alone. Mensah-Bonsu. IX:9:206.
Legal aid in Ghana. E. S. Aidoo. V:6:14.
Legon and the Legon Observer. K. A. K. Attobrah. VII:15:359.
Legon New Year School. M. Assimeng. V:2:16.
Legon Observer warned us. G. M. K. Kpedekpo. IV:8:18.
Legon Observer's defeat. K. Agyare. II:25:29.
Legon Observer's shattering defeat. O. Agyemang. II:24:17.
Legon Probe. 1) Legonite. 2) Ex-Legonite. II:11:17; 3) D. Hereward.
    II:12:17.
Lessons from Exemptions Commission. K. Yeboah. III:25:20-21.
Lessons of the Mid-East War for Africa. E. K. Vorkeh. IX:5:112.
Let Nigeria leave Biafra alone. H. C. Daniel. IV:3:16.
Let Nkrumah come home! Owusu-Frempong. VI:13:19-20.
Let sureties produce their picture. O. Kantanka. VIII:15:362.
Let them miss one election! K. A. Taylor. III:16:19.
Let there be light. K. Enu. VIII:21:504.
Let us be realistic. Y. Agyarko-Appea. VIII:4:93.
Let us now praise humorous men. K. Blankson. IX:8:185.

Correspondence

Let us protect our constitution. K. Atobrah. VI:27:19.
Let's forget about Nkrumah. K. Kwatelai-Quartey. VI:15:19-20.
Let's mind our own problems. S. A. Bukari. VIII:2:42.
Letters to the Editor. A. Amuzu-Kpeglo. II:15:19.
Leyland buses and Apartheid. B. O. Laryea. VIII:8:187.
Liberty of the majority. O. Awuku. IV:14:19.
Libraries and dancers. R. Greenfield. V:7:14.
LIMANN, H. Lack of courtesy in a public officer. II:26:17.
Limestone deposits at Nawule. A. J. Kwofie. VIII:16:384-385.
Lip-service to press freedom? G. Goka.
LIVERPOOL, N. O. Military tattoo. II:9:21.
Loans for cars in the Civil Service. K. A. Omari-Wadie. III:3:11.
Local government and the economy in post-coup Ghana. A. T. K. Nanor.
    VIII:1:22.
Local soaps. M. Yeboah. V:24:23.
LOGGO, K. White paper and Apaloo Commission. II:5:10-11.
Logistic fiasco. J. Amissah. VIII:17:410.
Long vacation period should change. E. M. Kumaga. VI:15:20-22.
LONGMAN, J. The public executions. II:11:16-17.
_____. Unnecessary imports. III:1:16.
LONGMAN, K. A. Economic development and the training of scientists.
    II:2:15.
Lost opportunity of the Hutchful incident. W. K. Ansah. V:26:18.
LOTSU, S. Biafra has come to stay. IV:12:12.
_____. Doctors' salaries. III:26:25-26.
_____. The O. A. U., Nigeria and Biafra. IV:10:16.
_____. The significance of 24th February. V:9:20-21.
Love-hate psychosis and the rest. J. Lartey. VIII:11:262.
Low-Cost housing projects. F. C. Essandoh. VII:7:169.
Low Local production: Its remedy. P. S. Acheampong. III:20:22-24.
Low-Wage earners housing scheme. F. C. Essandoh. VII:16:380.
Luxury and sacrifice. E. Osei. V:13:26.
LYNCH-ROBINSON, H. A. "American intervention." II:23:18.
M. A. Courses in Journalism. VIII:1:20.
McCASKIE, T. C. Frantz Fanon. III:10:11-12.
McCLEAN, G. O. National Union of Seamen. II:26:17.
McFALL, R. G. World cocoa prices and underdevelopment in Ghana--A
    rejoinder. VII:23:552.
Made in Ghana goods. 1) C. C. T. Blankson. II:2:15-16; 2) K. A.
    Sasu. II:2:16; 3) Y. Piesieh. VII:15:357-358.
Made in Ghana products. A. Darko. IV:13:17.
Madjitey and the dialogue question. K. N. Hanson. VI:2:13-14.
MAHAMA, E. A. Firestone agreement. III:16:18-19.
Making profits or doing charity? E. Kwenuah. IX:8:185.
Making the Observer "lively." Ampadu-Mari. V:15:17.
Malam Shitta case. G. E. Twum. VIII:10:237-238.
Malefactors in our society. B. Attumbu. III:19:14.
Manpower planning. VII:17:407-408.
MANSO, FREMPONG. See Frempong-Manso.
MANSO, P. Agricultural Loans. VI:19:15.

MANTE, F. G. Open letter to the P. M. V:25:19-20.
MANTE, G. A. No interference with the Army? VI:12:20-22.
MANTEAW, A. K. The Observer language. V:5:22.
MANU, J. On family planning. V:24:22-23.
MANU, K. Import licensing and St. John's. II:10:16.
MANU, O. Col. Bernasko and the O. F. Y. programme. IX:4:87-90.
MANU, OBENG. See Obeng-Manu.
MANU, S. A. O. Non-Aggression Jokes? V:22:25.
MANU-ACHEAMPONG, K. Reconciliation and not revival. VIII:6:134.
Manufacturing and servicing of electric equipment. D. M. Eyah.
   IX:1:13.
MANUH, F. Why not put Ghana's Army to farm work? VI:8:18.
MARAIS, G. Kwame Nkrumah as "we" knew him: Genoveva and Ofosu-Appiah.
   VII:26:626.
MARCELLE, M. School nurses. IV:12:12-14.
MARFO, K. The citizen and the police. IV:7:22.
_____. Crime in Ghana. III:14:24.
_____. The Nigerian Civil War. III:12:14.
_____. Single women in Ghana. III:19:17.
_____. Support for the Federal Government. III:25:21-22.
MARI, AMPADU. See Ampadu-Mari.
MARK, S. D. The O. S. A. and Pensioners. VIII:8:186-187.
MARKHAM, J. The African scene. II:1:15-16.
MARSHALL, B. The Gibbs review--Another rejoinder. IV:13:17.
Mass education. M. Onyina-Appea. IX:9:206.
Mass transfer of teachers. B. J. L. Kumasi. VI:23:20.
Massacres in Burundi. C. K. Minta. VIII:16:387.
Mathematics and the generation gap. P. A. V. Ansah. VIII:26:626-628.
MATTHEWS, M. Trauma over Legon Crisis. III:24:12-13.
MAVERICK, R. Dilemma of a patriot. III:25:18.
MAXWELL, P. W. C. Anti-Apartheid movement in Ghana. II:13:14-15.
_____. Kwesi Armah's extradition. II:3:15.
_____. The public executions. II:12:15.
MBRAH, K. Freedom and the State Press. VII:13:306.
Meddling with mass media? M. Bonnie. V:4:18.
Medical education. G. A. Ashitey. III:8:13.
Medium-sized batteries. 1) I. Nkansah. VII:22:526; 2) J. K. A.
   Mensah. VII:24:574.
MENSAH, A. The Prah Report. II:26:18.
MENSAH, A. A. Nkrumah, the Nzimas and the election. IV:20:16-18.
MENSAH, A. ACKAH. See Ackah-Mensah, A.
MENSAH, A. K. Prestige projects and retrenchment. IV:6:18-20.
MENSAH, A. N. The denizens of the street. VII:3:60.
_____. Doctors to be sacked? VII:20:480.
_____. The earthquake at Kumasi--Essentially a paradox. VIII:3:66.
_____. University entrance and guidance in schools--A comment.
   VIII:24:580.
MENSAH, ADDAE. See Addae-Mensah.
MENSAH, C. E. Banning Echo and Pioneer. VII:15:359.
_____. A nation of hypocrites. VII:11:264.
_____. Our National Papers. VII:12:286.

MENSAH, E. Working in the Rural areas. V:9:21.
MENSAH, E. OBENG. See Obeng-Mensah, E.
MENSAH, E. Y. BROBE. See Brobe-Mensah, E. Y.
MENSAH, E. Y. FREMPONG. See Frempong-Mensah, E. Y.
MENSAH, I. A. Ghana Sports. III:16:21.
_____. The Mills-Odoi Salaries Report. IV:12:11.
_____. Whither Ghana? II:25:30.
MENSAH, I. ACKOM. See Ackom-Mensah, I.
MENSAH, I. K. Ministry of Agriculture to be abolished? VII:25:603.
MENSAH, J. The old guard again? VIII:3:67.
MENSAH, J. K. Ghanaian Times and Busia's speech. II:8:13.
MENSAH, J. K. A. Medium sized batteries. VII:24:574.
MENSAH, J. P. AMANKWA. See Amankwa-Mensah, J. P.
MENSAH, K. Ministry of education and promotion examinations.
    II:12:16.
_____. That was amusing. II:21:15.
_____. Traffic at Liberation Circle. II:2:17.
MENSAH, K. KUTTIN. See Kuttin-Mensah, K.
MENSAH, K. T. The bungalow syndrome. VII:7:170.
MENSAH, O. On external debts. VII:1:15.
MENSAH, T. B. Ghana and Nigerian crisis. II:16:17.
Mensah and Odumase farms. J. Apronti. VI:25:20.
MENSAH-BONSU. Leave the Artiste fee alone. IX:9:206.
Mental hospital. A. P. Twumasi. A. Bystander. III:15:28.
Mentally retarded children. G. M. K. Kpedekpo. III:11:16-18.
Message to the "Legon Observer." J. C. Quaye. II:15:18-19.
Method of spelling words. E. Boateng. VII:11:266.
MFODWO, S. B. Disqualification of C. P. P. officials. II:20:19.
Mid-term break for schools. B. Milliyar. IV:24:25.
Mid-term break in schools. T. H. Tawiah. V:1:20-21.
Middle East crisis. A comment. E. Obeng-Mensah. 1) VIII:24:576-578;
    2) A. Ackah-Mensah. VII:26:626.
Military custody for suspects. VIII:18:438.
Military intervention in politics. E. K. A. Ninsin. III:24:11.
Military tattoo. N. O. Liverpool. II:9:21.
Military training for students. K. N. Hanson. VII:25:603-604.
Military training in our Varsities. K. S. Basilide. VIII:8:185.
Military training in the universities. 1) R. Bekoe-Dawson.
    VIII:12:284; 2) A. O. Adjei. VIII:12:284-285.
Milk more valuable than blood. K. Ahia. VIII:6:137.
MILLIAR, B. Up North and Down South. VIII:3:68.
MILLIYAR, B. Mid-term break for Schools. IV:24:25.
MILLS, A. O. Santrofi, Kontopiaat...and all that. IX:1:10.
_____. A tribute to courage and honesty. VII:6:142.
MILLS, C. M. The Classics. IV:19:11.
MILLS, K. A. Mini-beer in State Hotels. VII:18:432.
Mills-Odoi and P. and T. Technicians. P. C. T. Achina. V:11:26-28.
Mills-Odoi Report and Civil Servants. J. Welsing. III:19:12-14.
Mills-Odoi Salaries Report. I. A. Mensah. IV:12:11.
Minerals Industry. A. F. J. Smit. II:11:15; B. D. G. Folson.
    II:18:15.

Correspondence

Minerals industry--A correction. A. F. J. Smit. II:13:13.
Mini-Beer in State Hotels. K. A. Mills. VII:18:432; P. K. Adjei.
   VII:21:500.
Mini-budget unfair to rural folks? K. Asuah. VII:6:140; Rejoinder.
   K. Owusu-Kyei. VII:8:195.
Ministerial peregrinations. A. A. Odame. VI:26:20.
Ministers' salaries. E. M. Kumaga. IV:26:24.
Ministry of Agriculture to be abolished? I. K. Mensah. VII:25:603.
Ministry of education and promotion examinations. K. Mensah.
   II:12:16.
MINTA, C. K. The Massacres in Burundi. VIII:16:387.
MINTA, I. Cecil Rhodes and Rhodesia. V:11:25.
_____. Exams Council and G. C. E. fees. IV:5:16-17.
_____. The exemptions Commission. III:12:16.
_____. Ghanaian culture retrieved. V:7:14.
_____. Kontopiaat: the Party. III:15:29.
_____. Legon Observer Editor Again--A rejoinder. VII:12:287.
_____. Peace prospects in Nigeria. III:2:10.
_____. "The politics of intolerance." IV:19:12.
_____. Transport for non-resident students. VIII:22:527.
_____. University entrance examination. IV:26:25.
MINTA, I. K. The Abbott-Ghana controversy. II:24:11.
_____. Critics, Counter-critics and the future of Ghana.
   III:1:15.
MINTA, K. K. Who is an imperialist? IX:3:69.
Miss Hereward and Western liberalism. K. Bosque. V:5:22.
Missionary Schools and liberalism. D. Hereward. V:3:12.
Mr. Abedi's explanation. K. Amoakoh. VI:6:19.
Mr. Gyandoh writes. S. O. Gyandoh. VII:6:142.
Mr. Judicial Secretary, action not threats please. Kontopiaat.
   II:19:21.
Mr. Kontopiaat. K. Hemang. III:2:15.
Mr. Ollenu and Kotoka's statue. E. Bruku-Samuels. IV:24:24-25.
MITCHELL, L. E. Fan Milk. III:7:14-16.
MOBBS, D. R. Anti-Apartheid movement. II:14:28.
_____. Anti-Apartheid movement in Ghana. II:12:15-16.
Mobutu and Nigeria. N. T. Ward-Brew. III:11:14.
MOLAH, G. S. Foodstuff allowances. VIII:5:111.
_____. Price differentials. VIII:15:362.
_____. What price, sycophancy? VII:8:195.
MOUBARAK, A. "Another electronics industry?" II:16:18.
Moral corruption in Ghana. S. Brookes. V:17:21.
Moral courage and Mr. Victor Owusu. K. Yankon. II:14:29.
Moral turpitude in public hospitals. G. Odarlai. VII:24:574. Re-
   joinder. V. E. O. Portuphy-Lamptey. VIII:1:19.
More action and less rhetoric needed. F. O. Nkansah. VIII:2:41-42.
More "Banned" books? K. Ankomah. IV:5:16.
Moscow diary. W. Anti-Taylor. III:6:13.
MOSS, B. Student power of sorts. III:24:12.
MPRAH, K. Tampering with parcels. V:18:17.

Correspondence

_____. To the Director of P. and T. Accra. Pilfering at the Post
Office. VI:6:18.
MUANGE, E. A. Wasting talent. III:2:14-15.
Much to rejoice about. A. Tsikata. VIII:7:162.
MUSAH, J. Teachers and transportation. III:8:12.
N. L. C. and future politics. C. Agezo. III:18:20.
N. L. C. rulers and imminent retirement. 1) F. A. Asiedu. III:26:22;
2) Obeng-Manu. IV:1:10.
N. L. C. should inform the public. F. C. Essandoh. IV:1:10.
N. R. C. and our "Essential Goods." Obeng-Manu. VII:8:192-193.
N. R. C. and rural development. F. A. Asiedu. VII:6:140.
N. R. C. and rural development. R. Kakrabah-Quarshie. VII:8:193.
N. R. C. and temporary solutions. L. Koi-Larbi. VIII:5:109.
N. R. C. declares Assets. A. Tsikata. VII:15:359.
N. R. C. determined to feed and clothe Ghana. J. A. Yankson.
VII:22:529.
N. R. C. must not fail. K. Kyere. VII:9:214-216.
N. U. G. S. have a right to speak. G. K. Owens-Dey. VI:10:19.
NANOR, A. T. K. Local Government and the economy in post-coup Ghana.
VIII:1:22.
_____. Sekesua Health Centre. V:9:21.
NARH, A. K. Competitive examination--What about syllabuses?
III:22:21.
Nation of hypocrites. C. E. Mensah. VII:11:264. Rejoinder--1)
H. B. Augusto. VII:13:306; 2) J. Amankwa. VII:13:307.
National anthem turning commonplace? R. Kiya-Hinidza. VII:13:307.
National Committee on Apartheid. F. Hesse. V:2:15.
National Executive Council. K. A. II:14:26.
National flag. N. K. Preku. IV:8:20.
National Government. E. Edusei. VII:17:406.
National Government for Ghana. K. Abakah. VII:15:358.
National Holidays Decree. S. K. Oduro-Denkyi. IX:14:344.
National honours. E. S. Aidoo. IX:4:87.
National house of Chiefs. K. Frimpong. VIII:1:22.
National Self respect. K. A. Opoku. II:23:15-16.
National Service. P. B. Arthiabah. VIII:17:410.
National Service and salary increases. Badu-Yeboah. IX:7:160-161.
National Service and the state transport. K. Yankah. VIII:25:606.
National Union of Seamen. G. O. McClean. II:26:17.
Nationalised babies? K. Bruce. IV:6:22.
NATTEY, S. Too much criticism. III:16:19.
NATTEY, S. W. Farms or social centre? IV:3:17-18.
NEE OKINE, D. Soft and not so straight. VIII:1:262.
Need for a Press Trust--Rejoinder. S. K. Dzorkpe. VII:15:356-357.
VII:17:406.
Need for press council. E. Addy. V:26:18-19.
NELSON, W. Big Dada's histrionics--A rejoinder. VIII:25:606.
_____. Intellectual M...and all that--A subsequent rejoinder.
VIII:23:556.
Neo-colonialism and the future of Ghana. H. D. Arthur. II:26:14.
NEOGY, R. Public executions. II:15:13.

132

Correspondence

Neon-glamour vs. cheap basic needs. A. Quansah-Quaye. II:6:19.
Neon signs and foreign currency. Tax-Payer. II:12:16-17.
Neutrality run riot! J. Alarah. III:16:20.
New cedi. E. K. Sarpey. II:5:10; C. N. Wadia. II:7:18; G. Asare.
    II:8:14.
New changes. Busumafi. II:15:17.
New era? K. Opare. III:3:11.
New farmer. J. Gordon. III:4:12-13.
New mathematics and the generation gap. P. A. V. Ansah.
    VII:26:626-628.
New Order. Y. Owusu. V:10:20. S. Akwaboah. V:11:25.
New police order. J. B. Assani. VII:13:309.
New Press Decree. P. C. Pyne. VIII:6:136.
New status symbol? T. Eshun. VIII:19:461.
New University Institute of Journalism--A rejoinder. N. Okereke.
    VIII:1:19-20.
New working hours. K. Kyere. VII:7:170.
Newspapers and public speakers. B. D. G. Folson. III:8:12.
Newsprint used for wrapping. T. K. Sarpong. VIII:21:503.
NGYEDUAM, K. Explaining government policies. V:5:21.
_____. The facts about Kaleidescope. V:7:14.
NIBOI, J. A. A. Contracts for the S. C. C. IV:2:18.
Nigeria. D. A. Bekoe. II:23:17. B. I. Chukwukere. II:23:17-18.
Nigeria and Biafra. K. Ameyaw-Akwabi. IV:3:16-17.
Nigeria, Biafra and the relief problem. A. R. El-Alawah. V:4:19.
Nigeria-Biafra conflict. IV:5:18.
Nigeria-Biafra crisis. A. Graves. IV:8:21.
Nigeria-Biafra war and capitalist interests. E. Christian.
    IV:13:16-17.
Nigeria, Rhodesia and Biafra. N. Nwigwe. IV:1:13-14.
Nigerian Civil War. 1) R. Gbobi. III:10:10; 2) D. Droulers. K.
    Marfo. C. N. Wadia. III:12:14; 3) O. Quartey. III:12:16; 4)
    E. Tandoh. III:26:24; 5) F. A. Asiedu. IV:2:18-20.
Nigerian crisis. K. A. B. Jones-Quartey. II:7:16-17.
Nigerian war. P. Adu-Gyamfi. V:3:12.
Nigerian War: Chance for a solution? C. K. Gadzekpo. Ifezulike.
    N. Nwigwe. III:14:22.
Nigeria's final rush. O. Ogum. III:19:14-16.
NII ADDY, M. D. Is the closure necessary? VIII:11:261.
NIMAKO, C. B. "Party brigandage and the spoils system."--Rejoinder.
    IX:6:140.
NINSIN, E. K. A. Military intervention in politics. III:24:11.
NIVEN, A. Student power of sorts. III:23:16-17.
_____. Students largely vindicated. III:26:23.
Nixon said it. J. Apronti. VII:6:141.
NKANSAH, A. BADU. See Badu-Nkansah, A.
NKANSAH, F. O. More action and less rhetoric needed. VIII:2:41-42.
_____. Posting of the Agriculturist. VIII:5:110.
NKANSAH, I. Medium-sixed batteries. VII:22:526.
NKANSAH, S. SAGOE. See Sagoe-Nkansah, S.

Correspondence

NKANSAH, Y. On price increases of the National Papers. VIII:3:67.
NKRUMAH, I. K. Relative sizes of religious groups in Ghana.
    III:15:29.
NKRUMAH, K. Social Security and businessmen. VI:24:19-20.
NKRUMAH, O. K. When to learn English. IX:9:206.
Nkrumah and the building of socialism. P. K. Acheampong. VII:11:267.
Nkrumah: "Good" or "Bad?" E. Vorkeh. VIII:7:162-163.
Nkrumah passes away--Rejoinder. 1) Addae-Mensah. VII:10:240-241; 2)
    J. Kodzo. K. Yankah. VII:10:241. 3) A. Addo. J. Addo.
    VII:10:241-242; 4) A. K. Acheampong. Y. Boafo. VII:11:264.
Nkrumah! Rise and fall. S. Ryan. III:5:25.
Nkrumah, the Nzimas and the election. A. A. Mensah. IV:20:16-18.
Nkrumah's role in history. K. Dake. V:8:17.
NLARY, S. G. A. Radio R. S. A. Propaganda. VIII:8:187.
No Bridge-crossing, this time. P. Gamesu. III:24:11-12.
No certificates from S. I. C.? A. Darko. V:11:28.
No interference with the Army? G. A. Mante. VI:12:20-22.
No more "Adanko" business. S. Amina. IV:1:11.
No need to change Ghana flag. T. K. Amoako. IV:6:23.
No newspapers "as such." VIII:9:214.
No Sir, Sir Alec! D. Adjei-Brenya. IX:4:90.
No truth in B. B. C. Statement. P. J. Obebe. IV:6:22.
NOAGBEDZI, G. A. K. The plight of ex-convicts. V:17:22.
NOKWARE, K. Foreign foods in the bush. VIII:7:164.
Nominations. P. Gamesu. IV:17:17-18.
Non-Aggression jokes? S. A. O. Manu. V:22:25.
'Non-Education' for Africans? D. Hereward. V:13:27.
"Non-farming" Saltpondites. P. Ansah. VI:27:19.
Not another Jibowu Commission, please. K. Oti. IV:11:16-17.
Not "Drs." but honoured gentlemen. C. N. Wadia. VI:12:22.
Not one better than another. N. Aboagye-Akyea. IV:23:19.
Not the major but more food. VIII:5:110.
NTIM, A. Dr. Busia and the Judges. V:9:18.
NTIRI, A. A. Elmina and Cape Coast Castles. III:14:24.
NUKAFO, J. Incentive for teachers. VI:21:16.
NUKPE, J. M. Open letter to testing officers. II:7:18.
Nunoo Affair. A. Kwame. IV:12:11.
NWIGWE, F. N. Banda betrays Africa. II:9:21.
NWIGWE, N. Nigeria, Rhodesia and Biafra. IV:1:13-14.
_____. The Nigerian War: Chance for a solution? III:14:22.
_____. The O. A. U., Nigeria and Biafra. IV:10:16.
_____. The O. A. U. Summit. III:21:17.
_____. Support for the Federal Government. III:26:24.
NYAHO-DARTI, K. S. The registration of voters. IV:12:11.
NYAMEKYE, K. Who should wear what (in Cape Coast)? VIII:3:65.
NYAMIKE, K. The Nzimas and the P. A. P. IV:22:24.
NYAMIKEH, M. N. Ghana's external relations. II:6:18.
_____. Giving and accepting gifts. II:24:16.
NYMPHA, I. N. G. N. T. C. selling Portuguese goods? IX:1:12.
NYARKO, K. The Chairman of the Constitutional Commission and the
    Critics. III:8:10-11.

Correspondence

Nzimas and the P. A. P. K. Nyamike. IV:22:24.
O. A. U. and the Mercenaries. A. Fiadjoe. 1) II:26:15; 2) III:2:18.
O. A. U. Liberation Committee. E. A. Dzima. II:18:16.
O. A. U. Monrovia Meeting. W. Ockiya. IV:11:17.
O. A. U., Nigeria and Biafra. S. Lotsu. IV:10:16. N. Nwigwe.
    IV:10:16.
O. A. U. Summit. N. Nwigwe. III:21:17.
O. C. Wake up, Ministry of Agriculture. II:19:21.
O. F. Y. and the bush fires. A. Iddrisu. VIII:4:92.
O. S. A. and pensioners. S. D. Mark. VIII:8:186-187.
OBEBE, P. J. No truth in B. B. C. statement. IV:6:22.
OBENG-MANU. Another kind of Revolution. IV:6:18.
_____. "Big Talk" and unemployment. IV:4:29.
_____. Civil Servants under Nkrumah's rule. IV:26:24.
_____. Col. Bernasko and the O. F. Y. Programme. IX:4:87-90.
_____. Corruption and economic progress. V:9:21-22.
_____. Exaggerated claims of O. F. Y. VII:23:554-555.
_____. "Gapping Sycophants" again? IV:22:24.
_____. L. O. Editor again--A rejoinder. VII:11:265.
_____. N. L. C. Rulers and imminent retirement. IV:1:10.
_____. The N. R. C. and our "Essential Goods." VII:8:192-193.
_____. Our rural population and the price of kerosene. IX:6:137-138.
_____. A ray of hope. IV:21:16.
_____. Rotten meat, soaked sugar and all that. VIII:16:386.
_____. Roving ambassadors and national self-reliance. VII:9:214.
_____. This is our chance. IV:10:14.
_____. "Why should we let sleeping dogs lie?" IV:24:22-24.
_____. The withdrawn ¢30 million subsidy: An act of redemption or
    just another example of economic mismanagement? VIII:3:64.
OBENG-MENSAH, E. The Middle East crisis--A comment. VIII:24:576-578.
OBENG-SASU, D. Breach of contract by Legon Observer? VIII:7:164.
OBENG-YEBOAH, G. The check off system. VI:18:18.
_____. The same story will be told, unless.... VII:7:170-172.
OBETSEBI-LAMPTEY, O. Americans in Ghana. II:7:17-18.
OBINIM, K. High cost of living. VI:11:21.
_____. Just what is provocation? VI:21:16.
Obscene revolution. F. Amoakohene. IX:3:67.
Observer language. A. K. Manteaw. V:5:22; H. S. M. Atieku.
    V:9:21.
Observer Notebook--A rejoinder. J. K. Boateng. VI:25:22.
Observer Standard. 1) S. Q. Adibi. E. Boateng. V:7:16.
Observer unfair to G. B. C.? F. Awuku. VI:3:10.
Observer's language. J. E. Domfeh. V:26:19.
Observer's stand. B. Adjei. VI:10:18-19.
Obstacles to reform in Ghana. G. K. Asante. IV:15:14.
Oburoni Muntu and African ideology. K. B. Forge. V:3:12.
Oburoni Muntu: Congrats! J. Gyinayeh. V:9:21.
OCANSEY, S. The fuel policy of Ghana. III:3:11.
Occult significance of Kotoka's death. 1) A. Buckley. II:14:29;
    2) H. K. Akyeampong. II:15:19-20.
OCKIYA, W. O. A. U. Monrovia meeting. IV:11:17.

Correspondence

_____. Red-cross must give way to O. A. U. IV:14:19-20.
_____. The visa and the entry permit. IV:16:17.
_____. When genocide is no genocide. IV:1:13.
OCLOO, V. M. Bouncing Cheques. V:24:22.
OCRAN, T. Our stand in the Arab-Israeli conflict--A rejoinder.
    VIII:24:574-576.
ODAME, A. A. Ministerial peregrinations. VI:26:20.
ODARLAI, G. Moral turpitude in public hospitals. VII:24:574.
ODOI, T. P. Kwesi Armah's extradition. II:4:22-23.
ODURO, K. K. Criticising the Government. IX:2:42.
_____. Save our cocoa from drink! VIII:6:134.
_____. Too busy to play games. VIII:5:109-110.
ODURO-DENKYI, S. K. Gulder bottles. VIII:5:112.
_____. National holidays decree. IX:14:344.
_____. Postal system. VII:26:628.
_____. Prices of foodstuffs. VIII:3:66.
Of grammatical rules and literary habits. S. K. Acquaye. IV:19:12.
OFEI, K. OSEI. See Osei-Ofei, K.
OFFEI, J. D. ASANTE. See Asante-Offei, J. D.
Official Cars. II:4:23.
OFORI, D. "Politics of Political Detention." VI:26:20.
OFORI, E. K. Accra-Tema City Transport. II:24:17.
OFORI, I. M. Are Ghanaians different or just indifferent? VI:26:20-21.
_____. Shelter versus automobiles in the economic war. VII:5:119.
_____. Society wives. III:13:12.
OFORI, K. "Fires next time?" VIII:2:43.
_____. The voice of which revolution? VII:12:286.
OFORI-ATTA, E. E. B. The effects of surcharges. V:26:17-18.
OFOSU-APPIAH, L. H. Report of the University of Science & Technology.
    III:10:12.
_____. University accounts. II:7:16.
_____. Visitation Committee. IV:2:17.
OGUM, O. Horror in Crescendo. III:18:17.
_____. Nigeria's final rush. III:19:14-16.
_____. "Peace prospects in Nigeria." III:2:15-16.
"Oh Dunia." R. A. Davis. IX:12:288.
OHENE OKAI. Who gets what. VII:10:243.
Oil and the economy. J. Adu. V:16:22.
Oil drilling in Ghana. N. K. Bannerman. II:14:27.
OKAI, J. Happy birthday. III:15:29.
OKAI, O. Taxi rates: A bad case of capitulation. VIII:11:261.
OKEEM, E. O. Identity of writers. VI:9:24.
OKEREKE, N. New University Institute of Journalism--A rejoinder.
    VIII:1:19-20.
OKORLEY, R. Cecil Rhodes and Rhodesia. V:11:25-26.
OKRAKU, D. Y. A. Free education. III:20:22.
OKUM, K. Ghana and the Nigeria crisis. II:19:22.
Old guard again? J. Mensah. VIII:3:67.
"Old order changeth...." F. A. Asiedu. IV:19:10.
O'MALLY, R. J. The role of the Middle Easterners in our economy.
    II:20:21.

Correspondence

OMARI, T. P. Kwame Nkrumah revisited. V:17:21.
OMARI-WADIE, K. A. Loans for cars in the Civil Service. III:3:11.
Ominibus politics. J. Abiri. II:22:14.
On asking for help. S. A. A. Djoleto. III:3:10.
On drafting for the public. 1) K. Baah. III:9:12; 2) T. G. Kumi.
    III:10:12-13.
On external debts. O. Mensah. VII:1:15.
On family planning. 1) V. N. Blankson. V:23:21; 2) C. Owusu.
    V:23:21-22; 3) J. Manu. V:24:22-23.
On military training. B. A. Gogo. VIII:16:387.
On opting out. J. Apronti. VI:2:15-16.
On party discipline. S. K. O. Denkyi. V:18:17.
On price increases of the national papers. Y. Nkansah. VIII:3:67.
On students. D. Hereward. V:21:22.
On teachers' uniforms. J. H. K. Fiafor. V:14:24.
On the extinction of the "Biafra Republic." F. A. Asiedu. V:3:10-12.
On "The Illustrated Indian Weekly." 1) S. B. Shah. VII:22:525; 2)
    M. Charles. C. N. Wadia. VII:23:554.
On the question of experts. A. P. Twumasi. IV:4:29.
On the Soyinka night. M. B. Davies. IV:7:22-24.
On the treatment of "Benzosis." A. Van Dantzig. VII:5:119-120.
On training accountants. A rejoinder. VIII:22:529-530.
On "Utopia and education." D. Hereward. VII:17:407.
One can apportion blame. B. Adjei. VII:16:383-384.
One way traffic highway for Accra. K. A. K. Atobra and J. E. Frempong.
    III:4:14.
One year of the N. R. C. Rejoinder. A. K. Sarpong. VIII:2:41.
ONIFADE, T. O. A. The debate on the return to civilian rule. II:10:15.
Onward with the revolution. Y. A. Opoku. IX:10:234-236. Rejoinder.
    1) E. S. Aidoo. IX:11:252; 2) B. Charlie. IX:12:286; 3) E. S.
    Garbrah. IX:12:288.
ONWUKA, R. R. Whether Ojukwu fails or not. III:1:15-16.
ONYINA-APPEA, M. Mass education. IX:9:206.
OPARE, K. Fairer distribution of teachers. VII:21:500.
_____. Justice, man's fallibility, and the people. III:14:23.
_____. A new era? III:3:11.
_____. P. W. D. Mathematics. VIII:13:310.
_____. Postal Service and place names. III:11:16.
_____. S. O. S.--Matchets! VIII:2:43.
_____. Testing of vehicles. VII:25:603.
Open letter to F. G. Mante. K. Frimpong. VI:2:13.
Open letter to Maternity Hospital Doctors at Korle-Bu. G. A. Ashitey.
    III:1:17-18.
Open letter to testing officers. J. M. Nukpe. II:7:18.
Open letter to the Managing Director of Ghana Airways--Hand-baggage
    surcharge. IX:5:112.
Open letter to the P. M. F. G. Mante. V:25:19-20.
Operation Asutsuare--A rejoinder. P. H. K. Johnson. VII:9:216.
"Operation Feed Yourself." A. Adu-Sarkodie. VII:13:307.
"Operation Feed Yourself" Campaign. I. Y. Frempong-Mensah.
    VII:9:216-217.

Correspondence

Operation Feed Yourself gone awry? A. Kwansima. VII:21:501.
Opinion polls. 1) G. M. K. Kpedekpo. III:1:14; 2) G. K. Osei.
    III:1:14; 3) L. B. Akainyah. III:3:8; 4) A. Hore. III:5:24-25;
    5) S. Akida. III:26:23.
OPOKU, J. K. Congrats "Legon Observer." VII:15:360.
OPOKU, K. A. National self respect. II:23:15-16.
OPOKU, S. K. The ghost of the "Lincolnite." II:21:15.
_____. Opposition paper. V:11:26.
OPOKU, Y. A. Onward with the revolution. IX:10:234-236.
OPONG, Y. Allowance for Commissioners. VIII:5:111.
OPPONG-AGYARE, J. To Kontopiaat. III:4:14.
Opposition--blessing or curse? E. Y. Frempong-Mensah. IV:21:16.
Opposition in the Second Republic. A. A. Hammond. IV:14:18.
Opposition paper. S. K. Opoku. V:11:26.
Order of precedence or of priority. A. R. Taylor. II:8:14.
Organisational problems of Opposition. J. E. Domfeh. VI:3:10-11.
Organising Mass Education. A. P. Achampong. VII:23:552.
Organising problems of Opposition. J. E. Domfeh. VI:3:10-11.
OSAFO, K. Archaeology and African history. V:12:15.
_____. China and the United Nations. V:22:25.
_____. The Christmas spirit. IV:26:22.
_____. Corruption and economic progress. V:9:22.
_____. Ghana's housing problems. V:8:18.
_____. Ghana's tax structure. V:18:13.
_____. Our culture, tradition and foreign visitors. V:6:14-15.
_____. Public telephone booths. V:15:17.
_____. To the Editor. V:12:15.
OSAFO-ATTA, K. Ghana's privileged few. V:21:18.
OSAFO-KANTANKA. The Engineer and the Mills-Odoi Report. IV:9:16-18.
OSAKWE, B. "The Abe Fortas Affair"--A reply. IV:13:14-16.
OSEI, A. Ghana and the N. L. C. II:9:21.
OSEI, C. Kwame Nkrumah: hero or villain? VIII:6:136.
OSEI, E. Corruption among the clergy. V:18:17.
_____. Luxury and sacrifice. V:13:26.
_____. Passport Torture-Chamber. III:10:13.
OSEI, G. K. Opinion polls. III:1:14.
OSEI-KWAME, P. Restoring the balance? VIII:11:259-260.
OSEI-OFEI, K. Promoting the arrest or liquidation of Kwame and Co.
    II:1:18.
OSEI-TUTU, J. O. Towards a common Ghanaian language. IV:6:20-21.
OSEI-TUTU, T. Political virtues and our new Republic. IV:12:10-11.
_____. Should we all be farmers? IV:5:18.
Osofo Dadzie and the graduate. A. Adu Sarkodie. VIII:7:163.
OTI, K. Not another Jibowu Commission, please! IV:11:16-17.
OTU, M. A. Accidents--Macchi jet Aircraft. II:6:16.
Our culture, tradition and foreign visitors. K. Osafo. V:6:14-15.
Our educational system. D. Hereward. VIII:12:285.
Our leaders and wealth. J. H. K. Fiafor. VII:7:169.
Our National papers. C. E. Mensah. VII:12:286.
Our rural population and the price of Kerosene. Obeng-Manu.
    IX:6:137-138.

Correspondence

Our Secondary Schools revisited. K. B. Dickson. II:20:20.
Our stand in the Arab-Israeli conflict--A rejoinder. T. Ocran.
    VIII:24:574-576.
Our youth and the budget. 1) E. Tandoh. III:17:11; 2) Semenya.
    III:17:11-12.
"Out of bounds to civilians?" S. Ditto. VII:20:480.
Ovambo revolt. A. Anaglate. VII:2:41.
Overburdened Commissioner. K. Akwabi-Ameyaw. VIII:20:484.
Overhauling the passport office. Kwaku-Safo. II:22:26.
OWENS-DEY, G. K. The N. U. G. S. have a right to speak. VI:10:19.
OWENS-DEY, T. Gen. Afrifa and the Constitution. V:18:14.
OWENS-DEY, T. G. K. Kwame Nkrumah--hero or villain? VIII:8:186.
OWIAFE, E. K. Political demonstrations. V:10:20.
OWUSU, C. On family planning. V:23:21-22.
OWUSU, K. O. Why another 50p. increase? VIII:7:162.
OWUSU, M. F. Ghana Air Force accidents. II:2:16.
OWUSU, S. Learn to respect. VI:3:11-14.
OWUSU, Y. The new order. V:10:20.
_____. The Sallah case. V:11:25.
OWUSU-ACHEAW, W. Traders and the regime. VIII:6:136.
OWUSU-ANSAH, G. J. A. Exaggerated claims of O. F. Y. Rejoinder.
    VII:24:576.
OWUSU-ASANTE. Eastern Region projects--Akim-Wenchi. VI:15:22.
OWUSU-FREMPONG. Let Nkrumah come home! VI:13:19-20.
OWUSU-FREMPONG, Y. The prophet in his own country. VIII:10:236.
OWUSU-KYEI, K. Mini-Budget unfair to rural folks?--A rejoinder.
    VII:8:195.
OWUSU-SARPONG, A. Who is accountable for this? VII:11:265-266.
OWUSU-YAW, J. A. Afro-Arab solidarity? IX:14:344.
Oxford first for Ghana's President? R. Greenfield. VI:11:21.
P. M. and the Sallah case. M. Charles. V:10:20.
P. P. P. still going strong? B. O. Laryea. VIII:3:67.
P. W. D. Mathematics. K. Opare. VIII:13:310.
Parents should advise students. A. C. Coleman. III:23:17.
PARKER, C. Why Mr. Harlley's resignation? IV:22:24.
PARKER, N. Leadership in rural development. V:26:18.
Parking at the airport. C. N. Wadia. VIII:11:262.
Parliament and the N. U. G. S. K. A. B. Jones-Quartey. VI:11:20-21.
Parodoxes and contradictions. S. T. Boafo. IX:2:42.
"Party brigandage and the spoils system."--Rejoinder. 1) E. Edusei.
    IX:6:138; 2) P. B. Arthiabah. IX:6:138-140; 3) C. B. Nimako.
    IX:6:140.
Passport Torture--Chamber. E. Osei. III:10:13.
PAYIDA, D. S. Exaggerated claims of O. F. Y.--Rejoinder. VII:24:576.
Peace prospects in Nigeria. 1) I. Minta. III:8:10; 2) O. Ogum.
    III:2:15-16.
Peace with cultural honour. K. A. B. Jones-Quartey. VIII:10:230.
PEARSON, R. E. Salary increase. II:8:16-17.
PEASAH, J. A. The Ashanti Goldfields-Lonrho deal. III:23:14.
_____. Decrees 230 and 233. III:7:12.
_____. Dr. Gardiner and Abbott. III:3:8.
_____. Science and Arts education. II:17:22.

Correspondence

Pendulum of change. II:2:14.
Pepper bandits again. L. A. Tetteh. V:21:22.
Personal Assistants. C. Addae. IV:26:24.
Personal attack? F. C. Essandoh. III:4:14.
Personality cult again? P. C. K. Achina. IV:16:16.
Personality cult--true or false? O. Koranteng. IV:20:19-20.
PHILIPS, A. K. The thieves of Teshie-Nungua. VIII:22:530.
PHILLIPS, A. Exaggerated claims of O. F. Y.--Rejoinder.
     VII:24:576-578.
PHILLIPS, I. B. Housing the people. II:8:16.
_____. Safety devices for night driving. III:11:14.
Pick pocket extraordinary. W. Y. Twum. V:15:17.
PIESIEH, Y. Made-in-Ghana Goods. VII:15:357-358
"Pioneer." K. Bretuo. VII:20:480.
Pito Brewery at Tamale. E. M. K. Amenya. IV:19:12-14.
Plea to future politicians! J. Amoako-Addo. III:23:17-18.
Please, Mr. Electoral Commissioner. F. A. Asiedu. IV:17:18.
Please--Take a Ghanaian child. P. C. G. Berale. IV:22:24-26.
Plight of ex-convicts. G. A. K. Noagbedzi. V:17:22.
Plight of poverty. C. Ahiabor. V:19:21-22.
Plight of the low-paid worker. O. Kantanka. VIII:11:260.
Plight of the photographer here. C. O. Quarcoopome. V:13:27-28.
POBEE, J. Kontopiaat and Oguaa gods. V:21:20.
POKU, F. Single women in Ghana. III:22:22-24.
Police and the public. 1) D. Tulloch and M. Dummett. II:15:18; 2)
     B. Dapaah. II:17:19; 3) J. K. Adarkwaa. IV:19:10.
Political Assassinations. K. Antepim. IV:15:16.
Political demonstration. E. K. Owiafe. V:10:20.
Political detainees and national reconciliation. A. Adu-Gyamfi.
     VII:25:602.
Political parties and centre for Civic Education. M. S. Braimah.
     III:18:18-20.
Political parties in Ghana. K. G. Konuah. IV:9:18.
Political virtues and our new Republic. T. Osei-Tutu. IV:12:10-11.
Politicians and their pronouncements. S. K. O. Denkyi. IV:16:17.
Politicians' promises. K. N. Hanson. IV:14:18.
"Politics of intolerance." I. Minta. IV:19:12.
"Politics of Political detention." D. Ofori. VI:26:20.
Polygamy in Ghana. F. C. Essandoh. III:21:18.
Pope and birth control. A. Cockra. III:21:17.
Pope and contraception. A. R. C. Van Fleischer. III:17:10.
Population and planning. D. A. Ampofo. II:2:17.
Population growth and family planning. F. D. Tweneboah. V:9:20.
PORTUPHY-LAMPTEY, V. E. O. Moral turpitude in public hospitals--A
     rejoinder. VIII:1:19.
Post Office Sorting Division. C. Blankson. VIII:3:67.
Postal Service and place names. K. Opare. III:11:16.
Postal system. S. K. Oduro-Denkyi. VII:26:628.
Posting of the Agriculturist. F. O. Nkansah. VIII:5:110.
Postponing the inevitable. Y. Brenya. IX:8:184.
Posh cars. A. Boateng. VII:4:91.

Correspondence

POSNANSKY, M. Archaeology and African History. V:12:14-15.
Postmen and mosquitoes. Y. M. Agble. II:7:19.
Power from Akosombo. E. A. K. Akuoko. II:11:13-14.
Powerful-but-not gods. K. A. B. Jones-Quartey. VII:25:600.
PRAH, F. K. Devouring the Revolution. IV:17:18-20.
Prah report. A. Mensah. II:26:18.
PREKU, N. K. The National Flag. IV:8:20.
Preserving Ghana's Monuments. K. B. Forge. V:12:15.
Presidency under the Proposed Constitution. D. Reynolds. III:7:12.
Press. O. Afrane. VII:9:217.
Press and students demonstration. S. T. Boafo. IX:4:87.
Press freedom. K. A. Sasu. III:9:13.
Press, the people and the government. A rejoinder. K. Kuttin.
    IX:8:184.
Prestige project and retrenchement. A. K. Mensah. IV:6:18-20.
Price differentials. 1) K. Enu. VII:2:40. 2) G. S. Molah.
    VIII:15:362.
Price of arrogance and complacency. A-Lashie. VII:3:58-59.
Price of foodstuff. P. E. Ackom. IX:4:87.
Price of newspapers. P. A. V. Ansah. VIII:13:305. Rejoinders. 1)
    K. Dake. VIII:15:364; 2) P. A. V. Ansah. VIII:15:364-366.
Prices of foodstuffs. S. K. Oduro-Denkyi. VIII:3:66.
Prices of petrol and kerosene. K. Gyefuor. IX:7:161.
Prime Minister's New Year Message. S. W. K. Akwayena. VI:3:10.
Private Schools. D. Hereward. IV:26:25.
Probing the Assets of Certain persons. J. A. Schandorf. IV:9:16.
Problem of Shortages--A Personal note. K. Kuttin. VIII:26:628.
Prof. Bretton's book on Nkrumah. H. O. Williams. II:17:20.
Promoting the arrest or liquidation of Kwame and Co. K. Osei-Ofei.
    II:1:18.
Promotion of teachers. 1) E. O. Yeboah. V:12:16; 2) A. K. Tsetse.
    V:13:26.
Prophet in his own country. Y. Owusu-Frempong. VIII:10:236.
Proposed ¢3 million palace. J. K. Atta. VIII:13:306-308.
Protecting the consumer. Y. Agble. VII:25:603. Rejoinder. H. C.
    Lane. VIII:1:19.
"Provocation" indeed. S. K. O. Denkyi. VI:22:17.
Public executions 1) G. Annobil. II:11:16-17; 2) J. Longman.
    II:11:17; 3) P. W. C. Maxwell. II:12:15; 4) A. Badu-Nkansah.
    II:12:15; 5) R. Neogy. II:15:13.
Public holidays. O. Dwamena. IX:5:112.
Public telephone booths. K. Osafo. V:15:17.
Public transport: Another prestige project? A. Van Dantzig.
    II:6:17-18.
Purge in the Public Service. P. A. V. Ansah. V:6:13.
Purpose of University education. V. Amponsah. VIII:24:580. Re-
    joinder. K. Bonnah-Koomson. VIII:26:625-626.
PYNE, P. C. The new Press decree. VIII:6:136.
Quality control and made-in-Ghana goods. S. Adotey. VII:17:406.
Quality of teachers. J. H. K. Fiafor. V:18:16-17.

141

Correspondence

QUANSAH, J. C. Is the Otumfuo's N¢3 million palace really necessary? VI:12:22-23.
QUANSAH, W. A. The report on the U. S. T. Kumasi. III:7:13-14.
QUANSAH-QUAYE, A. Neon-glamour vs. Cheap basic needs. II:6:19.
QUAO, A. Radio Ghana, Brazil and Africa--A rejoinder. VII:25:600.
QUAO, E. Students for training Colleges. VII:19:454.
QUARCOO, E. Q. Commemorative gold coin. III:9:14.
QUARCOOPOME, C. O. The plight of the photographer here. V:13:27-28.
QUARSHIE, C. The tragedy of protocol. II:8:12-13.
QUARSHIE, R. KAKRABAH. See Kakrabah-Quarshie, R.
QUARTEY, J. KWARTELAI. See Kwartelai-Quartey, J.
QUARTEY, K. Street names in Accra. VIII:12:285.
QUARTEY, K. A. B. JONES. See Jones-Quartey, K. A. B.
QUARTEY, L. Scrap for metal works. II:2:16.
QUARTEY, O. The Nigeria Civil War. III:12:16.
QUAYE, A. QUANSAH. See Quansah-Quaye, A.
QUAYE, E. M. Taking chances again? III:11:12-14.
QUAYE, J. C. The Constitutional Commission. II:3:16.
_____. A message to the "Legon Observer." II:15:18-19.
QUAYE, J. V. The Ghana Airways mess! VII:6:141.
QUAYSON, J. ATTA. See Atta-Quayson, J.
Question of vocabulary. VIII:2:42.
QUIST, C. Soliciting at our Hotels. III:16:20-21.
QUIST, C. E. Is the problem salaries or high cost of living? II:12:17.
Quo Vadis Ghana? E. D. Kemevor. IV:1:12.
Radicalism. N. Khenchard. VII:4:91.
Radio Ghana, Brazil and Africa. M. Brown. VII:24:573-574. Rejoinder. A. Quao. VII:25:600.
Radio R. S. A. Propaganda. S. G. A. Nlary. VIII:8:187.
Ratifying the Constitution. E. Vorkeh. IV:17:17. B. D. G. Folson. IV:19:9-10.
RAY, P. A. The C. O. S. and Mfum. III:17:12-13.
Ray of hope. Obeng-Manu. IV:21:16.
READER. The Budget and public morality. VI:22:16.
_____. Educational reforms in Ghana. VII:22:526-528.
_____. Ghana's passports! V:17:22.
_____. An open letter to the Managing Director of Ghana Airways--Hand Baggage surcharge. IX:5:112.
_____. Too much foreign worship. V:24:21-22.
Real progress? K. B. Anokye. VII:11:266.
Recent changes....--A rejoinder. B. L. J. Kumasi. VIII:12:284.
Recent changes--Regional Commissioners. G. A. Gogo. VIII:10:234.
Reckless driving of motor cars at Christmas. E. W. Awadie. III:24:14.
Recognition of Biafra. 1) M. O. Ebegare. II:15:19; 2) K. G. Koto. III:10:10-11.
Recognition of Chiefs. K. A. Addo. III:1:17.
Reconciliation and future politics. K. Anso. II:1:18.
Reconciliation and not revival. 1) K. Manu-Acheampong. VIII:6:134; 2) K. Buadu. VIII:10:236.

Correspondence

Recording Nkrumah's ideas. K. Karikari. VII:25:602. Rejoinder.
    A. Sekyire. VIII:1:22.
Red-Cross must give way to O. A. U. W. Ockiya. IV:14:19-20.
Redeployment of C. C. E. Staff. F. Atsiogbe. VII:19:454-456.
Redeployment of Ex-C. C. E. Officers. 1) K. Sakyi. VII:17:407; 2)
    C. K. Agbelengor. VII:18:432.
Re-establish the G. C. E. P. E. Ackom. VIII:21:504-506.
Reflective number plates. 1) R. S. Kwakwa. III:5:27; 2) H. B. Roth.
    III:6:13-14.
Reform of Ghana Constitution. K. B. Bresi-Ando. II:6:18.
Registered mail. M. Bossman. II:14:27.
Registration of voters. 1) K. Archampong. III:21:17; 2) K. S.
    Nyaho-Darti. IV:12:11.
Relative sizes of religious groups in Ghana. I. K. Nkrumah.
    III:15:29.
Release of political detainees. M. Assimeng. VII:11:266-267.
Relevance of Ancient history. D. Hereward. VIII:5:112.
Religious discrimination in Ulster. E. Christian. V:21:20-24.
Remittance to students abroad. J. R. Birnie. IV:14:19.
Rent cuts. K. Akwabi-Ameyaw. VII:17:407.
Repairing car at R. T. Briscoe. K. B. Dickson. V:4:19.
Repeating our forebearers' mistakes? E. Christian. IV:5:16.
Reply to Abiri Kwabena. A. A. Enninful. VIII:12:284.
Report from Brong Ahafo. L. K. Appaw. VII:17:408.
Report of Auditor-General: Character of Ghanaian elite. A-Lashie.
    VI:24:19.
Report of the Auditor-General. J. B. Catwright. VI:25:21-22.
Report on the U. S. T. Kumasi. 1) W. A. Quansah. III:7:13-14; 2)
    L. H. Ofosu-Appiah. III:10:12.
Repudiation and Washington. K. Bempah. VII:7:168.
Restore the Subsidy on examination fees. Y. Gyasehene-Yeboah.
    IX:7:158.
Restoring the balance? P. Osei-Kwame. VIII:11:259-260.
Retrenchment and political exercise? F. C. Essandoh. IV:6:20.
Return to the barracks. C. Baddoo. III:14:24.
Return to civilian rule. 1) K. A. Taylor. II:21:15-16; 2) P.
    Adu-Gyamfi. III:12:16 and VII:21:501; 3) K. Bosompem. IX:3:67.
Return to civilian rule--A Footnote. P. Adu-Gyamfi. VII:22:525.
Returning exiles. VIII:2:41.
Revive the Ghana Consumers Association. G. A. Boal. VI:18:18-19.
Reviving Pan-Africanism. M. Chandler. V:10:21.
Revolution with a human face. V. Foli. IX:1:13.
Reward to N. L. C. K. Abakah. II:24:16.
Rewards to N. L. C. K. A. Taylor. II:22:14.
REYNOLDS, J. D. The Presidency under the proposed constitution.
    III:7:12.
Rhodesian independence issue. Y. M. Agble. VI:25:21.
Rhodesian issue. 1) E. Vorkeh. III:11:18; 2) F. A. Asiedu.
    III:26:24-25.
Rice in financial crisis. G. K. Agbengu. V:8:20.

Rich men. K. A. Taylor. II:17:20-22.
RIDDEN, G. M. Utopian Legon. VIII:20:483-484.
Rise and fall of Nkrumah. H. L. Bretton. III:4:12.
Road safety and word games. K. Kuttin-Mensah. VIII:1:23.
Roadworthiness: Prosecute the authorities too! 1) J. W. A. Boateng.
    VIII:9:214; 2) M. Charles. VIII:9:214.
Roadworthy cars and car worthy roads. P. A. V. Ansah. VIII:7:161.
ROBINSON, H. A. LYNCH. See Lynch-Robinson, H. A.
Role of the Middle Easterners in our economy. R. J. O'Mally.
    II:20:21.
ROTH, H. R. Reflective number plates. III:6:13-14.
Rotten meat, Soaked Sugar and all that. Obeng-Manu. VIII:16:386.
ROURKE, B. E. Agricultural revolution in Northern Ghana. VII:1:15.
_____. Strategy for inducing cocoa processing factories to locate in
    Ghana. IX:11:252.
Roving Ambassadors and national self-reliance. Obeng-Manu. VII:9:214.
"Rubbish Thrash!" K. A. B. Jones-Quartey. VIII:13:310.
Rural development programme and the economy. A. Laryea. VII:4:90-91.
Russian trained doctors. K. Boateng. II:20:21-22.
RYAN, S. Nkrumah! Rise and fall. III:5:25.
S. O. S. Matchets! K. Opare. VIII:2:43.
Safety devices for night driving. I. B. Phillips. III:11:14
Safety on our roads. Rejoinder. 1) I. Addae-Mensah. IX:10:232-234;
    2) A. Van Dantzig. IX:11:251-252.
SAFO, K. Foreign Banks and their employees. V:4:18-19.
SAFO, KWAKU. See Kwaku-Safo.
SAGOE-NKANSAH, S. Strategy for inducing cocoa processing factories
    to locate in Ghana--rejoinder. IX:11:252.
SAI, F. T. "Administrative arrogance?" II:25:8.
"St. John's International" import licensing. A. B. B. Kofi.
    II:9:20-21.
SAKYI, K. Redeployment of Ex-C. C. E. officers. VII:17:407.
Salaries for N. R. C. men. K. N. Hanson. VII:12:286-287.
Salary incentives for honesty? A. F. J. Smit. II:18:15.
Salary increases. 1) B. Hughes. II:1:18-19; 2) R. E. Pearson.
    II:8:16-17; 3) E. King. V:11:26.
Salary increases for the lower income group. III:11:16.
Salary review and the budget. F. C. Essandoh. III:6:14.
Sale of land in Ashanti. O. Attrams. VI:15:20.
Sallah case. Y. Owusu. V:11:25.
Sallah judgment. A. Larbi. V:10:20.
SAM, Y. ASSAH. See Assah-Sam, Y.
Same story will be told unless.... G. Obeng-Yeboah. VII:7:170-172.
SAMPSON, M. K. Sewerage works and traffic. VII:19:453.
SAMUELS, E. BRUKU. See Bruku-Samuels, E.
Sanitation in Accra. E. W. Awudie. III:11:14.
[Santrofi]: A. Ackah-Mensah. IX:1:10.
Santrofi and the professors of literature. K. Blankson. IX:11:254.
Santrofi, Kontopiaat and all that. 1) A. O. Mills. IX:1:10; 2) A.
    Ackah-Mensah. IX:1:10.
SAPE, K. M. The Budget and public morality. VI:22:16.

SARFOH, S. K. Speed checks. II:13:14.
SARKODIE, A. ADU. See Adu-Sarkodie, A.
SARPEY, E. K. To draft or not to draft. III:13:12.
_____. The new cedi. II:5:10.
_____. Social Security benefits. VIII:16:386.
SARPONG, A. K. One year of the N. R. C. A rejoinder. VIII:2:41.
SARPONG, A. OWUSU. See Owusu-Sarpong, A.
SARPONG, T. K. Newsprint used for wrapping. VIII:21:503.
SASU, D. OBENG. See Obeng-Sasu, D.
SASU, K. A. Accra-Tema City Council. II:14:27.
_____. Akosombo Power. II:9:21.
_____. Ambassador and Continental Hotels. IV:7:20-21.
_____. The counter-coup attempt. II:10:15.
_____. Made in Ghana goods. II:2:16.
_____. Press freedom. III:9:13.
_____. V. R. A. has bilharzia. II:21:15.
_____. Why worship the rich. VI:23:20-21.
Save our cocoa from drink. K. K. Oduro. VIII:6:134.
Save six from "Free" text book trap. B. Forson. VII:22:524.
Save us from Makola women. L. Koi-Larbi. VIII:7:163.
SAWYERR, G. F. A. The killing of Karume. VII:10:244.
SCHANDORF, J. A. Probing of Assets of certain persons. IV:9:16.
SCHNEIDER, P. Uncontrolled pricing. II:11:14.
Scholarships. F. Ackah. III:4:12.
Scholarships for University students. Y. A. Dodoo. III:22:21-22.
School curricula. A. P. Twumasi. II:26:15-16.
School holidays. B. J. L. Kumasi. VIII:16:387-388.
School nurses. M. Marcelle. IV:12:12-14.
Science and arts education. J. A. Peasah. II:17:22.
Scramble for Africa—Twentieth Century. R. Y. T. Defoe. III:26:24.
Scrap for metal works. L. Quartey. II:2:16.
Scrap this project. J. K. Adarkwa. VIII:14:336.
Seamy side of industrial civilization. F. B. Barnwell. V:24:23.
SEBUAVA, J. K. Britain and Kwesi Armah. II:4:23.
Second Medical School. K. Hayford. IX:7:158-160.
Secondary Day-Schools. K. Forge. IV:13:17.
Seidu, B. The Tamale hospital. IX:5:113.
Sekesua Health Centre. A. T. K. Nanor. V:9:21.
Sekou Toure and Nkrumah's body. K. Akom. VII:11:264-265.
SEKYIRE, A. Recording Nkrumah's ideas—A rejoinder. VIII:1:22.
Selection of the National Soccer Team. F. C. Essandoh. VII:26:629.
Self-reliance and expatriate missionaries. Rejoinder. 1) H. Senoo.
      VIII:22:526-527; 2) D. Hereward. VIII:22:527; 3) R. A. Amponsah.
      VIII:23:555-556; 4) E. S. Aidoo and P. A. V. Ansah. VIII:23:556.
Self-reliance and expatriate missionaries—the last word. H. Senoo.
      VIII:24:578.
Self-reliance and trade surplus. J. D. Asante-Offei. VIII:1:20-22.
SEMANYA, K. The Kotoka Trust Fund. II:23:19.
SEMENYA, E. K. Our youth and the budget. III:17:11-12.
SEMORDZI, K. C. P. P. and blows—A reply. II:4:23-24.
SENAKE, E. K. Help! V:1:20.

Correspondence

SENANU, K. E. The Aliens' Order. IV:26:24.

_____. The Armed Forces military parade. IX:2:40-42.

Senator Kennedy and "Caesar's Wife." P. Gamesu. IV:16:14-16.

SENOO, H. Self-reliance and expatriate missionaries--rejoinder.
    VIII:22:526-527.

_____. Self-reliance and expatriate missionaries--the last word.
    VIII:24:578.

SENYO, K. Who wants civilian rule now? VIII:16:387.

Sergeant and the salesgirl. J. K. Eshun. VII:24:575.

Services of Accra-Tema City Council. A. Forson. II:21:15.

"Servitude?" Has Dr. Busia said that? Editor. V:24:21.

SERWAH, A. Bus service report. II:22:13-14.

Sewerage works and traffic. 1) E. S. Aidoo. VII:16:380; 2) M. K.
    Sampson. VII:19:453.

SEYIRE, A. An ideal ruler in Africa. VI:24:19.

SHAH, S. B. On "the Illustrated Indian Weekly." VII:22:525.

Shelter versus automobiles in the economic war. I. M. Ofori.
    VII:5:119.

Shopping: S. C. O. A. Technoa. M. Yeboah. VII:21:504. Reply. B.
    Bedane. VII:526.

Shortcomings of intellectuals. H. N. Daniel. V:6:14.

Should Nkrumah be pardoned? E. G. Atta-Appiah. V:11:25.

Should we all be farmers. T. Osei-Tutu. IV:5:18.

SIBIDOW, S. M. Developing the North. V:15:17.

SIBUNDVSKI, E. Ghana's privileged few. V:18:13-14.

Significance of Guru Nanak. J. E. B. Adu. V:3:14-16.

Significance of 24th February. S. Lotsu. V:9:20-21.

Single women in Ghana. 1) K. Marfo. III:19:17; 2) F. Poku.
    III:22:22-24.

Sir Eric vs. Dr. Kofi on Cocoa. E. Vorkeh. VII:26:624-626.

Slot machines and all that. K. Afedzi. VII:26:628.

Slow justice in Ghana. L. E. D. Aduonum. V:9:18-20.

"Sly corner." S. K. Amoah. VII:24:574-575.

Small step for Parliament: big disaster for nation. M. Y. Turkpe.
    VI:19:14.

SMIT, A. F. J. The future of our mines. VIII:1:19.

_____. The Minerals industry. II:11:15.

_____. "The Minerals industry"--A correction. II:13:13.

_____. Salary incentives for honesty? II:18:15.

SMITH, F. K. This dependence on cocoa. V:18:14-16.

SMITH, H. J. An American reaction to "import licensing." II:8:12.

Smuggling at the borders. F. C. Essandoh. V:7:14.

Soccer incentives. B. Forson. IX:3:69.

Social Security and businessmen. K. Nkrumah. VI:24:19-20.

Social Security benefits. E. K. Sarpey. VIII:16:386.

Socialist re-emergence? B. George? VI:16:20-21.

Socialist revolution due in Ghana. M. A. Attopley. VI:6:18-19.

Society wives. 1) A. Danso. III:11:14; 2) I. M. Ofori. III:13:12.

"Soft and not so straight." D. Nee Okine. VIII:11:262.

Soliciting at our Hotels. C. Quist. III:16:20-21.

Correspondence

Some are more equal than others. III:24:14.
Some problems for the next civilian government. F. A. Asiedu.
    IV:15:14-16.
Somersault in logic. K. Dake. IV:12:11-12.
Southern Rhodesia--case of British hypocrisy. 1) R. A. Afful.
    III:7:11; 2) K. O. Asamani. III:7:11-12.
Soviet-trained Ghanaian Doctors. M. S. Braimah. VIII:3:66.
Specialist Teachers' salaries. S. Bruku. VI:6:19-20.
Specialist Teachers' salary. L. Donyuo. VI:3:14-15.
Speed checks. S. K. Sarfoh. II:13:14.
SPIO, J. B. Hughes and salary increase. II:6:18-19.
SPIO, J. B. Government white paper on Cargo Handling Co. III:21:17.
Spirit of tolerance. A. Borquaye. VII:25:602-603. Rejoinder. S.
    Ditto. VIII:2:42.
Split in the Volta Region. 1) J. H. K. Fiafor. V:17:22; 2) C. Y.
    Khra. V:23:22; 3) J. K. S. Akpanya. V:26:19.
State enterprise and the G. C. B. J. Apronti. VII:24:575.
Stealing at the ports. O. Laryea. VIII:16:387.
Stealing at the Ports--A correction. O. Laryea. VIII:21:504.
STEWART, J. M. The language question in School. IV:6:22.
Stop preaching tribalism. M. A. S. Wormenor. V:15:16-17.
Stop these unnecessary arrests. D. Kofison. II:22:14.
Stop this bullying now. P. A. V. Ansah. VII:5:120. Rejoinders.
    1) G. B. Akuffo. VII:6:141; 2) P. H. K. Johnson. VII:8:194; 3)
    P. A. V. Ansah. VII:8:194-195.
Stop this drilling. D. A. Brenyah. VIII:3:64-65.
Strategy for inducing cocoa processing factories to locate in Ghana.
    Rejoinders. 1) B. E. Rourke. IX:11:252; 2) S. Sagoe-Nkansah.
    IX:11:252.
Street names in Accra. K. Quartey. VIII:12:285. Rejoinders. 1)
    B. Awua-Kyeretwie. VIII:15:362-364; 2) F. F. Addae. VIII:15:364.
Strength of African culture. J. Amoako-Addo. V:8:18-20.
Strong need for an Opposition Press. P. K. Anhwere. VI:7:18.
STUCKRAD VON, H. See Von Stuckrad, H.
Student power of sorts. 1) A. Niven. III:23:16-17; 2) B. Moss.
    III:24:12.
Students and politics. J. Alarah. III:4:15.
Students and self-interest. K. O. Adinkrah. IX:1:10.
Students and the salary review. M. A. Fie. IX:3:68.
Students at customs. Antwi-Boadi. III:12:17.
Students for training colleges. E. Quao. VII:19:454.
Students largely vindicated. A. Niven. III:26:23.
Students loan scheme. 1) C. Addy. VI:16:21; 2) A. Van Dantzig.
    VI:18:18; 3) D. Adjei-Brenya. VI:2:15; 4) D. Hereward. VI:6:18.
Study of classics. E. Boateng. IV:17:20.
Study of Ghanaian languages. E. Boateng. II:26:16.
Subversion Decree. E. S. Aidoo. VII:16:380.
Success at what price? J. H. Fiafor. VI:25:21.
Support for the Federal Government. 1) K. Marfo. III:25:21-22; 2)
    N. Nwigwe. III:26:24; 3) V. Ezenwinginya. IV:1:13.

T. U. C.--Rise up or Pack up! K. Ameyibor. VI:17:22.
T. V. Tortures. M. Johnson. III:2:18.
Taking chances again? E. M. Quaye. III:11:12-14.
Talking point. Y. M. Agble. VII:18:432.
TAMAKLOE, W. Fire outbreak in factories. VIII:7:164.
Tamale Hospital. B. Seidu. IX:5:113.
Tampering with parcels. K. Mprah. V:18:17.
TANDOH, E. Britain, Nigeria and Rhodesia. III:8:10.
_____. Nigerian civil war. III:26:24.
_____. Open letter to Gen. Gowon. III:26:24.
_____. Our youth and the budget. III:17:11.
TANO, I. Ghana's unemployment problems. V:13:28.
TANYEGBE, F. K. The exploited and lowly headteacher. VIII:5:111.
TARCHIE, J. C. Ten seconds of English please--Another rejoinder.
    VIII:23:558.
The task ahead for the youth. G. A. Ashitey. IV:1:11-12.
Tasteless crisis. G. A. Frempong. IV:26:25.
TAVIRA, J. Equatorial Guinea. III:23:17.
TAWIAH, J. K. Football. II:14:28-29.
TAWIAH, T. H. Mid-term break in Schools. V:1:20-21.
Tax on Rest-houses. E. Appiah. VII:21:501.
TAX-PAYER. Neon signs and foreign currency. II:12:16-17.
Taxation and the Ghanaian tax-payer. K. G. Konuah. IV:7:20.
Taxi rates: a bad case of capitulation. O. Okai. VIII:11:261.
TAYLOR, A. R. Order of precedence or of priority. II:8:14.
TAYLOR, K. A. Czech invasion by Russians. III:20:25.
_____. Great men. III:2:18.
_____. Let them miss one election! III:16:19.
_____. Return to civilian rule. II:21:15-16.
_____. Rewards for N. L. C. II:22:14.
_____. Rich men. II:17:20-22.
TAYLOR, W. ANTI. See Anti-Taylor, W.
Teachers and incentives. A. De Beck Asare. VI:6:20.
Teachers and the Ministry. G. H. K. Amehia-Adugu. VIII:11:261-262.
Teachers and transportation. J. Musah. III:8:12.
Teachers uniforms. S. Bruku. V:12:16.
Teaching of Classics. D. Hereward. III:15:29.
Teaching service decree. B. J. L. Kumasi. IX:3:68.
TEKYI, K. Ghanaian economic enterprise. III:12:16.
Ten seconds of English, please. 1) [Anonymous.] VIII:21:506. 2)
    J. K. Ampah. VIII:22:529. 3) J. C. Tarchie. VIII:23:558.
Testing of vehicles. K. Opare. VII:25:603.
TETTEH, G. N. Building the new National Soccer Team. III:19:16.
_____. Compensation for N. L. C. members. IV:16:17.
_____. Hail Kontopiaat. V:1:21.
TETTEH, K. O. The African deal. IX:13:318.
TETTEH, L. A. Pepper bandits again. V:21:22.
Thanks for rescue. K. Kent. VIII:8:186.
That Black Star. P. A. V. Ansah. VII:2:40-41.
That Black Star again. C. Krahene. VII:4:89.

Correspondence

That expensive day. G. A. Frempong. II:26:17.
"That Pele Match." H. Daniels. IV:5:18.
That shocking editorial. I. K. Gyasi. II:25:8.
That was amusing. K. Mensah. II:21:15.
Theatre at Legon. A. Dankwa. IV:8:20.
There are revolts and revolts. M. B. Davies. III:26:23-24.
These military promotions. M. Y. Agbosu. V:18:14.
These multiple taxes. J. M. Agble. V:11:28.
These pot-holes. J. A. Agyare. III:14:24.
These promises! C. C. T. Blankson. V:5:21.
Thieves of Teshie-Nungua. A. K. Philips. VIII:22:530.
This changing of sides. M. Charles. V:17:22.
This dependence on Cocoa. F. K. Smith. V:18:14-16.
This foreign exchange. 1) Y. M. Ashle. C. N. Wadia. IV:8:20; 2)
    G. M. K. Kpedekpo. IV:9:20.
This is our chance. Obeng-Manu. IV:10:14.
THOMAS, R. G. A. E. C. must act. VII:9:217.
Time and energy wasted. D. W. Ewer. VIII:19:461.
"Times and Dr. Busia." H. B. Yusif. II:10:15.
To draft or not to draft. E. K. Sarpely. III:13:12.
To Kontopiaat. 1) J. Oppong-Agyare. III:4:14; 2) E. Darko.
    III:4:14-15.
To the Director of P. and T. Accra--Pilfering at the Post Office. K.
    Mprah. VI:6:18.
To the editor. 1) T. Owens-Dey. V:18:14; 2) C. Owusu. V:23:21-22.
To what extent can a man sacrifice? E. D. Kemevor. III:14:24.
Too busy to play games. K. K. Oduro. VIII:5:109-110.
Too much criticism. S. Nattey. III:16:19.
Too much foreign worship. Reader. V:24:21-22.
Top civil servants and politicians. E. M. Kumaga. IV:24:24.
Tourism in Ghana. J. Gyinayeh. VI:2:16.
Towards a common Ghanaian language. 1) J. O. Osei-Tutu. IV:6:20-21;
    2) K. Forge. IV:6:21-22.
Trade Union Congress. K. Asmah. III:12:16.
Trade with South Africa. K. Addae-Mensah. VI:11:21.
Trade with South Africa? C. Addae. III:11:14.
Traders and the regime. W. Owusu-Acheaw. VIII:6:136.
Traffic and Ghana V. I. Ps. E. A. Boateng. II:18:15.
Traffic at Liberation Circle. K. Mensah. II:2:17.
Tragedy in Burundi. D. Adjei-Brenya. VII:12:288.
Tragedy of protocol. C. Quarshie. II:8:12-13.
Training of Certificate 'B' teachers. 1) T. K. Amoako. IV:17:20;
    2) E. A. Afiapa. IV:20:16.
Training our intellectuals. K. Arhin. V:3:10.
Transfer fees in Soccer. B. Akutteh. V:12:16.
Translate and be read! D. Hereward. IV:23:19.
Transport for non-resident students. I. Minta. VIII:22:527.
Trauma over Legon crisis. M. Matthews. III:24:12-13.
Tribal names and surnames. 1) K. J. L. Kumasi. VI:20:14; 2) G. K.
    Godi. VI:22:17-18.

Correspondence

Tribalism and the new politics. 1) O. Kantanka. IV:11:16; 2) F. A.
    Asiedu. IV:12:10.
Tribalism in its true perspective. K. G. Konuah. IV:3:17.
Tribute to courage and honesty. A. O. Mills. VII:6:142.
Tribute to Mr. E. Y. Amedekey. C. Dompreh. VII:18:433.
Tribute to Mr. B. A. Yakubu. E. A. Kwei. VI:14:22.
Tro-tro fares. Frempong-Mensah. V:2:17.
Trouble with Ghanaians. E. Asare. VIII:9:213-214.
TRUTENAU, H. Farmers' money: what for? II:15:18.
_____. We do need a Press Trust--Think again. IV:14:18-19.
TRUTENAU, H. M. J. An African in Latin America. V:13:27.
_____. Ghana's art treasures. V:19:22.
TRUTENAU, H. T. The unspeakable sin. III:8:12-13.
Truth about Biafra. A. C. Adiele. II:8:10.
TSETSE, A. K. Promotion of teachers. V:13:28.
TSIKATA, A. Declaration of Assets. VII:9:214.
_____. Much to rejoice about. VIII:7:162.
_____. N. R. C. declares Assets. VII:15:359.
TSIKATA, F. S. Unlimited power for the Vice-Chancellor? VI:12:22.
TUEKPE, M. Y. Small step for parliament, big disaster for nation.
    VI:19:14.
TUEKPE, Y. Where was Ofosu-Appiah's sting? VII:19:454.
TULLOCH, D. and DUMMETT, M. The police and the public. II:15:18.
TURKSON, J. Who deserves scholarship? IX:5:113.
_____. Who is Mr. Saki Scheck? III:21:18.
Turmoil in Ghana schools and colleges. J. W. Abroquah. II:18:16.
Tut-tut-tut--"Legon Observer." III:16:19.
TUTU, J. O. OSEI. See Osei-Tutu, J. O.
TWENEBOAH, F. D. Population growth and family planning. V:9:20.
25 years of Adult Education. P. B. Arthiabah. IX:2:40.
TWUM, G. Graduate employment. VIII:5:111.
TWUM, G. E. The Malam Shitta case. VIII:10:237-238.
TWUM, W. Y. Pick pocket extraordinary. V:15:17.
TWUMASI, A. P. The mental hospital. III:15:28.
_____. On the question of experts. IV:4:29.
_____. School curricula. II:26:15-16.
TWUMASI, Y. Calculated public deception? IV:14:20.
U. A. C. and Guinea Bissau. J. A. Eghan. VIII:25:606.
U. C. C. C. Science results. P. A. V. Ansah. IV:16:14.
UKACHUKWU, A. O. "When Genocide is no Genocide." IV:2:20.
Unacceptable substitute. H. Anokye. IV:24:25-26.
Uncertainty of future politics. N. Kuenyhia. III:13:10.
Uncontrolled pricing. 1) E. Attaku. II:10:15-16; 2) P. Schneider.
    II:11:14.
Uncritical Ghanaians. G. Danso. VI:19:14.
Undercurrents and Abbott. E. Dumor. II:26:13-14.
Underground railway for Accra? K. A. Kumi Attobrah and J. E.
    Frimpong. II:1:16.
Underpriviledged Schools. D. Hereward. VIII:6:133-134.
Unedifying newspaper attacks. E. Daniel. V:5:22.
Unemployment. W. Y. Aidoo. III:5:26.

Correspondence

Unemployment and crime. A. Kepler. III:3:8-10.
Unidentified accident victims. A. K. Annan. VII:22:524-525.
United Nations has defeated its aims. M. Bombande. IV:2:18.
University accounts. L. H. Ofosu-Appiah. II:7:16.
University admission requirements. P. B. Abanyie. IX:7:160.
University and Society--rejoinder. 1) [Anonymous.] VII:26:629. 2)
    D. Hereward. VIII:1:18-19.
University appeal funds. E. Y. Frempong-Mensah. V:7:14.
University Cafeteria. P. A. V. Ansah. III:22:22.
University entrance and guidance in schools--A comment. A. N. Mensah.
    VIII:24:580.
University entrance examination. I. Minta. IV:26:25.
University Loan Scheme. 1) D. Adjei-Brenya. VI:2:15; 2) D. Hereward.
    VI:6:18; 3) C. Addy. VI:16:21; 4) A. Van Dantzig. VI:18:18.
University of Ghana Examinations. A. S. Amevor. II:21:14.
University of Ghana External Degrees. A. Boateng. VII:26:628.
University students and military discipline. G. Dua-Boakye.
    VIII:13:308-309.
Unlimited power for the Vice-Chancellor? F. S. Tsikata. VI:12:22.
Unnecessary imports. J. Longman. III:1:16.
Unspeakable sin. H. T. Trutenau. III:8:12-13.
Up North and Down South. B. Milliar. VIII:3:68.
Urgently needed--A genuine revolution. M. Attopley. VI:25:20.
Utopian Legon. G. M. Ridden. VIII:20:483-484.
V. R. A. has bilharzia. K. A. Sasu. II:21:15.
VAN DANTZIG, A. See Dantzig, A. Van.
Victor Owusu and varsity education. T. N. Ward-Brew. III:17:10.
Violation of territorial waters. K. Adu. III:24:12.
Visa and the entry permit. W. Ockiya. IV:16:17.
Visitation Committee. L. H. Ofosu-Appiah. IV:2:17.
Voice of which revolution? K. Ofori. VII:12:286.
Volunteer is a volunteer. P. Eshun. VIII:14:336.
Volunteers to America and the Ministry of Education. D. A. Brown.
    II:11:15-16.
VON FLEISCHER, A. R. C. The Pope and contraception. III:17:10.
VON STUCKRAD, H. Conflict of Idealism and Realism. III:1:16.
VORKEH, E. The basic attitude--Legon Varsity unrest. III:24:13.
_____. Gardiner on intellectuals in politics. VIII:1:20.
_____. Nkrumah: "Good or bad?" VIII:7:162-163.
_____. Ratifying the Constitution. IV:17:17.
_____. The Rhodesian issue. III:11:18.
_____. Sir Eric vs. Dr. Kofi on Cocoa. VII:26:624-626.
VORKEH, E. K. Lessons of the Mid-East War for Africa. IX:5:112.
WADDIE, K. A. OMARI. See Omari-Waddie, K. A.
WADIA, C. N. British justice and Kwesi Armah. II:5:10.
_____. Does it make sense? IV:6:20.
_____. The new cedi. II:7:18.
_____. The Nigerian Civil War. III:12:14.
_____. Not "Drs." but honoured gentlemen. VI:12:22.
_____. On the "Illustrated Weekly of India." VII:23:554.

_____. Parking at the Airport. VIII:11:262.
_____. This foreign exchange. IV:8:20.
Wake up A. T. C. C.! B. Laryea. IX:3:67.
Wake up, Ministry of Agriculture. O. C. II:19:21.
Walls: Architectural craze or fortresses? A. Kwamena. III:2:17-18.
Wanted: African self-help. A. I. L. Alhassan. VI:4:16.
Wanted: Ghana's social history. P. M. Desewu. VIII:10:236.
Wanted: quality teachers. J. B. Amoafo. VI:20:14.
War clouds in Nigeria. M. Bossman. II:13:15.
WARD-BREW, T. N. Biafra: A second Kantanga? III:18:18.
_____. Czech invasion by Russians. III:20:24.
_____. Mobutu and Nigeria. III:11:14.
_____. Victor Owusu and Varsity education. III:17:10.
Warning to public officers. N. L. Yartey. VII:16:381-382.
Was it a reward or a punishment? K. Enu. VIII:4:93.
Was this necessary or just big? K. Abiri. VIII:10:237.
Waste of public funds on drugs. Y. Bediako. VI:17:20-22.
Wasting talent. E. A. Muange. III:2:14-15.
Watch Tower Prophecies. E. Douglas-Djarbeng. V:3:14.
We do need a Press Trust--think again. H. Trutenau. IV:14:18-19.
We must examine ourselves. M. A. Adu. VIII:14:336.
We should cater for their children too. K. N. Bame. II:12:16.
WEIDEN, P. Another electronic industry for Ghana. II:13:13.
WEINER, L. K. What becomes of his dream. IV:10:15.
Welfare state in Ghana? Afari-Gyan. V:25:19.
WELSING, J. Mills-Odoi Report and Civil Servants. III:19:12-13.
West Indians and British Services. Y. M. Agble. VIII:9:214.
What are the facts. E. S. Larverh. VIII:6:137.
What becomes of his dream. L. K. Weiner. IV:10:15.
What boring stuff. J. Apronti. VIII:26:625.
What is wrong with Ghanaian Agriculturist? J. Gyinayeh. VII:6:141.
What is wrong with the University? C. R. Whittaker. III:9:13.
What kind of candidates for the next Parliament? 1) K. Haligah.
    III:7:12-13; 2) K. Kwakutse. III:9:13.
What next, Mr. Wilson? P. Adu-Gyamfi. IV:14:20.
What price sycophancy? G. S. Molah. VII:8:195. Rejoinder. S. G.
    Larbi. VII:11:266.
What price tribalism? R. T. Defoe. IV:20:19.
What went wrong? IV:7:20.
What went wrong.... C. G. Baeta. II:1:16-17.
"What--Went--Wrong" Lectures. P. A. V. Ansah. IV:17:20.
Whatever happened to "Talking Point." P. A. V. Ansah. VII:3:60.
What's our reserve position now? F. C. Essandoh. IV:10:15.
What's wrong with Africa? M. N. F. Ashu. III:26:22.
What's wrong with Manya-Krobo local council? E. B. Kpabitey.
    IV:11:18.
When genocide is no genocide. 1) W. Ockiya. IV:1:13; 2) A. O.
    Ukachukwu. IV:2:20.
When to learn English. O. K. Nkrumah. IX:9:206.
Where is Kontopiaat? 1) K. Addae. IV:15:16; 2) H. K. Akuffo.
    V:7:14-16; 3) Y. Bekoe. VI:26:21.

Correspondence

Where is the Editor of the Graphic? S. K. O. Denkyi. VI:3:15.
Where was Ofosu-Appiah's sting? Y. Tuekpe. VII:19:454.
Whether Ojukwu fails or not. R. R. Onwuka. III:1:15-16.
Which is more worthy--the car or the road? Aduonum-Darko. VIII:8:187.
White paper and Apaloo Commission. 1) K. Apeagyei. II:3:16; 2) K.
    Loggo. II:5:10-11.
Whither Ghana? R. A. Afful. I. A. Mensah. II:25:30.
Whither is the Bus Service drifting? K. Asempa. II:22:13.
Whither Red China? E. Y. Frempong-Mensah. IV:25:17.
WHITTAKER, C. R. What is wrong with the University? III:9:13.
Who authorized higher rates? S. Antwi-Badu. VIII:13:309.
Who deserves scholarships? 1) J. Turkson. IX:5:113; 2) J. Atta-
    Quayson. IX:6:137.
Who gets what? Ohene Okai. VII:10:243.
Who is a rebel in Nigeria? H. C. Daniel. III:6:12.
Who is accountable for this? A. Owusu-Sarpong. VII:11:265-266.
Who is an imperialist? K. K. Minta. IX:3:69.
Who is an intellectual? K. Asante. VII:7:168.
Who is Mr. Saki-Scheck? J. Turkson. III:21:18.
Who is to do what? B. K. Dankwa. IX:8:184.
Who or what incites the workers to strike? M. C. Charles. VI:10:19.
Who really needs help? J. B. Essandoh. VIII:17:410.
Who should wear what (in Cape Coast)? K. Nyamekye. VIII:3:65.
Who should wear what (in Cape Coast)--A footnote. VIII:4:93.
Who wants civilian rule now? K. Senyo. VIII:16:387.
Who was in contempt? S. K. Afful. VII:26:629.
Who will escape the hanging? P. A. V. Ansah. VII:13:307. Rejoinder.
    W. K. Ansah. VII:15:358-359.
Who will go to heaven? A. Ackon. VII:23:555.
Who's telling the truth? K. Amoako-Crentsil. IX:1:10.
Whose freedom of the Press? Rejoinder. 1) B. Bretuo. VIII:19:458-460;
    2) Charlie-Boye. VIII:20:483.
Why another 50p. increase? K. O. Owusu. VIII:7:162.
Why bother the lady? IV:20:18.
Why Mr. Harlley's resignation? C. Parker. IV:22:24.
Why not put Ghana's Army to farm work? F. Manuh. VI:8:18.
"Why should we let sleeping dogs lie?" Obeng-Manu. IV:24:22-24.
Why the Hurry. J. E. Armah. III:24:11.
Why the Mission schools? J. K. Frimpong. 1) IV:25:18; 2) V:2:15-16.
Why this soccer fanaticism? S. K. O. Denkyi. V:2:17.
Why we study Classics. D. Hereward. IV:16:16.
Why worship the rich? K. A. Sasu. VI:23:20-21.
Will to apologise. J. E. Wiredu. III:1:14-15.
WILLIAMS, H. O. Prof. Bretton's book on Nkrumah. II:17:20.
WILLS, J. B. Crop production in Ghana. II:23:18-19.
WIREDU, J. E. How to revive the one party system in Ghana.
    VII:6:139-140.
_____. The will to apologise. III:1:14-15.
Withdrawal of Scholarships. 1) G. K. Benson. II:11:14-15; 2) K.
    Arhin. II:13:13.

Correspondence

Withdrawal of ¢30 million subsidy--Rejoinder. 1) L. Blay-Amihere. B. O. Laryea. VIII:4:90; 2) K. Arye. VIII:4:90-92.

Withdrawn ¢30 million subsidy: An act of redemption or just another example of economic mismanagement? Obeng-Manu. VIII:3:64.

Wives. K. James. III:10:10.

Women and the nation. 1) P. A. V. Ansah. V:8:20-21; 2) C. O. Kissiedu. V:12:15-16.

Working hours. 1) V. Kwami. II:17:20; 2) P. A. F. Amankwa. II:19:22.

Working in mysterious ways. K. Blankson. IX:9:208.

Working in the Rural areas. V:9:21.

World cocoa prices and under-development in Ghana. A note. T. A. Kofi. VII:22:528. Rejoinders. R. G. McFall. VII:23:552. See also VII:23:578 (580); VII:23:580-581; VII:26:624.

World prices of exportable goods. F. K. Buor. IX:14:342.

WORMENOR, M. A. S. Stop preaching tribalism. V:15:16-17.

YAKUBU, A. A. Administration of the Kusasi district. II:18:15-16.

YANKAH, K. A deep seated conspiracy? IX:4:87.

_____. Explanation please, N. L. C.! IV:20:18.

_____. National Service and the state transport. VIII:25:606.

_____. Nkrumah passes away--Rejoinder. VII:10:241.

YANKOM, K. Moral courage and Mr. Victor Owusu. II:14:29.

_____. Youth at our night clubs. III:13:12.

YANKSON, J. A. N. R. C. determined to feed and clothe Ghana. VII:22:529.

YARTEY, N. L. Warning to public officers. VII:16:381-382.

YAW, J. A. OWUSU. See Owusu-Yaw, J. A.

YAW, O. The Beaver aircraft accident. V:12:14.

_____. British Arms sales. VI:9:23-24.

YEBOAH, BADU. See Badu-Yeboah.

YEBOAH, E. ANTWI. See Antwi-Yeboah, K. E.

YEBOAH, E. O. Promotion of teachers. V:12:16.

YEBOAH, G. O. Interplay of reasoning. VII:2:40.

YEBOAH, G. OBENG. See Obeng-Yeboah, G.

YEBOAH, J. M. ASANTE. See Asante-Yeboah, J. M.

YEBOAH, K. Lessons from Exemptions Commission. III:25:20-21.

YEBOAH, M. Local soaps. V:24:23.

_____. Shopping: S. C. O. A. Technoa. VII:21:504.

YEBOAH, Y. GYASEHENE. See Gyasehene-Yeboah, Y.

Yendi skin probe. VIII:2:42-43.

YIADU, P. T. B. Hughes and salary increase. II:5:10.

YIRENKYI, S. A. Help me! I am in a dilemma. III:24:14.

Youth and the aged. A-Lashie. VII:4:89.

Youth Associations. P. Adu-Gyamfi. IV:1:12.

Youth at our night clubs. K. Yankom. III:13:12.

YUSIF, H. B. "The Times and Dr. Busia." II:10:15.

ZORMELO, S. K. The devaluation and economic recovery. II:16:16.

ZWENNES, J. L. Discrimination in our own country? II:2:14-15.

News Summary

A. D. B. loan for Ghana. VIII:21:511.
A. D. B. loan for Investment Bank. VIII:26:630.
A. D. B. to spend ¢3m. on food crops. IX:3:75.
Abidjan Conference. III:23:26.
Academy Report. II:2:22.
Accra gets 40 "Mini" Buses. VII:25:607.
Accra-Tema Water Supply project. VI:7:21.
Acheampong, (Col.) addresses Heads of Diplomatic Missions. VII:2:42.
Acheampong, (Col.) honoured. VIII:11:263.
Acheampong, (Col.) on return to civilian rule. VII:18:435.
Acheampong, (Col.) requests Brazilian coach. VIII:13:310.
Activists released. VII:2:42.
Addoquaye Laryea, (death of). VI:8:22.
Adomako on the economy. II:7:23.
Adult Education Institute. V:1:23.
Advisory Committee. IX:2:50.
Africa and Electric power. III:26:30.
Africa loses a great goal-keeper. VI:24:22.
African Airlines Association formed. III:9:22.
African Bank Governors. III:17:22.
African Bank ready to assist. III:17:21.
African Groundnut Council. III:23:26.
African Press. II:8:22-23.
African States must be objective. VI:13:22.
Afrifa and Disqualification Decree. III:24:22.
Afro-Asian Rural Reconstruction Organization. III:11:21.
Agama, (Dr.) gets new post. VII:25:607.
Agreement on Ghana's debts. IX:9:218.
Agricultural and Industrial Company Project. II:13:18-19.
Agricultural Council. II:11:23.
Agricultural Development Bank. III:11:20-21.
Agricultural/Industrial Project. II:14:17.
Agricultural Ministry, changes in. VIII:4:95.
Agricultural Ministry, Probe offices for. VI:9:26.
Agriculture, boost for. III:23:26.
Aid agreements with U. S. and W. Germany. II:14:16.
Aid to peasant farmers. VII:16:386.

155

Aid to stranded Ghanaians. II:2:20.
Air taxi service for Ghana. VI:11:22.
Aircraft: only two models to be used. IX:1:23.
Airlift of tomatoes. VIII:5:119.
Aliens barred from retail trade. V:1:23.
Aliens, statement on. IX:1:22.
Aliens to be issued permits. IV:3:22.
Aluminium production in Ghana. II:7:22.
Ambassadorial appointments. II:13:18.
Ambassadors. III:16:25.
American firm to prospect for diamonds. VIII:20:487.
Ammunition Depot burgled. II:10:22.
Amnesty for Prisoners. VIII:5:119.
Ankrah, (Lt.-Gen.) in Togo. III:8:22.
Ankrah, (Gen.) returns from Ivory Coast. III:20:25.
Anlo investigations. II:13:18.
Another Aid Pact. III:26:30.
Anti-Brucellosis campaign. III:9:22.
Anti-mosquito campaign. II:1:23.
Apaloo Commission, Report of. II:3:22.
Appiah, Gbedemah appointed envoys. VII:7:174.
Applications for exemption. III:13:20.
Appointment of Commission of Inquiry into the Samreboi incident.
   VI:24:22.
Appointment of Judges, body to advise N. L. C. on. III:14:28.
Appointment of Technical Committees. VI:9:26.
Armed forces magazine. II:6:23.
Army appointments. II:2:22.
Army, promotions. II:8:22.
Army recruitment suspended. II:13:18.
Army to cultivate farms. VII:7:174.
Arrests after April 17. II:11:23.
Asante, (Major) resigns. IX:8:195.
Ashanti Goldfields, 1967. III:9:22.
Assets of Botsio and others frozen. VIII:21:511.
Assets, new probe. VII:13:315.
Assets Report. III:14:28.
Assistance to small business. VIII:6:143.
Association of Ghanaian Importers and Exporters. II:3:22.
Attempted coup foiled. VII:15:361.
Attempted coup trial. VII:16:386.
Atu-Mensah, S. sentenced. II:5:22.
Auditor-General's report. II:6:23.
Australian "Droughtmaster" for Ghana? VIII:13:310.
Balance of payments. III:18:22.
Ban on politics lifted (Togo). IV:3:22.
Bank for Housing and Construction. VIII:26:630.
Batteries. II:13:18.
Bearer Premium bonds reintroduced. VIII:15:367.
Bechemhene released. II:13:18.
Benni, (Lt.-Col.) C. D. in new position. VIII:1:23.

Chiefs, new bill proposed. VI:12:26.
Chieftaincy in Volta Region to be probed. VIII:9:215.
Chinese envoy arrives. VII:20:482.
Chinese gifts. IX:14:347.
Churches to merge. VIII:1:23.
Circulation of currency. III:23:26.
Citizenship Identity Cards. VII:10:246.
Citrus farm for Adansi. VIII:12:287.
Civic Education Centre. II:13:18.
Civil Service and trade unions. II:4:31.
Civil war in Pakistan. VI:8:22.
Cocoa. III:12:21-22.
Cocoa. III:18:22.
Cocoa. III:21:22.
Cocoa, hold up of. VIII:7:166.
Cocoa, mass spraying abolished. VIII:6:143.
Cocoa price raised. VIII:21:510.
Cocoa purchasing. II:6:23.
Cocoa Report. II:13:18.
Cocoa sales to be held up. VI:10:22.
Cocoa to be sold in London. VII:9:222.
Combined Transport Agreement Confab opens. IX:7:170.
Commercial Library. II:8:22.
Commission on Ghana Prisons. II:2:21.
Commission to probe award of contracts. VII:7:174.
Commissioner for Information addresses the Press. VII:7:174.
Commissioners appointed. VII:3:66.
Commissioners reshuffled. VIII:9:215.
Committee for projects. VII:7:173.
Committee on Atomic Reactor. VII:20:482.
Committee on Timber formed. VIII:22:535.
Committee to probe students demonstration. IX:4:99.
Committees on development. VI:11:22.
Common staff for Ghana's Universities. VII:20:482.
Commonwealth Conference. IV:2:26.
Company's contract cancelled. IX:1:23.
Complaints, body to investigate. VII:20:482.
Conference on West African Regional Economic Co-operation. II:10:22.
Conference opens. IX:4:99.
Conferences: Agriculture and Industry. III:8:22.
Congo. III:22:26.
Congolese Military Delegation. III:9:22.
Constituent Assembly. IV:2:26.
Constituent Assembly set up. III:24:22.
Constitution (new) Chiefs on party politics. II:14:16-17.
Constitution (new) Questionnaire on. II:1:23.
Constitutional Commission goes into the Regions. II:2:22.
Constitutional proposals, campaign to publicise. III:10:15.
Contractors demand formation of disciplinary Committee. III:15:30.
Corned beef delayed at Bolga. VIII:12:287.
Corporation reduces rent. VIII:12:287.

Corporation to buy Manganese. VIII:20:487.
Cotton. III:13:20.
Cotton Development, I. B. R. D. loans for. VIII:11:263.
Cotton gets aid too. III:26:30.
Cotton, Growing more. VII:11:270.
Cotton, producer price raised. VIII:22:533.
Course in food storage. III:19:20.
Court Bill, new published. VI:13:22.
Courts (Amendment) Decree, 1972 (N. R. C. D. 101). VII:19:458.
Crime wave. III:20:26.
Curing Cancer with "Sarodua." VI:22:18.
Curriculum Committee. VIII:6:143.
Customs and Excise Collection [1967-68]. III:17:20.
Dahomey. III:9:22.
Dahomey. III:21:22-23.
Dahomian Government, new. III:17:22.
Danquah, (the late Dr.). V:4:22.
Danquah, (Dr. J. B.), Memorial for. V:6:18.
Data processing unit. III:10:15.
Dawhenya Irrigation Project work begins. VIII:10:239.
Death of new Ambassador. III:16:25.
Death penalty for robbery with violence in Sierra Leone. VI:22:18.
Death sentences commuted. II:12:24.
Death sentences commuted. VII:26:631.
Debt repayment, the Netherlands. II:13:18.
Debts, new moratorium on. III:23:26.
Decree on Ghanaian enterprise. IV:2:25.
Decree on Newspapers. VIII:5:119.
Decree on rumours. VIII:14:342.
Decree on slot machines. VIII:10:239.
Decree on statutory corporations. VIII:19:463.
Decree prohibiting communication with Nkrumah and Co. II:1:22.
Decrees on "Newspapers" and "Prohibition of Rumours" repealed.
    III:10:15.
Deportation of Soviet Correspondents, etc. II:13:18.
Detainees, (final batch) released. VIII:14:342.
Detainees released. VIII:2:47.
Detector gift for Ghana. VII:23:559.
Development in the North. III:9:22.
Diamond marketing, new methods. IV:2:25.
Discipline in the police. III:11:21.
Disqualification. III:14:28.
Disqualified persons, list of. III:11:22.
Dock work. II:13:19.
Doctors and transfer. VII:20:482.
Doctors, (new graduates out). VI:15:26.
Donations from State Enterprises. II:13:19.
Drevici Complex to resume work. III:11:20.
Driving on the right. VI:22:18.
Driving on the right, date fixed for. VIII:17:415.
East and Central African Heads. V:4:22.

News Summary

Foreign foods, new distribution system. VIII:7:165.
Foreign foods rushed to Kumasi. VIII:2:47.
Foreign foods still in the news. VIII:19:463.
Former Chief Executives to be probed. VIII:11:263.
Former Minister jailed. III:17:20.
Former Security Officers freed. III:17:20.
¢41 million licences issued to 5 firms. VII:7:174.
¢43,000 for Arts Festival. VIII:17:415.
Foundation presents 100 TV sets for schools. VI:24:21.
N¢450,000 for new townships. VI:24:21.
France and Nigeria. III:17:22.
From Congo (Brazzaville). III:17:21.
Full pay for pensioners abolished. VII:4:94.
G. B. C. Commercial Service. II:6:23.
G. I. H. O. C. in search for markets. VI:24:22.
G. I. H. O. C., New Board. VI:19:16.
G. I. H. O. C. to make fridges. VIII:13:310.
G. N. T. C. II:3:22.
Gap in trade balance. III:26:30.
Gbedemah in exemption bid. III:23:26.
General mobilization ordered? III:17:22.
German ambassador, new. III:17:22.
German firm to buy Ghanaian cassava. VII:23:559.
Ghana and African F. A. III:18:22.
Ghana and Nigeria to co-operate in Tourism. VII:23:559.
Ghana and Poland sign pact. IX:14:347.
Ghana and the "Entente" states. III:16:24-25.
Ghana and U. K. Arms sales. VI:7:21.
Ghana and West Germany. III:17:21.
Ghana Armed Forces, changes in. II:10:22.
Ghana assists cattle breeding countries. VIII:11:263.
Ghana at the U. N. II:10:22.
Ghana bags ¢140 million from timber sales. IX:7:170.
Ghana Bar Association elects officers. II:1:22.
Ghana beat Nigeria in sports. VI:10:22.
Ghana Branch of the International Commission of Jurists. II:2:22.
Ghana breaks with Israel. VIII:22:535.
Ghana-Bulgaria Trade Agreement. II:5:22.
Ghana calls for probe. IX:8:195.
Ghana calls on Israel to quit Arab lands. VIII:21:511.
Ghana Commercial Bank employees not to engage in business. III:21:20.
Ghana condemns Russia. III:18:22.
Ghana-Czechoslovakia Trade Agreement. II:4:31.
Ghana electricity for Togo and Dahomey. VII:26:631.
Ghana Government and Agriculture. V:4:22.
Ghana-Guinea relations to be restored. VII:8:198.
Ghana Industrial Holding Corporation Board inaugurated. III:15:30.
Ghana invites U. S. Tourists. VI:24:22.
Ghana-Ivory Coast Border. III:21:20.
Ghana-Ivory Coast co-operation. VI:12:26.
Ghana-Malta establish ties. IX:5:123.

Ghana Press Release No. 390/72. VII:15:361.
Ghana Press release: Shortage of Dry-Cell Batteries. II:12:24.
Ghana Railways and Ports Authority. III:19:20-21.
Ghana ready to send troops. VIII:23:559.
Ghana receives grant. VIII:23:559.
Ghana recognises Cambodia Government. IX:10:243.
Ghana recognises Guinea-Bissau. VIII:20:487.
Ghana saves ¢1 million on sale of cocoa. VII:12:289.
Ghana signs pacts with Hungary. VIII:24:583.
Ghana suffers trade deficit. V:6:18.
Ghana to expand trade with Senegal. II:7:22.
Ghana to make motor cycles. VII:11:270.
Ghana to produce 25% of her edible oil. VII:13:315.
Ghana to spend ¢98 million more on crude oil. IX:5:123.
Ghana to step up Cotton Production. VII:22:535.
Ghana-Togo Agreement. VIII:7:166.
Ghana/Togo Air Pact. III:17:22.
Ghana-Togo Cement Project. IX:3:75.
Ghana-Togo to co-operate. VII:12:289.
Ghana Trade Fair, 2nd. VIII:18:22.
Ghana-U. N. D. P. agreement. III:8:22.
Ghana, Upper Volta Border talks. VII:7:174.
Ghana, Upper Volta Demarcation Commission. III:9:22.
Ghana urges U. S. to sign Cocoa Pact. IX:3:75.
Ghana-U. S. Tyre Agreement. II:13:18.
Ghana wants direct rule. VII:12:289.
Ghana will assist refugees. VII:7:174.
Ghana Youth Council. II:8:22.
Ghana-Yugoslavia Trade Agreement. II:7:22.
Ghanaian Business. III:26:30.
Ghanaian Business, policy to promote. III:15:30.
Ghanaian citizens' identity cards. VII:23:559.
Ghana contractors. III:14:28.
Ghanaian gets U. N. E. F. Post. IX:8:194.
Ghanaian journalists. II:1:22.
Ghanaian Nationals abroad. II:10:15.
Ghanaian poet elected fellow of U. K. Society. III:9:22.
Ghanaian solders in great performances at the Big Games. VI:24:22.
Ghanaian students overseas. III:9:22.
Ghanaians expelled from Kinshasa. VI:22:18.
Ghanaians trained abroad urged to return home. III:14:27.
Ghana's economy buoyant. III:23:25.
Ghana's external debts. II:6:23.
Ghana's Republic day. IX:8:194.
Ghana's request for World Bank loan. III:21:20-22.
Ghana's stamps abroad. III:26:30.
Ghana's stand on C'wealth. VII:11:270.
Ghana's team for Commonwealth Games. IX:1:22.
Ghana's "Warship." II:1:22-23.
Gold. III:14:27.
Gold ore, more discovered at Prestea. VII:20:482.

Golden Triangle. III:14:28.
"Golden Triangle" Road. II:8:22.
Goldsmith provides ¢15,000 Electricity Plant. VII:18:435.
Goodwill mission. VII:3:66.
Government acquires shares. VIII:11:263.
Government acquires shares in banks. VIII:2:47.
Government acquires shares in log firms. VIII:3:71.
Government acts on rents. VII:18:435.
Government commutes death sentences. IX:8:195.
Government issues warning. IX:7:170.
Government makes changes. IX:8:195.
Government of Ghana Treasury Bills Issue. VII:2:42.
Government orders rent cuts. VIII:2:47.
Government participates in Timber Industry. VIII:1:23.
Government participation in Mines. VII:25:607.
Government takes over Fuel firms. VI:15:26.
Government takes over Loyalty Companies. VII:26:631.
Government takes shares in Mim Timber Co. VIII:20:487.
Government to acquire lands for farming. VI:10:22.
Government to set up Ranches. VI:17:26.
Government to set up Settler farms. VII:9:222.
Government to spend N¢581.7 million. VI:18:22.
Government to spend ¢97 million. VII:16:386.
Government to take 55% shares in Bauxite Company. VIII:22:533.
Government urged to freeze vacation jobs. VIII:14:342.
Guinea Armed Forces in Sierra Leone. VI:8:22.
Harbour congested. VIII:9:215.
Harlley (Mr.) gets more responsibilities. II:7:22.
Harlley (Mr.) on civilian rule. II:8:23.
Helicopters to convey food. VIII:13:310-311.
HI-Y annual Congress. III:16:24.
Holland aids Togo school. IV:2:26.
Hospital (New). VI:11:22.
Hospital fees. III:15:30.
Hospital fees, exemption (new). VI:21:16-18.
Hospital, (new ¢4 million) opens. IX:4:99.
Houses for the workers. VIII:19:463.
Housing Corporation mounts crash project. VIII:6:143.
Housing loan for civil servants. VIII:16:391.
Housing Lottery. VIII:7:166.
Housing plan for Ghanaians abroad. VII:23:559.
Hungary gives medical equipment to Ghana. IX:9:216.
I. M. F. and Ghana. II:8:23.
I. M. F. assistance. II:12:23.
I. M. F. official praises N. L. C. III:17:21.
Ibos demand safeguards. V:3:19.
Ibos, new position. V:4:21-22.
Immigrants. III:11:22.
Import Control of certain goods. II:1:22.
Import Licence Fees due. III:19:22.

Importation of salted fish. III:20:26.
Improving meat supply. VII:25:606.
Industries at Takoradi. III:11:20.
Information officers told to be bold. VII:25:607.
Inkumsah, (Mrs.) and Mr. Osei jailed. III:11:20.
International Monetary System, new structure of operation. VI:22:18.
Invention by Ghanaian Doctor. III:17:21.
Irresponsible parents, Government urged to act. VI:21:18.
Italy gives credit facilities to Ghana. III:8:22.
Japanese Government to assist Ghana's Virology Project. IV:2:24-25.
Japanese Government to give medical aid to Ghana. III:15:30.
Joint State-Private cement enterprise. II:12:23-24.
Judge and Party supporters. V:2:19.
Jumu, (Major). III:23:25.
Jumu, (Major) freed. III:19:21-22.
Jurist pays respect to Danquah. II:3:22.
Juxon-Smith, (Brig.) Andrew, conviction quashed. VI:22:18.
Kade Match Factory. II:13:18.
Kaiser Engineers revisit Accra Plains. VIII:18:439.
Kattah, (Brig.) case against, withdrawn. VII:25:607.
Kaunda on Rhodesia. III:23:26.
Kenya. III:9:22.
Kerekou, (Col.) visits Ghana. VIII:14:342.
Kotoka Statue. III:20:26.
Kotoka Trust. II:10:22.
Kotoka Trust Fund, the Civil Service. II:12:24.
Kotoko qualifies for semi-finals. VI:22:18.
Kumasi University makes discoveries. IX:1:23.
The Kwesi Armah's case: Ghana protests against Britain's decision.
    II:3:23.
Labour Party to aid freedom fighter. VI:12:25.
Lake Transport Pact signed. VI:10:22.
Land problem, a hindrance to development. VI:24:21.
Land tenure report submitted. IX:9:216.
Launching of new Corps. V:1:23.
Law passed on One-Party State. VI:18:22.
Lawyers and Criminal proceedings. III:8:22.
Lawyers (new) enrolled. III:21:22.
Leaders of April 17 Insurrection executed. II:10:22.
Lecturers boycott lectures. VIII:7:165-166.
Legal Profession (Amendment) Decree 1967. II:5:22.
Legal scrutiny of government commercial agreements. II:2:20.
LEVI, H. G. III:26:30.
Life Insurance for farmers. VII:16:386.
Loan to Guinea. III:21:22.
Loans. III:13:19.
Loans for traders. VI:10:22.
Local Administration Bill. VI:7:21-22.
Local Cement Plant. III:26:30.
Local Council workers, back pay for. VI:11:22.
Local Councils, chiefs to serve on. VII:7:173.

Local Councils, reports on irregularities in. VI:9:26.
Local Government election next year. VI:9:26.
Logistics Committee suspended. VIII:16:391.
Louis Armstrong dies. VI:15:26.
Lower Volta Projects. III:23:25.
McNamara in Ghana. VI:12:26.
Manpower Conference. III:23:26.
Many join Corps. V:2:19.
Mao in good health. VI:21:18.
Mass Media Seminar. VI:16:22.
Matchets from Bibiani. VIII:14:342.
Mate, Casely retires. V:3:19.
Meat, further importation of. VIII:12:287.
Meat, more arrives. VIII:16:391.
Meat, New prices. VII:23:559.
Meat rots at Bolgatanga. VIII:15:367.
Mechanized fufu preparation. II:4:31.
Military Tribunal. VII:20:482.
Military Tribunal. VIII:22:535.
Military Tribunal. VIII:23:599.
Military Tribunal. IX:1:23.
Military Tribunal sits on November plot. II:10:22.
Military Tribunals. II:2:21.
Mining Operations (Government Participation) Decree, 1972.
    VII:25:604-606.
Ministerial appointments, changes in. VI:21:18.
Mirchandanis deported. VIII:15:367.
Mirchandanis, sentences reduced. VIII:13:311.
Mobutu. III:21:22.
Moon flight is a tremendous scientific achievement, Gen. Ankrah.
    IV:2:24.
More Judges promoted. VI:12:26.
More loans. III:11:21.
More trials promised. II:12:23.
Moroccan coup bid foiled. VI:15:26.
Motion on dialogue. VI:7:22.
Motor offences, on the spot fines for. VIII:21:510.
N. A. L., New leader. V:6:18.
N. A. L. write against Minister. V:4:22.
N. L. C. uncovers plot to stage counter-coup. II:3:23.
N. R. C. VII:2:41.
N. R. C., Chairman broadcasts to the Nation. VII:2:42.
N. R. C. Chairman meets Principal Secretaries and Head of Government
    Departments. VII:2:42.
N. R. C. Chairman's first press conference. VII:2:41-42.
N. R. C. Chairman's message to C'wealth Congress. VII:12:289.
N. R. C. Chiefs send message to. VII:15:363.
N. R. C. commended. IX:14:347.
N. R. C. declares stand on Lonrho. VIII:10:239.
N. R. C. demonstration in support of. VII:15:363.

N. R. C. gives house for Raffle. VIII:20:487.
N. R. C. gives priority to feeder roads. VII:10:246.
N. R. C. Head appointed Chief Commander. VII:7:173.
N. R. C. Head visits Lome. VII:8:198.
N. R. C. issues Charter. VIII:1:23.
N. R. C. members, four promoted. IX:8:195.
N. R. C. reshuffle. VII:21:506.
N. R. C. reshuffle. IX:1:22.
N. R. C. sworn in. VII:3:66.
N. R. C. to stay on. VIII:21:511.
N. S. C. dissolved. VII:7:174.
N. U. G. S. apologies to Speaker. VI:11:22.
N. U. G. S. Communique. VI:9:26.
N. U. G. S. disagree with Government decision. VIII:19:463.
N. U. G. S. Press release. IX:6:143-146.
Nana Kobina Nketsia. II:3:22.
National Advisory Committee suspended. VII:4:94.
National Development Bond. VII:4:94.
National Family Planning Council inaugurated. VI:7:22.
National Lotteries. III:16:25.
National Service for Varsity graduates. VIII:15:367.
National Standards Board. II:7:23.
Navy arrests two Russian vessels. III:22:26.
Netherlands Society donates money to Ghana Credit Union. III:11:20.
New appointments. VIII:2:47.
New Arab Federation. VI:19:16.
New Cedi. II:5:22.
New Committee set up. III:26:30.
New definition. III:26:30.
New Parliament opened. VI:15:26.
New price list out. VIII:19:463.
New rates of allowance for Public Service. VI:18:22.
New taxes on vehicles. VIII:3:71.
New Time Table in Ghana. III:23:25.
New trading agency. VII:20:482.
New Vice-Chancellor for Kumasi University. IX:1:22.
New Water Scheme for Accra. VIII:3:70.
Nigeria. III:9:22.
Nigeria. III:20:26.
Nigeria. III:21:22.
Nigeria and the E. C. M. III:21:23.
Nigeria: "No Genocide." III:21:23.
Nigerian Cattle, Regional allocation starts. VIII:13:311.
Nigerian Embassy denies. III:23:26.
Nigerian leaders hold talks in Ghana. II:2:20.
Nigerian's Sovereign prerogatives. V:4:22.
Nigeria's Terms. III:17:22.
Nima Affair before Court. II:7:23.
Nima, reconstruction at. VIII:9:215.
Nimeiry back to power. VI:17:26.
Nixon's curbs on inflation. VI:18:22.

P. M. presents Loans Scheme Bill. VI:15:26.
P. M. returns. VI:10:22.
P. P.'s external debts. VII:3:66.
Pacts with Israel and Poland. VIII:5:118.
Pakistan condemns Minority Regime. V:6:18.
Pakistani envoy (new). III:19:20.
Patriotic gesture. V:1:23.
Pay for workers (new). VIII:16:391.
Pay increase. II:5:22.
Pay, new structure for Ghana. VIII:15:367.
Pay rise for lower income group. VIII:17:415.
Peace in 1970. V:1:23.
Pencil factory to be re-opened. VIII:5:118.
Peoples' Educational Association meets. VIII:18:439.
Pharmaceutical factory opened. IX:8:194.
Philatelic Bureau planned. III:12:21.
Pill, an aid to the Church. VI:21:18.
Pledge to oust white rule. V:4:22.
Point and counter-point. III:18:22.
Police Exams leak. VIII:18:439.
Police Superintendent sacked. II:3:22.
Political Activities banned. VI:8:22.
Political education. II:2:21-22.
Population census. III:9:22.
Portugal urged to free colonies. IX:9:218.
Post Office Bank houses customers. VIII:10:239.
Preparations to welcome expelled fishermen. IV:2:25.
President gets Doctorate Degree. IV:10:22.
President returns home. VI:11:22.
President Tito's visit. V:4:22.
President Tubman buried. VI:17:26.
Press and the Judiciary. III:12:21.
Press conference by Lt.-Gen. Ankrah on the attempted coup on 17th
    April, 1967. II:9:23.
Press release: Police and Army to counter bribery and corruption.
    II:2:20-21.
Prices and Incomes Board. III:10:15.
Prices and Incomes Board. VII:25:607.
Prisons Commission. II:3:22.
Private Investigation Bureau. III:21:22.
Probe Committee. V:1:23.
Proceedings following Commission Reports. III:15:30.
Proclamation revoked. III:23:76.
Progress Party assets seized. VII:2:42.
Proscription of the P. P. P. IV:12:18.
Protective custody (final batch of releases from). III:10:15.
Qualifications from the East. VII:22:535.
R. C.s to distribute cattle. VII:9:246.
R. E. C.s take oath of office. V:2:19.
Rabbit production. VII:12:289.
Rail men end strike. VI:15:26.

Railway men on strike. VI:15:26.
Railway men return to work. III:20:25-26.
Railway strikers cause damage. III:19:22.
Railways will not be scrapped. VI:21:18.
Registration. III:22:26.
Registration Officers. VI:10:22.
Rehabilitating ex-detainees. VI:27:22.
Release of "Refugees" from Custody. II:3:23.
Re-negotiation of External debts. II:1:22.
Reported executions. III:23:26.
Representation Decree, Amendment to. III:18:22.
Rescheduling of debts, Israel. II:11:23.
Rescheduling of Ghana's debts. III:22:26.
Research Unit for Adult Learning. IV:2:25.
Reshuffle in the Civil Service. VII:7:174.
Retiring Awards for dismissed officers. V:6:18.
Revolutionary Radio. VII:11:270.
Rhodesia. III:20:26.
Rhodesia. III:23:26.
Rhodesian balance reduced. IV:3:22.
Rhodesian Judge rules. III:18:22.
Rhodesian Judges. III:18:22.
Rice in financial crisis. V:2:19.
Rice, Northern Region to plant ¢87,000 worth of paddy. VII:8:198.
Rice, producer price raised. VIII:21:511.
Rice production. III:11:20.
Rice, unsold in the North. III:9:22.
Roadworthiness Certificate, Date postponed. VII:26:631.
Roberto in Ghana. II:1:22.
Row between Kaunda and lawyers. VI:21:18.
Rowland at Obuasi. VIII:18:439.
Rowland to visit Ghana. VIII:14:342.
Rural Development Programme. VI:24:21.
Rural water projects to be reviewed. VII:12:289.
Saboteurs, arrest of. II:6:23.
Salary Review Committee inaugurated. VIII:17:415.
Salary Review, T. U. C. representation increased. VIII:19:463.
Sanctions. IV:2:25.
Schools, new directives on. VI:12:25-26.
Science for Training Colleges. III:16:25.
Seamen's boycott of the "Aureol." III:8:22.
Security Council and Rhodesia. III:17:22.
Sekou Toure greets N. R. C. VII:2:42.
Seminar on land problems. VII:18:435.
Seminars. II:4:31.
Senator Kennedy on his political future. V:10:22.
Senior Civil Servants' Association. III:13:19.
Senior Civil Servants' Association. III:16:25.
Settlement Farm for Peki. VI:27:22.
Seven envoys appointed. VII:9:222.
Seventh Battalion disbanded. VI:21:18.

Subversion trial, at the. VII:22:535.
Subversion trial ends. VII:23:559.
Subversion trial, new opens. VIII:26:630.
Subversion: Two seek to quash sentence. VIII:11:263.
Sudan President ousted. VI:16:22.
Sugar, cube banned. VII:9:222.
Sugar Factory in Kenya. III:23:26.
Sugar Industry to be re-vitalised. VII:26:631.
Sugar, move to resolve shortage. III:22:26.
Supplementary vote. VI:15:24.
Survey of movement of Ghanaians. III:19:21.
Suspension of school. II:2:22.
T. U. C. Assets, clamp down on. VI:19:18.
T. U. C. elections cancelled. VII:10:246.
T. U. C. men warned about strikes. VIII:7:165.
T. U. C. no longer a public body. II:11:21-22.
T. U. C. Polls in 1974. VII:13:315.
Taiwan willing to help Ghana. VI:24:22.
Tamale Hospital ready in January. VIII:23:559.
Taylor Assets Committee. VIII:13:311.
Taylor submits report. IX:8:194-195.
Teachers for Uganda. VIII:16:391.
Teaching Service Decree Published. IX:5:123.
Teaching Service Head appointed. IX:9:216.
Team reschedules debts in Italy. II:11:23.
Technical examinations localised. VII:22:535.
Tema sardines out next week. VIII:23:559.
Tema Shipyard and Dry-dock. III:11:20.
Textile factory. II:2:20.
Third phase of O. F. Y. launched. IX:4:99.
30,000 cattle from Gambia. VIII:5:118.
¢3 million for oil exploration. VII:8:198.
Three persons to die. VIII:26:630.
3,000 public officer to retire. VIII:5:118.
Timber firm banned. VIII:3:70.
Top C. P. P. men acquitted. III:13:20.
Top Police officers alleged to be in business. II:11:23.
Towards Civil rule. III:9:22.
Trade Fair Site, use of. II:5:22.
Trade Surplus. III:17:21.
Trade Surplus. VII:25:607.
Trade surplus of ¢11 million. VIII:9:215.
Trade Unionists to Israel. V:1:22-23.
Traffic offences, on the spot fines for. IX:1:23.
Trial begins today. VIII:21:511.
"Tribe" banned. VII:7:173.
25th Annual New Year School opens. IX:1:22.
24 Awarded Honours. VIII:5:119.
£20,000 Prize for the arrest of Busia. VII:18:435.
23 Members of P. P. Released. VIII:5:119.
2 factories for Central Region. VII:8:198.

¢250,000 loan to Upper Region Farmers. VIII:7:166.
Two million Dollars for Cattle Breeding. VIII:6:143.
¢2 million loan for Cattle. VII:20:482.
N¢2 million trade-surplus recorded. VI:19:18.
¢2.4 million farm tools ordered. VIII:7:166.
¢2.4 million Housing Pact signed. IX:1:22.
Two sentenced to death for subversion. VIII:3:71.
Tyres shortage to continue. VIII:21:510-511.
U Thant in Ghana. V:2:19.
U Thant on Peace prospects. V:2:19.
U. N. Consultant killed by thugs. V:10:22.
U. N. Secretary-General arrives. IX:5:123.
U. N. D. P. experts to study Keta Lagoon. III:21:20.
U. N. D. P. to aid Ghana. VII:7:174.
U. S. ambassador, new. III:19:22.
U. S. Bank to help develop Ghana's rubber resources. III:9:22.
U. S. Enterprise in Ghana. III:11:20.
U. S.-Ghana Aid Pact signed. VI:19:18.
U. S./Ghana Food Agreement. II:6:23.
U. S. International School in Ghana. III:14:28.
U. S. to triple assistance. IV:3:22.
Uganda wants Ghana Science Teachers.- VII:8:198.
Unemployment benefits. VII:18:435.
Union calls for probe into tyres shortage. VIII:20:487.
Universities closed down. IX:4:99.
University closed down. III:23:25.
University of Ghana Faculty of Law. III:8:22.
University re-opens. III:24:22.
Upper Volta. III:20:26.
Upper Volta President. III:18:22.
Used Cars, Statement on. VIII:24:583.
Vice-Chancellor arrives in Budapest. V:10:22.
Vice-Chancellor calls for scholarship review. VIII:10:239.
Vice-Chancellor (new) for Kumasi University. IX:1:22.
Vocational Training Unit. III:23:25.
Volta Dam Resettlement progress. V:4:22.
Volta Lake Research. VIII:26:630.
Vorster accuses Kaunda. VI:10:22.
Voters' Register. VI:7:22.
Voters' registration. III:17:20-21.
W. A. School Certificate. III:11:20.
Walk on hunger. VI:10:22.
Warning against strikes. II:1:22.
Water and Sewerage Corporation. III:16:26.
Water for Upper Region. VIII:7:166.
Weija Dam. III:14:27.
West African Common Market. III:10:15.
West African Historical Museum. IX:1:23.
West German Business Delegation in Ghana. III:10:15.
West German firm gives ¢4,000. IX:3:75.
West German Mark to be floated. VI:11:22.

News Summary

White paper on Workers Brigade. III:19:21.
White Paper on Yendi Skin Affairs. IX:9:216.
Woodwool banned. VII:21:506.
Work on canal begins. VIII:12:287.
Work starts on 600-acre Sugar Plantation. III:14:27-28.
Workers sign Agreement. V:1:23.
World Bank talks (first in Africa). VII:24:21.
World Cocoa Price. VII:18:435.

Reviews

ACHEBE, C. Girls at war. Rev. by G. Beyir. VIII:14:338.
_____. A man of the people. (Heinemann). Rev. by B. S. Kwakwa.
II:2:19-20.
ACKOM-MENSAH, I. Growth for developing countries through profit-sharing.
(Univ. of Wisconsin Press, 1967). Rev. by K. E. De Graft-Johnson.
III:2:19-20.
_____. Q. and A. Questions and Answers based on the Companies Code,
1963 (Act 179) of Ghana. Rev. by S. O. Gyandoh. II:1:19-20.
African deal (film). Rev. by M. D. Steuer. IX:12:290-294.
AGBODEKA, F. Ghana in the 20th Century. (Ghana Univ. Press, 1972).
Rev. by S. K. B. Asante. VII:23:555-559.
AIDOO, A. A. No Sweetness here. (Longman). Rev. by A. N. Mensah.
VI:16:21-22.
AINSLIE, R. The press in Africa, Communications, past and present.
(V. Gollancz, 1966). Rev. by K. A. B. Jones-Quartey. II:5:11-12.
ALLEN, C. and R. W. JOHNSON. African Perspectives (C. U. P.). Rev.
by R. Addo-Fening. VI:23:21-22.
AMEDEKEY, E. Y. The Culture of Ghana: A bibliography. (Ghana Univ.
Press.). Rev. by A. N. DeHeer. VI:27:21.
ANDRESKI, S. The African predicament (M. Joseph, 1968). Rev. by
Y. O. Saffu. III:24:19-22.
ANSAH, W. K. The denizens of the street. (Ghana Publishing Corp.,
1971). Rev. by A. N. Mensah. VII:1:17-18.
ANTI-TAYLOR, W. Moscow diary. (R. Hale, 1967). Rev. by S. Ryan.
III:4:16-17.
APPIAH, P. The Children of Ananse (Evans). Rev. by I. Ikiddeh.
III:18:20-21.
ARMAH, A. K. The beautyful ones are not yet born. (Heinemann, 1968).
Rev. by J. Apronti. IV:6:23-24.
BARTON, I. M. Africa in the Roman Empire. (Ghana Univ. Press, 1973).
Rev. by G. Adeleye. IX:11:265.
BEIER, U. Yoruba Poetry: (C. U. P. 1971). An anthology of traditional
Poems. Rev. by I. Ikiddeh. V:13:28-29.
BHAGWATI, J. and EUKANS, R. S. Foreign Aid: Selected readings.
(Penguin, 1970). Rev. by T. K. Cavanagh. V:25:21-22.
BING, G. Reap the Whirlwind. (McGibbon & Kee). Rev. by A. A. Boahen.
III:22:16-19.

Reviews

_____. Reap the Whirlwind. (McGibbon & Kee). Rev. by A. A. Boahen.
III:23:20-25.

Blood and tears (Play). Rev. by Yeboa-Nyamekye. VIII:5:116-118.

BRETTON, H. The Rise and Fall of Kwame Nkrumah: A study of personal
rule in Africa. (Praeger, 1966). Rev. by S. Ryan. II:22:18.

BROOKS, G. "A Broadside Treasury." (Broadside Press, 1971). Rev.
by A. Britwum. VII:16:382-384.

BRUTUS, D. Letters to Martha and other poems from a South African
prison. (Heinemann, 1968). Rev. by A. N. Mensah. IV:12:14-15.

BUSIA, K. A. Africa in Search of Democracy. (Routledge & K. Paul,
1967). Rev. by A. Irele. III:1:18-21.

CARMICHAEL, S. and C. V. HAMILTON. Black power--the politics of
liberation. (Random House). Rev. by J. Mawuse. III:9:16-17.

CERVENKA, Z. The Organization of African Unity and its charter.
(C. Hurst, 1969). Rev. by Y. O. Saffu. V:8:21-22.

CHRISTIE, A. Witness for prosecution. K. A. B. Jones-Quartey.
II:12:18-19.

CLARK. J. P. Casualties. (Longman, 1970). Rev. by E. Gunner.
VII:5:121-122.

COMMONWEALTH SECRETARIAT. Education in the developing countries of
the Commonwealth - Abstracts of Current Research, 1969. Rev. by
E. A. Haizel. V:20:26.

Corpse's comedy and Achimota School's enfant terrible. Rev. by K. E.
Senanu. VI:12:24-25.

CRABBE, JUSTICE A. The role of the lawyer in Society. A. review of
J. Mensah Sarbah, 1864-1910. His life and works. (Ghana Univ.
Press, 1971). Rev. by S. O. Gyandoh. VII:17:410-411.

Dancing with Ramblers, Jerry Hansen and the Ramblers Dance Band
(Record). Rev. by A. A. Aidoo. III:17:16-17.

DANQUAH, J. B. The third woman (Play, directed by G. Andoh Wilson).
Rev. by K. E. Senanu. VIII:15:366-367.

DANQUAH, M. Ghana Economic Review 1971/72. (Editorial and Publishing
Services). Rev. by J. B. Abban. VII:6:146.

DAVIDSON, B. The liberation of Guinea. (Penguin). Rev. by A. Irele.
IV:24:26-27.

DAVIES, I. African Trade Unions. (Penguin, 1966). Rev. by J. A.
Peasah. II:6:19-21.

DEBRAY, R. Revolution in the Revolution (Pelican, 1968). Rev. by
K. Nyarko. IV:5:20-22.

DEUTSCHER, I. The unfinished revolution: Russia 1917-1967.
(O. U. P. 1967). Rev. by S. Ryan. II:26:20-22.

DUNN, J. Modern revolutions: An introduction to the analysis of a
political phenomenon. (C. U. P., 1972). Rev. by K. Folson.
VII:13:308-311.

DUODU, C. The Gab boys. (Deutsch, 1967). Rev. by P. A. V. Ansah.
III:12:20-21.

EASMON, R. S. The burnt out marriage. (Nelson, 1967). Rev. by
H. Clarke. III:11:18.

_____. The burnt out marriage (Nelson, 1967). Rev. by A. A. Aidoo.
III:13:17-18.

Reviews

Education in the developing countries of the Commonwealth: Research
   Register 1970/71. Rev. by P. R. C. Williams. VII:12:288-289.
EDWARDS, P. Equiano's travels. (Heinemann). Rev. by I. Ikiddeh.
   III:5:27-29.
Efficiency in Road Construction (H. M. S. O. Publication, 1965). Rev.
   by J. W. S. de Graft-Johnson. II:12:17-18.
EPHSON, I. S. Ancient Forts and Castles of the Gold Coast (Ghana).
   (Ilen Publications). Review article by Barbara Priddy.
   VI:11:14-18.
FANON, F. Black skin white mask. (Grove 1967). Rev. by A Corre-
   spondent. III:8:15-17.
_____. The wretched of the earth. (MacGibbon & Kee, 1965). Rev.
   by K. Archampong. II:3:18-21.
FITCH, B. and M. Oppenheimer. Ghana, end of an illusion. (Monthly
   Rev. Press. 1966). Rev. by B. D. G. Folson. II:4:24-26.
FLECKER, J. E. Hassan of Baghdad (directed by G. Wilson). Rev. by
   L. Amissah-Arthur. IX:9:214-216.
FOSTER, P. Education and Social Change in Ghana. (Routledge and K.
   Paul 1965). Rev. by B. S. Kwakwa. II:18:19-21.
FYNN, J. K. Asante and its Neighbours, 1700-1807. (Longman, 1971).
   Rev. by S. Tenkorang. VII:20:481.
GANN, L. H. and P. DUIGNAN. Burden of empire: an appraisal of Western
   Colonialism in Africa South of the Sahara. (Pall Mall, 1968).
   Rev. by "New Critic." IV:20:22.
GARLICK, P. C. African traders and economic development in Ghana.
   (O. U. P., 1971). Rev. by J. B. Abban. VI:26:24-26.
Ghana Journal of Agricultural Science Vol. 1, No. 1. Rev. by Y.
   Ahenkora. IV:1:14-16.
GIBBS, J. African Radio (Plays for radio). VIII:16:390-391.
HALIBURTON, G. M. The Prophet Harris. (Longman, 1971). Rev. by
   K. Asare Opoku. VII:21:505-506.
HARVEY, W. B. Law and Change in Ghana. (Princeton Univ. Press, 1966).
   Rev. by B. D. G. Folson. II:4:24-26.
'Hassan'--A rejoinder to a review by K. Egyir. IX:11:258.
HENSHAW, J. E. Medicine for love (play). Rev. by J. Gibbs. IV:12:17.
Henshaw's medicine for love: A rejoinder to James Gibbs' Review by
   N. Daniels. IV:13:18.
High Level and skilled manpower survey in Ghana--1968 and assessment
   of manpower situation (1971). Rev. by A. Bulley. VII:15:360-361.
IKIDDEH, I. Drum beats. Rev. by J. Apronti. III:16:24.
JONES, P. Kwame Nkrumah. (H. Hamilton, 1965). Rev. by B. D. G.
   Folson. II:4:24-26.
KAFE, J. K. Ghana: An annotated bibliography of academic thesis,
   1920-1970 in the Commonwealth, Republic of Ireland and the United
   States of America. (G. K. Hall, 1973). Rev. by F. Fiadjoe.
   IX:3:73-75.
KAY, G. B. The political economy of Colonialism in Ghana: Documents
   and Statistics 1900-1960. (C. U. P., 1972). Rev. by P. Greenhalgh.
   VII:8:197-198.
KAYPER-MENSAH, A. W. The Dark Wanderer. (H. Erdmann Verlag). Rev.
   by G. Moore. V:26:22.

KHAN, M. A. Friends not masters: A political autobiography. (O. U. P.). Rev. by Y. Saffu. II:23:23-25.

KING, K. ed. Pan-Africanism from within. (O. U. P., 1973). Rev. by S. K. B. Asante. IX:5:120-123.

LANGLEY, J. A. Pan-Africanism and nationalism in West Africa 1900-1945. (Clarendon Press, 1973). Rev. by Y. Twumasi. IX:8:190-194.

LAURENCE, M. Long drums and cannons (MacMillan, 1968). Rev. by A. Niven. IV:12:15-17.

LEGUM, C. and DRYSDALE, J. Africa contemporary record: Annual Survey and documents 1968/69. (Africa Research Ltd., 1969). Rev. by F. Hesse. IV:23:20-22.

LENNOX, S. C. and M. CHADWICK. Mathematics for engineers and Applied Scientists. (Heinemann, 1976). Rev. by K. Kyiamah. VI:19:16.

LIYONG, J. Eating chiefs (Heinemann, 1970). Rev. by A. N. Mensah. VI:8:21-22.

MARAIS, G. Kwame Nkrumah as I knew him. (Janay). Rev. by L. H. Offosu-Appiah. VII:18:433-435.

MARKOVITZ, I. L. Leopold Sedar Senghor and the Politics of Negritude. (Heinemann, 1969). Rev. by Y. Saffu. V:16:20-22.

MAZRUI, A. A. The Anglo-African Commonwealth. (Pergamon Press, 1967). Rev. by J. A. Peasah. II:24:19-21.

Mikado (Play). Rev. by J. Apronti. V:11:28-30.

MILLEN, B. H. The political role of Labour in developing countries 1963. (Brooking Institution, 1963). Rev. by J. A. Peasah. II:6:19-21.

MONDLANE, E. The struggle for Mozambique: Rev. by A. Irele. IV:24:26-27.

MOORE, G. The chosen tongue. (Longmans, 1969). Rev. by E. O. Akyea. V:3:16.

_____. Wole Soyinka. (Evans, 1971). Rev. by J. Gibbs. VII:10:244-245.

Mother's tears. Rev. by Jawa Apronti. III:6:20-21.

MOXON, J. Volta: Man's greatest lake. (Deutsch, 1969). Rev. by F. Hesse. V:4:19-21.

MUNONYE, J. Obi. (Heinemann, 1969). Rev. by H. M. J. Trutenau. V:6:15-18.

NAMASIVAYAM, S. The drafting of legislature in Ghana. (Ghana Univ. Press). Rev. by G. K. A. Ofosu-Amaah. III:10:14.

NGUGI, J. A grain of wheat. (Heinemann, 1968). Rev. by J. Apronti. III:12:19-20.

Night with Senghor. Rev. by K. A. B. Jones-Quartey. III:8:17-19.

No tears for Ananse. (Ghana Film Corp.). Rev. by M. Bossman. II:10:17-18.

OCRAN, A. K. A myth is broken. (Longmans, 1968). Rev. by P. A. V. Ansah. IV:2:22-24.

OFOSU-APPIAH, L. H. The Life of Lt. Gen. Kotoka Hero of the 24th Feb. revolution. Rev. by G. Adali-Mortty. VII:8:196-197.

OKAI, J. Oath of the Fontomfrom and other poems. (Simon and Schuster, 1971). Rev. by J. Apronti. VI:24:20-21.

OMARI, T. P. Kwame Nkrumah, The anatomy of an African Dictatorship. (Moxon, 1970). Rev. by M. Assimeng. V:16:18-20.

Organization of Scientific research in Ghana. (Ghana Information
    Services, 1966). Rev. by F. Hesse. II:11:18-21.

PALANGYO, P. K. Dying in the Sun. (Heinemann, 1968). Rev. by A. N.
    Mensah. IV:5:22.

PALMER, E. An Introduction to the Africana novel. (Heinemann, 1972).
    Rev. by K. Britwum. VII:19:456-457.

Patterns of protest: A review article by M. Assimeng. VI:4:19-20.

PEIL, M. The Ghanaian factory worker; Industrial man in Africa.
    (C. U. P., 1972). Rev. by P. A. Twumasi. VII:11:267-268.

PIDGEON, G. W. F. Financial control in developing countries with
    particular reference to State Corporation. (Longman). Rev. by
    S. A. Nkrumah. VII:7:172-173.

PIKE, R. L. and M. L. BROWN. Nutrition: An integrated approach.
    (Wiley). Rev. by O. Andah. III:26:28.

POOLE, R. H. and P. J. SHEPHERD. D. H. Lawrence: A selection.
    (Heinemann, 1970). Rev. by A. N. Mensah. V:24:23-25.

ROSCOE, A. A. Mother is gold, a study of West African literature.
    (C. U. P., 1971). Rev. by A. N. Mensah. VI:18:19-22.

RUHUMBIKA, G. Village in Uhuru. Rev. by J. Apronti. V:7:16-17.

SAWER, G. Ombudsmen. (Melbourne Univ. Press, 1968). Rev. by
    S. O. Gyandoh. IV:10:16-18.

SCHATTEN, F. Communism in Africa. Rev. by B. D. G. Folson.
    II:8:17-18.

SHORT, P. Banda. (Routledge & K. Paul, 1974). Rev. by Y. Saffu.
    IX:11:266.

Soul to soul. (Musical night). Rev. by K. A. B. Jones-Quartey.
    VI:6:21-22.

SOYINKA, W. An evening with...Rev. by I. Irele. IV:5:18-20.

_____. Idanre and other poems. (Methuen, 1967). Rev. by B. Maccani.
    III:19:20.

_____. The man died. (Collings, 1972). Rev. by J. Gibbs.
    VIII:3:68-70.

_____. The swamp dwellers. Rev. by K. A. B. Jones-Quartey.
    II:12:18-19.

Soyinka and Ghana. Rev. by J. Gibbs. VI:15:22-24.

SUTHERLAND, E. T. Foriwa. Rev. by J. Apronti. IV:11:18-20.

THOMPSON, V. B. Africa and Unity: evolution of Pan-Africanism.
    (Longmans, 1969). Rev. by Y. O. Saffu. V:8:21-22.

Tributes to Dr. J. B. Danquah. Rev. by K. Mensah. II:14:15.

TUCKER, M. Africa in Modern Literature. (F. Ungar Pub. Co., 1967).
    Rev. by I. Ikiddeh. III:16:23-24.

Universitas. Vol. 1. Rev. by I. Ikiddeh. IV:11:20-22.

UWECHUE, R. Reflections on the Nigerian Civil War. (International
    Publishers, 1969). Rev. by I. Irele. IV:15:20-22.

What is on the Ghana? (Reindorf Public Relations Services). Rev.
    by A. N. Hakam. II:5:12-14.

Williamson's Akan religion and the Christian faith ed. by K. Dickson.
    (Ghana Univ. Press, 1965). Rev. by K. A. Opoku. III:5:29-30.

Wole Soyinka and radio. Rev. by J. Gibbs. VIII:21:508-510.

Reviews

WORONOFF, JON. West African wager: Houphouet Versus Nkrumah.
    (Metuchen, 1972). Rev. by S. K. B. Asante. VIII:6:140-141.
WRAITH, R. E. Guggisberg. (O. U. P., 1967). Rev. by K. A. B. Jones-
    Quartey. II:16:21-23.